George Gordon Byron Byron

# The Works of Lord Byron

Volume IV.

George Gordon Byron Byron

**The Works of Lord Byron**
*Volume IV.*

ISBN/EAN: 9783742829870

Manufactured in Europe, USA, Canada, Australia, Japa

Cover: Foto ©Andreas Hilbeck / pixelio.de

Manufactured and distributed by brebook publishing software (www.brebook.com)

George Gordon Byron Byron

**The Works of Lord Byron**

# COLLECTION
## OF
# BRITISH AUTHORS.
## VOL. XI.

---

THE WORKS OF LORD BYRON.

IN FIVE VOLUMES.

VOL. IV.

# THE WORKS
OF
# LORD BYRON

COMPLETE IN FIVE VOLUMES.

*Second Edition.*

VOL. IV.

LEIPZIG
BERNHARD TAUCHNITZ
1866.

# CONTENTS

## OF VOLUME IV.

| | Page |
|---|---|
| **HEBREW MELODIES.** Advertisement | 1 |
| She Walks in Beauty | 2 |
| The Harp the Monarch Minstrel swept | 2 |
| If that High World | 3 |
| The Wild Gazelle | 4 |
| Oh! Weep for Those | 4 |
| On Jordan's Banks | 5 |
| Jephtha's Daughter | 5 |
| Oh! Snatch'd away in Beauty's Bloom | 6 |
| My Soul is Dark | 7 |
| I saw Thee weep | 7 |
| Thy Days are Done | 8 |
| Song of Saul before his Last Battle | 9 |
| Saul | 9 |
| "All is Vanity, saith the Preacher" | 10 |
| When Coldness wraps this Suffering Clay | 11 |
| Vision of Belshazzar | 12 |
| Sun of the Sleepless! | 14 |
| Were my Bosom as False as thou deem'st it to be | 14 |
| Herod's Lament for Mariamne | 14 |
| On the Day of the Destruction of Jerusalem by Titus | 15 |
| By the Rivers of Babylon we sat down and wept | 16 |
| The Destruction of Sennacherib | 17 |
| A Spirit pass'd before me | 18 |
| **DOMESTIC PIECES—1816.** | 19 |
| Fare thee Well | 19 |
| A Sketch | 22 |
| Stanzas to Augusta | 25 |
| Stanzas to Augusta | 27 |
| Epistle to Augusta | 28 |
| Lines on hearing that Lady Byron was ill | 33 |

CONTENTS OF VOLUME IV.

|  | Page |
|---|---|
| OCCASIONAL PIECES. WRITTEN IN 1807—8 | 35 |
| The Adieu | 35 |
| To a Vain Lady | 39 |
| To Anne | 40 |
| To the Same | 40 |
| To the Author of a Sonnet | 41 |
| On finding a Fan | 42 |
| Farewell to the Muse | 42 |
| To an Oak at Newstead | 44 |
| On revisiting Harrow | 45 |
| Epitaph on John Adams, of Southwell | 46 |
| To my Son | 46 |
| Farewell! If ever Fondest Prayer | 47 |
| Bright be the Place of thy Soul | 48 |
| When we two parted | 48 |
| To a Youthful Friend | 49 |
| Lines inscribed upon a Cup formed from a Skull | 52 |
| WRITTEN IN 1809—10 | 53 |
| Well! Thou art happy | 53 |
| Inscription on the Monument of a Newfoundland Dog | 54 |
| To a Lady, on being asked my reason for Quitting England in the Spring | 55 |
| Remind me not, remind me not | 56 |
| There was a Time, I need not name | 57 |
| And wilt thou weep when I am Low? | 58 |
| Fill the Goblet again | 59 |
| Stanzas to a Lady, on leaving England | 60 |
| Lines to Mr. Hodgson | 61 |
| Lines written in an Album, at Malta | 64 |
| To Florence | 65 |
| Stanzas composed during a Thunderstorm | 66 |
| Stanzas written in Passing the Ambracian Gulf | 68 |
| The Spell is broke, the Charm is flown! | 69 |
| Written after swimming from Sestos to Abydos | 70 |
| Maid of Athens, ere we part | 71 |
| WRITTEN IN 1811—1812 | 72 |
| Lines written beneath a Picture | 72 |
| Substitute for an Epitaph | 72 |
| Translation of a famous Greek War Song | 73 |
| Translation of a Romaic Song | 75 |
| Lines in the Travellers' Book at Orchomenus | 76 |
| On Parting | 76 |
| Epitaph for Joseph Blackett, Late Poet and Shoemaker | 77 |
| On Moore's Last Operatic Farce, or Farcical Opera | 78 |
| Epistle to a Friend | 78 |
| To Thyrza | 80 |

## CONTENTS OF VOLUME IV.

|  | Page |
|---|---|
| Stanzas | 81 |
| Stanzas | 82 |
| Euthanasia | 84 |
| Stanzas | 85 |
| Stanzas | 87 |
| On a Cornelian Heart which was Broken | 89 |
| Lines to a Lady Weeping | 89 |
| The Chain I gave | 89 |
| Lines written on a Blank Leaf of the "Pleasures of Memory" | 90 |
| Address | 91 |
| To Time | 93 |
| Translation of a Romaic Love Song | 94 |
| Stanzas | 95 |
| On being asked what was the "Origin of Love" | 96 |
| Stanzas | 97 |
| On Lord Thurlow's Poems | 98 |
| To Lord Thurlow | 99 |
| To Thomas Moore | 100 |
| Impromptu, in Reply to a Friend | 101 |
| Sonnet, to Genevra | 101 |
| Sonnet, to the Same | 102 |
| From the Portuguese | 102 |
| 1814—1816 | 103 |
| The Devil's Drive | 103 |
| Windsor Poetics | 106 |
| Stanzas for Music | 106 |
| Address intended to be recited at the Caledonian Meeting | 107 |
| Fragment of an Epistle to Thomas Moore | 108 |
| Condolatory Address to Sarah, Countess of Jersey, on the Prince Regent's returning her Picture to Mrs. Mee | 109 |
| To Belshazzar | 110 |
| Elegiac Stanzas on the Death of Sir Peter Parker, Bart. | 111 |
| Stanzas for Music | 112 |
| Stanzas for Music | 113 |
| On Napoleon's Escape from Elba | 114 |
| Ode from the French | 114 |
| From the French | 118 |
| On the Star of "The Legion of Honour" | 119 |
| Napoleon's Farewell | 121 |
| Endorsement to the Deed of Separation, in the April of 1816 | 122 |
| Darkness | 122 |
| Churchill's Grave | 124 |
| Prometheus | 126 |
| A Fragment | 129 |
| Sonnet to Lake Leman | 130 |
| ROMANCE MUY DOLOROSO DEL SITIO Y TOMA DE ALHAMA | 131 |

|  | Page |
|---|---|
| A very Mournful Ballad on the Siege and Conquest of Alhama | 138 |
| Sonetto di Vittorelli | 140 |
| Translation from Vittorelli | 141 |
| Stanzas for Music | 142 |
| To Thomas Moore | 143 |
| Song for the Luddites | 144 |
| So we 'll go no more a Roving | 144 |
| On the Bust of Helen by Canova | 145 |
| Versicles | 145 |
| To Mr. Murray | 145 |
| Epistle from Mr. Murray to Dr. Polidori | 146 |
| Epistle to Mr. Murray | 148 |
| To Mr. Murray | 149 |
| To Thomas Moore | 150 |
| Epitaph for William Pitt | 151 |
| Sonnet to George the Fourth | 151 |
| Epigram | 151 |
| On my Wedding-Day | 152 |
| Epigram | 152 |
| Stanzas | 152 |
| Epigram | 152 |
| The Irish Avatar | 152 |
| On the Birth of John William Rizzo Hoppner | 157 |
| Stanzas | 157 |
| The Charity Ball | 160 |
| Epigram on my Wedding-Day | 161 |
| On my Thirty-Third Birth-Day | 161 |
| Epigram | 161 |
| To Mr. Murray | 161 |
| Stanzas to the Po | 163 |
| Stanzas written on the Road between Florence and Pisa | 165 |
| Stanzas: To a Hindoo Air | 165 |
| On this day I complete my Thirty-Sixth Year | 166 |
| APPENDIX. Farewell to Malta | 168 |
| To Dives | 170 |
| From the French | 170 |
| Parenthetical Address by Dr. Plagiary | 170 |
| Verses found in a Summer House at Hales-Owen | 172 |
| Martial, Lib. I. Epig. L | 173 |
| New Duet; Answer; Epigrams | 173 |
| Epitaph; The Conquest | 174 |
| MANFRED, A DRAMATIC POEM | 175 |
| CAIN, A MYSTERY. Dedication. Preface | 219 |
| THE DEFORMED TRANSFORMED, A DRAMA | 285 |
| HEAVEN AND EARTH, A MYSTERY | 337 |

# HEBREW MELODIES.

## ADVERTISEMENT.

The subsequent poems were written at the request of my friend, the Hon. D. Kinnaird, for a Selection of Hebrew Melodies, and have been published, with the music, arranged by Mr. Braham and Mr. Nathan.

January, 1815.

## HEBREW MELODIES.

### SHE WALKS IN BEAUTY.

#### I.

She walks in beauty, like the night
  Of cloudless climes and starry skies;
And all that's best of dark and bright
  Meet in her aspect and her eyes:
Thus mellow'd to that tender light
  Which heaven to gaudy day denies.

#### II.

One shade the more, one ray the less,
  Had half impair'd the nameless grace,
Which waves in every raven tress,
  Or softly lightens o'er her face;
Where thoughts serenely sweet express,
  How pure, how dear their dwelling-place.

#### III.

And on that cheek, and o'er that brow,
  So soft, so calm, yet eloquent,
The smiles that win, the tints that glow,
  But tell of days in goodness spent,
A mind at peace with all below,
  A heart whose love is innocent!

---

### THE HARP THE MONARCH MINSTREL SWEPT.

#### I.

The harp the monarch minstrel swept,
  The King of men, the loved of Heaven,
Which Music hallow'd while she wept
  O'er tones her heart of hearts had given,
  Redoubled be her tears, its chords are riven!

## HEBREW MELODIES.

It soften'd men of iron mould,
  It gave them virtues not their own;
No ear so dull, no soul so cold,
    That felt not, fired not to the tone,
    Till David's lyre grew mightier than his throne!

II.

It told the triumphs of our King,
  It wafted glory to our God;
It made our gladden'd valleys ring,
    The cedars bow, the mountains nod;
    Its sound aspired to Heaven and there abode!
Since then, though heard on earth no more,
  Devotion and her daughter Love,
Still bid the bursting spirit soar
    To sounds that seem as from above,
    In dreams that day's broad light can not remove.

---

### IF THAT HIGH WORLD.

I.

If that high world, which lies beyond
  Our own, surviving Love endears;
If there the cherish'd heart be fond,
    The eye the same, except in tears —
How welcome those untrodden spheres!
    How sweet this very hour to die!
To soar from earth and find all fears
    Lost in thy light — Eternity!

II.

It must be so: 'tis not for self
  That we so tremble on the brink;
And striving to o'erleap the gulf,
    Yet cling to Being's severing link.
Oh! in that future let us think
    To hold each heart the heart that shares,
With them the immortal waters drink,
    And soul in soul grow deathless theirs!

## THE WILD GAZELLE.

### I.

The wild gazelle on Judah's hills
    Exulting yet may bound,
And drink from all the living rills
    That gush on holy ground;
Its airy step and glorious eye
May glance in tameless transport by: —

### II.

A step as fleet, an eye more bright,
    Hath Judah witness'd there;
And o'er her scenes of lost delight
    Inhabitants more fair.
The cedars wave on Lebanon,
But Judah's statelier maids are gone!

### III.

More blest each palm that shades those plains
    Than Israel's scatter'd race;
For, taking root, it there remains
    In solitary grace:
It cannot quit its place of birth,
It will not live in other earth.

### IV.

But we must wander witheringly,
    In other lands to die;
And where our fathers' ashes be,
    Our own may never lie:
Our temple hath not left a stone,
And Mockery sits on Salem's throne.

---

## OH! WEEP FOR THOSE.

### I.

Oh! weep for those that wept by Babel's stream,
Whose shrines are desolate, whose land a dream;
Weep for the harp of Judah's broken shell;
Mourn — where their God hath dwelt the Godless dwell!

## HEBREW MELODIES.

### II.

And where shall Israel lave her bleeding feet?
And when shall Zion's songs again seem sweet?
And Judah's melody once more rejoice
The hearts that leap'd before its heavenly voice?

### III.

Tribes of the wandering foot and weary breast,
How shall ye flee away and be at rest!
The wild-dove hath her nest, the fox his cave,
Mankind their country — Israel but the grave!

## ON JORDAN'S BANKS.

### I.

On Jordan's banks the Arab's camels stray,
On Sion's hill the False One's votaries pray,
The Baal-adorer bows on Sinai's steep —
Yet there — even there — Oh God! thy thunders sleep:

### II.

There — where thy finger scorch'd the tablet stone!
There — where thy shadow to thy people shone!
Thy glory shrouded in its garb of fire:
Thyself — none living see and not expire!

### III.

Oh! in the lightning let thy glance appear;
Sweep from his shiver'd hand the oppressor's spear:
How long by tyrants shall thy land be trod!
How long thy temple worshipless, O God!

## JEPHTHA'S DAUGHTER.

### I.

Since our Country, our God — Oh, my Sire!
Demand that thy Daughter expire;
Since thy triumph was bought by thy vow —
Strike the bosom that's bared for thee now!

II.

And the voice of my mourning is o'er,
And the mountains behold me no more:
If the hand that I love lay me low,
There cannot be pain in the blow!

III.

And of this, oh, my Father! be sure —
That the blood of thy child is as pure
As the blessing I beg ere it flow,
And the last thought that soothes me below.

IV.

Though the virgins of Salem lament,
Be the judge and the hero unbent!
I have won the great battle for thee,
And my Father and Country are free!

V.

When this blood of thy giving hath gush'd,
When the voice that thou lovest is hush'd,
Let my memory still be thy pride,
And forget not I smiled as I died!

---

## OH! SNATCH'D AWAY IN BEAUTY'S BLOOM.

I.

Oh! snatch'd away in beauty's bloom,
On thee shall press no ponderous tomb;
  But on thy turf shall roses rear
  Their leaves, the earliest of the year;
And the wild cypress wave in tender gloom:

II.

And oft by yon blue gushing stream
  Shall Sorrow lean her drooping head,
And feed deep thought with many a dream,
  And lingering pause and lightly tread;
  Fond wretch! as if her step disturb'd the dead!

### III.

Away! we know that tears are vain,
  That death nor heeds nor hears distress:
Will this unteach us to complain?
  Or make one mourner weep the less?
And thou — who tell'st me to forget,
Thy looks are wan, thine eyes are wet.

---

## MY SOUL IS DARK.

### I.

My soul is dark — Oh! quickly string
  The harp I yet can brook to hear;
And let thy gentle fingers fling
  Its melting murmurs o'er mine ear.
If in this heart a hope be dear,
  That sound shall charm it forth again:
If in these eyes there lurk a tear,
  'Twill flow, and cease to burn my brain.

### II.

But bid the strain be wild and deep,
  Nor let thy notes of joy be first:
I tell thee, minstrel, I must weep,
  Or else this heavy heart will burst;
For it hath been by sorrow nursed,
  And ached in sleepless silence long;
And now 'tis doom'd to know the worst,
  And break at once — or yield to song.

---

## I SAW THEE WEEP.

### I.

I saw thee weep — the big bright tear
  Came o'er that eye of blue;
And then methought it did appear
  A violet dropping dew:

## HEBREW MELODIES.

I saw thee smile — the sapphire's blaze
  Beside thee ceased to shine;
It could not match the living rays
  That fill'd that glance of thine.

II.

As clouds from yonder sun receive
  A deep and mellow dye,
Which scarce the shade of coming eve
  Can banish from the sky,
Those smiles unto the moodiest mind
  Their own pure joy impart;
Their sunshine leaves a glow behind
  That lightens o'er the heart.

---

### THY DAYS ARE DONE.

I.

Thy days are done, thy fame begun;
  Thy country's strains record
The triumphs of her chosen Son,
  The slaughters of his sword!
The deeds he did, the fields he won,
  The freedom he restored!

II.

Though thou art fall'n, while we are free
  Thou shalt not taste of death!
The generous blood that flow'd from thee
  Disdain'd to sink beneath:
Within our veins its currents be,
  Thy spirit on our breath!

III.

Thy name, our charging hosts along,
  Shall be the battle-word!
Thy fall, the theme of choral song
  From virgin voices pour'd!
To weep would do thy glory wrong;
  Thou shalt not be deplored.

---

## HEBREW MELODIES.

### SONG OF SAUL BEFORE HIS LAST BATTLE.

#### I.

Warriors and chiefs! should the shaft or the sword
Pierce me in leading the host of the Lord,
Heed not the corse, though a king's, in your path:
Bury your steel in the bosoms of Gath!

#### II.

Thou who art bearing my buckler and bow,
Should the soldiers of Saul look away from the foe,
Stretch me that moment in blood at thy feet!
Mine be the doom which they dared not to meet.

#### III.

Farewell to others, but never we part,
Heir to my royalty, son of my heart!
Bright is the diadem, boundless the sway,
Or kingly the death, which awaits us to-day!

---

### SAUL.

#### I.

Thou whose spell can raise the dead,
  Bid the prophet's form appear.
"Samuel, raise thy buried head!
  King, behold the phantom seer!"
Earth yawn'd; he stood the centre of a cloud:
Light changed its hue, retiring from his shroud.
Death stood all glassy in his fixed eye;
His hand was wither'd, and his veins were dry;
His foot, in bony whiteness, glitter'd there,
Shrunken and sinewless, and ghastly bare;
From lips that moved not and unbreathing frame,
Like cavern'd winds, the hollow accents came.
Saul saw, and fell to earth, as falls the oak,
At once, and blasted by the thunder-stroke.

## II.

"Why is my sleep disquieted?
Who is he that calls the dead?
Is it thou, O King? Behold,
Bloodless are these limbs, and cold:
Such are mine; and such shall be
Thine to-morrow, when with me:
Ere the coming day is done,
Such shalt thou be, such thy son.
Fare thee well, but for a day,
Then we mix our mouldering clay.
Thou, thy race, lie pale and low,
Pierced by shafts of many a bow;
And the falchion by thy side
To thy heart thy hand shall guide:
Crownless, breathless, headless fall,
Son and sire, the house of Saul!"

## "ALL IS VANITY, SAITH THE PREACHER."

### I.

FAME, wisdom, love, and power were mine,
    And health and youth possess'd me;
My goblets blush'd from every vine,
    And lovely forms caress'd me;
I sunn'd my heart in beauty's eyes,
    And felt my soul grow tender;
All earth can give, or mortal prize,
    Was mine of regal splendour.

### II.

I strive to number o'er what days
    Remembrance can discover,
Which all that life or earth displays
    Would lure me to live over.
There rose no day, there roll'd no hour
    Of pleasure unembitter'd;
And not a trapping deck'd my power
    That gall'd not while it glitter'd.

## HEBREW MELODIES.

### III.

The serpent of the field, by art
   And spells, is won from harming;
But that which coils around the heart,
   Oh! who hath power of charming?
It will not list to wisdom's lore,
   Nor music's voice can lure it;
But there it stings for evermore
   The soul that must endure it.

---

## WHEN COLDNESS WRAPS THIS SUFFERING CLAY.

### I.

When coldness wraps this suffering clay,
   Ah! whither strays the immortal mind?
It cannot die, it cannot stay,
   But leaves its darken'd dust behind.
Then, unembodied, doth it trace
   By steps each planet's heavenly way?
Or fill at once the realms of space,
   A thing of eyes, that all survey?

### II.

Eternal, boundless, undecay'd,
   A thought unseen, but seeing all,
All, all in earth, or skies display'd,
   Shall it survey, shall it recall:
Each fainter trace that memory holds
   So darkly of departed years,
In one broad glance the soul beholds,
   And all, that was, at once appears.

### III.

Before Creation peopled earth,
   Its eye shall roll through chaos back;
And where the furthest heaven had birth,
   The spirit trace its rising track.

And where the future mars or makes,
  Its glance dilate o'er all to be,
While sun is quench'd or system breaks,
  Fix'd in its own eternity.

### IV.

Above or Love, Hope, Hate, or Fear,
  It lives all passionless and pure:
An age shall fleet like earthly year;
  Its years as moments shall endure.
Away, away, without a wing,
  O'er all, through all, its thought shall fly;
A nameless and eternal thing,
  Forgetting what it was to die.

---

## VISION OF BELSHAZZAR.

### I.

The King was on his throne,
  The Satraps throng'd the hall;
A thousand bright lamps shone
  O'er that high festival.
A thousand cups of gold,
  In Judah deem'd divine —
Jehovah's vessels hold
  The godless Heathen's wine.

### II.

In that same hour and hall,
  The fingers of a hand
Came forth against the wall,
  And wrote as if on sand:
The fingers of a man; —
  A solitary hand
Along the letters ran,
  And traced them like a wand.

### III.

The monarch saw, and shook,
   And bade no more rejoice;
All bloodless wax'd his look,
   And tremulous his voice.
"Let the men of lore appear,
   The wisest of the earth,
And expound the words of fear,
   Which mar our royal mirth."

### IV.

Chaldea's seers are good,
   But here they have no skill;
And the unknown letters stood
   Untold and awful still.
And Babel's men of age
   Are wise and deep in lore;
But now they were not sage,
   They saw — but knew no more.

### V.

A captive in the land,
   A stranger and a youth,
He heard the king's command,
   He saw that writing's truth.
The lamps around were bright,
   The prophecy in view;
He read it on that night, —
   The morrow proved it true.

### VI.

"Belshazzar's grave is made,
   His kingdom pass'd away,
He, in the balance weigh'd,
   Is light and worthless clay.
The shroud, his robe of state,
   His canopy the stone;
The Mede is at his gate!
   The Persian on his throne!"

## SUN OF THE SLEEPLESS!

Sun of the sleepless! melancholy star!
Whose tearful beam glows tremulously far,
That show'st the darkness thou canst not dispel,
How like art thou to joy remember'd well!
So gleams the past, the light of other days,
Which shines, but warms not with its powerless rays;
A night-beam Sorrow watcheth to behold,
Distinct, but distant — clear — but, oh how cold!

## WERE MY BOSOM AS FALSE AS THOU DEEM'ST IT TO BE.

### I.

Were my bosom as false as thou deem'st it to be,
I need not have wander'd from far Galilee;
It was but abjuring my creed to efface
The curse which, thou say'st, is the crime of my race.

### II.

If the bad never triumph, then God is with thee!
If the slave only sin, thou art spotless and free!
If the Exile on earth is an Outcast on high,
Live on in thy faith, but in mine I will die.

### III.

I have lost for that faith more than thou canst bestow,
As the God who permits thee to prosper doth know;
In his hand is my heart and my hope — and in thine
The land and the life which for him I resign.

## HEROD'S LAMENT FOR MARIAMNE.

### I.

Oh, Mariamne! now for thee
  The heart for which thou bled'st is bleeding;
Revenge is lost in agony,
  And wild remorse to rage succeeding.

Oh, Mariamne! where art thou?
  Thou canst not hear my bitter pleading:
Ah! couldst thou — thou wouldst pardon now,
  Though Heaven were to my prayer unheeding.

## II.

And is she dead? — and did they dare
  Obey my frenzy's jealous raving?
My wrath but doom'd my own despair:
  The sword that smote her's o'er me waving. —
But thou art cold, my murder'd love!
  And this dark heart is vainly craving
For her who soars alone above,
  And leaves my soul unworthy saving.

## III.

She's gone, who shared my diadem;
  She sunk, with her my joys entombing;
I swept that flower from Judah's stem,
  Whose leaves for me alone were blooming;
And mine's the guilt, and mine the hell,
  This bosom's desolation dooming;
And I have earn'd those tortures well,
  Which unconsumed are still consuming!

---

# ON THE DAY OF THE DESTRUCTION OF JERUSALEM BY TITUS.

## I.

From the last hill that looks on thy once holy dome
I beheld thee, oh Sion! when render'd to Rome:
'Twas thy last sun went down, and the flames of thy fall
Flash'd back on the last glance I gave to thy wall.

## II.

I look'd for thy temple, I look'd for my home,
And forgot for a moment my bondage to come;
I beheld but the death-fire that fed on thy fane,
And the fast-fetter'd hands that made vengeance in vain.

### III.

On many an eve, the high spot whence I gazed
Had reflected the last beam of day as it blazed;
While I stood on the height, and beheld the decline
Of the rays from the mountain that shone on thy shrine.

### IV.

And now on that mountain I stood on that day,
But I mark'd not the twilight beam melting away;
Oh! would that the lightning had glared in its stead,
And the thunderbolt burst on the conqueror's head!

### V.

But the Gods of the Pagan shall never profane
The shrine where Jehovah disdain'd not to reign;
And scatter'd and scorn'd as thy people may be,
Our worship, oh Father! is only for thee.

---

## BY THE RIVERS OF BABYLON WE SAT DOWN AND WEPT.

### I.

We sate down and wept by the waters
  Of Babel, and thought of the day
When our foe, in the hue of his slaughters,
  Made Salem's high places his prey;
And ye, oh her desolate daughters!
  Were scatter'd all weeping away.

### II.

While sadly we gazed on the river
  Which roll'd on in freedom below,
They demanded the song; but, oh never
  That triumph the stranger shall know!
May this right hand be wither'd for ever,
  Ere it string our high harp for the foe!

III.

On the willow that harp is suspended,
  Oh Salem! its sound should be free;
And the hour when thy glories were ended
  But left me that token of thee:
And ne'er shall its soft tones be blended
  With the voice of the spoiler by me!

### THE DESTRUCTION OF SENNACHERIB.

I.

The Assyrian came down like the wolf on the fold,
And his cohorts were gleaming in purple and gold;
And the sheen of their spears was like stars on the sea,
When the blue wave rolls nightly on deep Galilee.

II.

Like the leaves of the forest when Summer is green,
That host with their banners at sunset were seen:
Like the leaves of the forest when Autumn hath blown,
That host on the morrow lay wither'd and strown.

III.

For the Angel of Death spread his wings on the blast,
And breathed in the face of the foe as he pass'd;
And the eyes of the sleepers wax'd deadly and chill,
And their hearts but once heaved, and for ever grew still!

IV.

And there lay the steed with his nostril all wide,
But through it there roll'd not the breath of his pride:
And the foam of his gasping lay white on the turf,
And cold as the spray of the rock-beating surf.

V.

And there lay the rider distorted and pale,
With the dew on his brow, and the rust on his mail
And the tents were all silent, the banners alone,
The lances unlifted, the trumpet unblown.

#### VI.

And the widows of Ashur are loud in their wail,
And the idols are broke in the temple of Baal;
And the might of the Gentile, unsmote by the sword,
Hath melted like snow in the glance of the Lord!

### A SPIRIT PASS'D BEFORE ME.
#### FROM JOB.

#### I.

A spirit pass'd before me: I beheld
The face of immortality unveil'd —
Deep sleep came down on every eye save mine —
And there it stood, — all formless — but divine:
Along my bones the creeping flesh did quake;
And as my damp hair stiffen'd, thus it spake:

#### II.

"Is man more just than God? Is man more pure
Than he who deems even Seraphs insecure?
Creatures of clay — vain dwellers in the dust!
The moth survives you, and are ye more just?
Things of a day! you wither ere the night,
Heedless and blind to Wisdom's wasted light!"

# DOMESTIC PIECES — 1816.

### FARE THEE WELL.

> "Alas! they had been friends in Youth;
> But whispering tongues can poison truth;
> And constancy lives in realms above;
> And Life is thorny; and youth is vain:
> And to be wroth with one we love,
> Doth work like madness in the brain;
> \* \* \* \* \*
> But never either found another
> To free the hollow heart from paining —
> They stood aloof, the scars remaining,
> Like cliffs, which had been rent asunder;
> A dreary sea now flows between,
> But neither heat, nor frost, nor thunder
> Shall wholly do away, I ween,
> The marks of that which once hath been."
> <div align="right">COLERIDGE's <i>Christabel</i>.</div>

Fare thee well! and if for ever,
  Still for ever, fare *thee well:*
Even though unforgiving, never
  'Gainst thee shall my heart rebel.

Would that breast were bared before thee
  Where thy head so oft hath lain,
While that placid sleep came o'er thee
  Which thou ne'er canst know again.

Would that breast, by thee glanced over,
   Every inmost thought could show!
Then thou would'st at last discover
   'Twas not well to spurn it so.

Though the world for this commend thee —
   Though it smile upon the blow,
Even its praises must offend thee,
   Founded on another's woe:

Though my many faults defaced me,
   Could no other arm be found,
Than the one which once embraced me,
   To inflict a cureless wound?

Yet, oh yet, thyself deceive not;
   Love may sink by slow decay,
But by sudden wrench, believe not
   Hearts can thus be torn away:

Still thine own its life retaineth —
   Still must mine, though bleeding, beat;
And the undying thought which paineth
   Is — that we no more may meet.

These are words of deeper sorrow
   Than the wail above the dead;
Both shall live, but every morrow
   Wake us from a widow'd bed.

And when thou would solace gather,
   When our child's first accents flow,
Wilt thou teach her to say "Father!"
   Though his care she must forego?

When her little hands shall press thee,
   When her lip to thine is press'd,
Think of him whose prayer shall bless thee,
   Think of him thy love had bless'd!

Should her lineaments resemble
    Those thou never more may'st see,
Then thy heart will softly tremble
    With a pulse yet true to me.

All my faults perchance thou knowest,
    All my madness none can know;
All my hopes, where'er thou goest,
    Wither, yet with *thee* they go.

Every feeling hath been shaken;
    Pride, which not a world could bow,
Bows to thee — by thee forsaken,
    Even my soul forsakes me now:

But 'tis done — all words are idle —
    Words from me are vainer still;
But the thoughts we cannot bridle
    Force their way without the will. —

Fare thee well! — thus disunited,
    Torn from every nearer tie,
Sear'd in heart, and lone, and blighted,
    More than this I scarce can die.

                          March 17. 1816.

## A SKETCH.

> "Honest — honest Iago!
> If that thou bo'st a devil, I cannot kill thee." — SHAKSPEARE.

Born in the garret, in the kitchen bred,
Promoted thence to deck her mistress' head;
Next — for some gracious service unexpress'd,
And from its wages only to be guess'd —
Raised from the toilet to the table, — where
Her wondering betters wait behind her chair.
With eye unmoved, and forehead unabash'd,
She dines from off the plate she lately wash'd.
Quick with the tale, and ready with the lie —
The genial confidante, and general spy —
Who could, ye gods! her next employment guess —
An only infant's earliest governess!
She taught the child to read, and taught so well,
That she herself, by teaching, learn'd to spell.
An adept next in penmanship she grows,
As many a nameless slander deftly shows:
What she had made the pupil of her art,
None know — but that high Soul secured the heart,
And panted for the truth it could not hear,
With longing breast and undeluded ear.
Foil'd was perversion by that youthful mind,
Which Flattery fool'd not — Baseness could not blind,
Deceit infect not — near Contagion soil —
Indulgence weaken — nor Example spoil —
Nor master'd Science tempt her to look down
On humbler talents with a pitying frown —
Nor Genius swell — nor Beauty render vain —
Nor Envy ruffle to retaliate pain —
Nor Fortune change — Pride raise — nor Passion bow,
Nor Virtue teach austerity — till now.
Serenely purest of her sex that live,
But wanting one sweet weakness — to forgive,

Too shock'd at faults her soul can never know,
She deems that all could be like her below:
Foe to all vice, yet hardly Virtue's friend,
For Virtue pardons those she would amend.

But to the theme: — now laid aside too long,
The baleful burthen of this honest song —
Though all her former functions are no more,
She rules the circle which she served before.
If mothers — none know why — before her quake;
If daughters dread her for the mothers' sake;
If early habits — those false links, which bind
At times the loftiest to the meanest mind —
Have given her power too deeply to instil
The angry essence of her deadly will;
If like a snake she steal within your walls,
Till the black slime betray her as she crawls;
If like a viper to the heart she wind,
And leave the venom there she did not find;
What marvel that this hag of hatred works
Eternal evil latent as she lurks,
To make a Pandemonium where she dwells,
And reign the Hecate of domestic hells?
Skill'd by a touch to deepen scandal's tints
With all the kind mendacity of hints,
While mingling truth with falsehood — sneers with — [smiles
A thread of candour with a web of wiles;
A plain blunt show of briefly-spoken seeming,
To hide her bloodless heart's soul-harden'd scheming;
A lip of lies — a face form'd to conceal;
And, without feeling, mock at all who feel:
With a vile mask the Gorgon would disown;
A cheek of parchment — and an eye of stone.
Mark, how the channels of her yellow blood
Ooze to her skin, and stagnate there to mud,
Cased like the centipede in saffron mail,
Or darker greenness of the scorpion's scale —

(For drawn from reptiles only may we trace
Congenial colours in that soul or face) —
Look on her features! and behold her mind
As in a mirror of itself defined:
Look on the picture! deem it not o'ercharged —
There is no trait which might not be enlarged:
Yet true to "Nature's journeymen," who made
This monster when their mistress left off trade —
This female dog-star of her little sky,
Where all beneath her influence droop or die.

Oh! wretch without a tear — without a thought,
Save joy above the ruin thou hast wrought —
The time shall come, nor long remote, when thou
Shalt feel far more than thou inflictest now;
Feel for thy vile self-loving self in vain,
And turn thee howling in unpitied pain.
May the strong curse of crush'd affections light
Back on thy bosom with reflected blight!
And make thee in thy leprosy of mind
As loathsome to thyself as to mankind!
Till all thy self-thoughts curdle into hate,
Black — as thy will for others would create:
Till thy hard heart be calcined into dust,
And thy soul welter in its hideous crust.
Oh, may thy grave be sleepless as the bed, —
The widow'd couch of fire, that thou hast spread!
Then, when thou fain wouldst weary Heaven with prayer,
Look on thine earthly victims — and despair!
Down to the dust! — and, as thou rott'st away,
Even worms shall perish on thy poisonous clay.
But for the love I bore, and still must bear,
To her thy malice from all ties would tear —
Thy name — thy human name — to every eye
The climax of all scorn should hang on high,
Exalted o'er thy less abhorr'd compeers —
And festering in the infamy of years.

March 29. 1816.

## STANZAS TO AUGUSTA.

["WHEN ALL AROUND," &c.]

### I.

When all around grew drear and dark,
   And reason half withheld her ray —
And hope but shed a dying spark
   Which more misled my lonely way;

### II.

In that deep midnight of the mind,
   And that internal strife of heart,
When dreading to be deem'd too kind,
   The weak despair — the cold depart;

### III.

When fortune changed — and love fled far,
   And hatred's shafts flew thick and fast,
Thou wert the solitary star
   Which rose and set not to the last.

### IV.

Oh! blest be thine unbroken light!
   That watch'd me as a seraph's eye,
And stood between me and the night,
   For ever shining sweetly nigh.

### V.

And when the cloud upon us came,
   Which strove to blacken o'er thy ray —
Then purer spread its gentle flame,
   And dash'd the darkness all away.

### VI.

Still may thy spirit dwell on mine,
   And teach it what to brave or brook —
There's more in one soft word of thine
   Than in the world's defied rebuke.

VII.

Thou stood'st, as stands a lovely tree,
    That still unbroke, though gently bent,
Still waves with fond fidelity
    Its boughs above a monument.

VIII.

The winds might rend — the skies might pour,
    But there thou wert — and still would'st be
Devoted in the stormiest hour
    To shed thy weeping leaves o'er me.

IX.

But thou and thine shall know no blight,
    Whatever fate on me may fall;
For heaven in sunshine will requite
    The kind — and thee the most of all.

X.

Then let the ties of baffled love
    Be broken — thine will never break;
Thy heart can feel — but will not move;
    Thy soul, though soft, will never shake.

XI.

And these, when all was lost beside,
    Were found and still are fix'd in thee;
And bearing still a breast so tried,
    Earth is no desert — ev'n to me.

## STANZAS TO AUGUSTA.

[" THOUGH THE DAY OF MY DESTINY'S," &c.]

I.

Though the day of my destiny's over,
  And the star of my fate hath declined,
Thy soft heart refused to discover
  The faults which so many could find;
Though thy soul with my grief was acquainted,
  It shrunk not to share it with me,
And the love which my spirit hath painted
  It never hath found but in *thee*.

II.

Then when nature around me is smiling,
  The last smile which answers to mine,
I do not believe it beguiling,
  Because it reminds me of thine;
And when winds are at war with the ocean,
  As the breasts I believed in with me,
If their billows excite an emotion,
  It is that they bear me from *thee*.

III.

Though the rock of my last hope is shiver'd,
  And its fragments are sunk in the wave,
Though I feel that my soul is deliver'd
  To pain — it shall not be its slave.
There is many a pang to pursue me:
  They may crush, but they shall not contemn —
They may torture, but shall not subdue me —
  'Tis of *thee* that I think — not of them.

IV.

Though human, thou didst not deceive me,
  Though woman, thou didst not forsake,
Though loved, thou forborest to grieve me,
  Though slander'd, thou never couldst shake, —

Though trusted, thou didst not disclaim me,
  Though parted, it was not to fly,
Though watchful, 'twas not to defame me,
  Nor, mute, that the world might belie.

### V.

Yet I blame not the world, nor despise it,
  Nor the war of the many with one —
If my soul was not fitted to prize it,
  'Twas folly not sooner to shun:
And if dearly that error hath cost me,
  And more than I once could foresee,
I have found that, whatever it lost me,
  It could not deprive me of *thee.*

### VI.

From the wreck of the past, which hath perish'd,
  Thus much I at least may recall,
It hath taught me that what I most cherish'd
  Deserved to be dearest of all:
In the desert a fountain is springing,
  In the wide waste there still is a tree,
And a bird in the solitude singing,
  Which speaks to my spirit of *thee.*

July 24. 1816.

## EPISTLE TO AUGUSTA.

["MY SISTER! MY SWEET SISTER!" &c.]

### I.

My sister! my sweet sister! if a name
Dearer and purer were, it should be thine.
Mountains and seas divide us, but I claim
No tears, but tenderness to answer mine:
Go where I will, to me thou art the same —
A loved regret which I would not resign.
There yet are two things in my destiny, —
A world to roam through, and a home with thee.

## DOMESTIC PIECES.

### II.

The first were nothing — had I still the last,
It were the haven of my happiness;
But other claims and other ties thou hast,
And mine is not the wish to make them less.
A strange doom is thy father's son's, and past
Recalling, as it lies beyond redress;
Reversed for him our grandsire's fate of yore, —
He had no rest at sea, nor I on shore.

### III.

If my inheritance of storms hath been
In other elements, and on the rocks
Of perils, overlook'd or unforeseen,
I have sustain'd my share of worldly shocks,
The fault was mine; nor do I seek to screen
My errors with defensive paradox;
I have been cunning in mine overthrow,
The careful pilot of my proper woe.

### IV.

Mine were my faults, and mine be their reward,
My whole life was a contest, since the day
That gave me being, gave me that which marr'd
The gift, — a fate, or will, that walk'd astray;
And I at times have found the struggle hard,
And thought of shaking off my bonds of clay:
But now I fain would for a time survive,
If but to see what next can well arrive.

### V.

Kingdoms and empires in my little day
I have outlived, and yet I am not old;
And when I look on this, the petty spray
Of my own years of trouble, which have roll'd
Like a wild bay of breakers, melts away:
Something — I know not what — does still uphold
A spirit of slight patience; — not in vain,
Even for its own sake, do we purchase pain.

## DOMESTIC PIECES.

### VI.

Perhaps the workings of defiance stir
Within me, — or perhaps a cold despair,
Brought on when ills habitually recur, —
Perhaps a kinder clime, or purer air,
(For even to this may change of soul refer,
And with light armour we may learn to bear,)
Have taught me a strange quiet, which was not
The chief companion of a calmer lot.

### VII.

I feel almost at times as I have felt
In happy childhood; trees, and flowers, and brooks,
Which do remember me of where I dwelt
Ere my young mind was sacrificed to books,
Come as of yore upon me, and can melt
My heart with recognition of their looks;
And even at moments I could think I see
Some living thing to love — but none like thee.

### VIII.

Here are the Alpine landscapes which create
A fund for contemplation; — to admire
Is a brief feeling of a trivial date;
But something worthier do such scenes inspire:
Here to be lonely is not desolate,
For much I view which I could most desire,
And, above all, a lake I can behold
Lovelier, not dearer, than our own of old.

### IX.

Oh that thou wert but with me! — but I grow
The fool of my own wishes, and forget
The solitude which I have vaunted so
Has lost its praise in this but one regret;
There may be others which I less may show; —
I am not of the plaintive mood, and yet
I feel an ebb in my philosophy,
And the tide rising in my alter'd eye.

### X.

I did remind thee of our own dear Lake,*
By the old Hall which may be mine no more.
Leman's is fair; but think not I forsake
The sweet remembrance of a dearer shore:
Sad havoc Time must with my memory make
Ere *that* or *thou* can fade these eyes before;
Though, like all things which I have loved, they are
Resign'd for ever, or divided far.

### XI.

The world is all before me; I but ask
Of Nature that with which she will comply —
It is but in her summer's sun to bask,
To mingle with the quiet of her sky,
To see her gentle face without a mask,
And never gaze on it with apathy.
She was my early friend, and now shall be
My sister — till I look again on thee.

### XII.

I can reduce all feelings but this one;
And that I would not; — for at length I see
Such scenes as those wherein my life begun.
The earliest — even the only paths for me —
Had I but sooner learnt the crowd to shun,
I had been better than I now can be;
The passions which have torn me would have slept;
*I* had not suffer'd, and *thou* hadst not wept.

### XIII.

With false Ambition what had I to do?
Little with Love, and least of all with Fame;
And yet they came unsought, and with me grew,
And made me all which they can make — a name.
Yet this was not the end I did pursue;
Surely I once beheld a nobler aim.
But all is over — I am one the more
To baffled millions which have gone before.

* The Lake of Newstead Abbey.

#### XIV.

And for the future, this world's future may
From me demand but little of my care;
I have outlived myself by many a day;
Having survived so many things that were;
My years have been no slumber, but the prey
Of ceaseless vigils; for I had the share
  Of life which might have fill'd a century,
Before its fourth in time had pass'd me by.

#### XV.

And for the remnant which may be to come
I am content; and for the past I feel
Not thankless, — for within the crowded sum
Of struggles, happiness at times would steal,
And for the present, I would not benumb
My feelings farther. — Nor shall I conceal
  That with all this I still can look around
And worship Nature with a thought profound.

#### XVI.

For thee, my own sweet sister, in thy heart
I know myself secure, as thou in mine;
We were and are — I am, even as thou art —
Beings who ne'er each other can resign;
It is the same, together or apart,
From life's commencement to its slow decline
  We are entwined — let death come slow or fast,
The tie which bound the first endures the last!

---

**LINES**

ON HEARING THAT LADY BYRON WAS ILL.

AND thou wert sad — yet I was not with thee;
    And thou wert sick, and yet I was not near;
Methought that joy and health alone could be
    Where I was not — and pain and sorrow here!
And is it thus? — it is as I foretold,
    And shall be more so; for the mind recoils
Upon itself, and the wreck'd heart lies cold,
    While heaviness collects the shatter'd spoils.
It is not in the storm nor in the strife
    We feel benumb'd, and wish to be no more,
    But in the after-silence on the shore,
When all is lost, except a little life.

I am too well avenged! — but 'twas my right;
    Whate'er my sins might be, *thou* wert not sent
To be the Nemesis who should requite —
    Nor did Heaven choose so near an instrument.
Mercy is for the merciful! — if thou
Hast been of such, 'twill be accorded now.
Thy nights are banish'd from the realms of sleep! —
    Yes! they may flatter thee, but thou shalt feel
    A hollow agony which will not heal,
For thou art pillow'd on a curse too deep;
Thou hast sown in my sorrow, and must reap
    The bitter harvest in a woe as real!
I have had many foes, but none like thee;
    For 'gainst the rest myself I could defend,
    And be avenged, or turn them into friend;
But thou in safe implacability
Hadst nought to dread — in thy own weakness shielded,
And in my love, which hath but too much yielded,

And spared, for thy sake, some I should not spare —
And thus upon the world — trust in thy truth —
And the wild fame of my ungovern'd youth —
　On things that were not, and on things that are —
Even upon such a basis hast thou built
A monument, whose cement hath been guilt!
　The moral Clytemnestra of thy lord,
And hew'd down, with an unsuspected sword,
Fame, peace, and hope — and all the better life
　Which, but for this cold treason of thy heart,
Might still have risen from out the grave of strife,
　And found a nobler duty than to part.
But of thy virtues didst thou make a vice,
　Trafficking with them in a purpose cold,
　For present anger, and for future gold —
And buying other's grief at any price.
And thus once enter'd into crooked ways,
The early truth, which was thy proper praise,
Did not still walk beside thee — but at times,
And with a breast unknowing its own crimes,
Deceit, averments incompatible,
Equivocations, and the thoughts which dwell
　In Janus-spirits — the significant eye
Which learns to lie with silence — the pretext
Of Prudence, with advantages annex'd —
The acquiescence in all things which tend,
No matter how, to the desired end —
　All found a place in thy philosophy.
The means were worthy, and the end is won —
I would not do by thee as thou hast done!

　　　　　　　　　　　　September, 1816.

# OCCASIONAL PIECES.

### WRITTEN IN 1807—8.

---

#### THE ADIEU.

##### WRITTEN UNDER THE IMPRESSION THAT THE AUTHOR WOULD SOON DIE.

Adieu, thou Hill!\* where early joy
  Spread roses o'er my brow;
Where Science seeks each loitering boy
  With knowledge to endow.
Adieu my youthful friends or foes,
Partners of former bliss or woes;
  No more through Ida's paths we stray;
Soon must I share the gloomy cell,
Whose ever-slumbering inmates dwell
  Unconscious of the day.

Adieu, ye hoary Regal Fanes,
  Ye spires of Granta's vale,
Where Learning robed in sable reigns,
  And Melancholy pale.
Ye comrades of the jovial hour,
Ye tenants of the classic bower,
  On Cama's verdant margin placed,
Adieu! while memory still is mine,
For, offerings on Oblivion's shrine,
  These scenes must be effaced.

\* Harrow.

Adieu, ye mountains of the clime
  Where grew my youthful years;
Where Loch na Garr in snows sublime
  His giant summit rears.
Why did my childhood wander forth
From you, ye regions of the North,
  With sons of pride to roam?
Why did I quit my Highland cave,
Marr's dusky heath, and Dee's clear wave,
  To seek a Sotheron home?

Hall of my Sires! a long farewell —
  Yet why to thee adieu?
Thy vaults will echo back my knell,
  Thy towers my tomb will view:
The faltering tongue which sung thy fall,
And former glories of thy Hall
  Forgets its wonted simple note —
But yet the Lyre retains the strings,
And sometimes, on Æolian wings,
  In dying strains may float.

Fields, which surround yon rustic cot,
  While yet I linger here,
Adieu! you are not now forgot,
  To retrospection dear.
Streamlet! along whose rippling surge,
My youthful limbs were wont to urge
  At noontide heat their pliant course;
Plunging with ardour from the shore,
Thy springs will lave these limbs no more,
  Deprived of active force.

And shall I here forget the scene,
  Still nearest to my breast?
Rocks rise, and rivers roll between
  The spot which passion blest;

Yet, Mary*, all thy beauties seem
Fresh as in Love's bewitching dream,
　To me in smiles display'd:
Till slow disease resigns his prey
To Death, the parent of decay,
　Thine image cannot fade.

And thou, my Friend!** whose gentle love
　Yet thrills my bosom's chords,
How much thy friendship was above
　Description's power of words!
Still near my breast thy gift I wear
Which sparkled once with Feeling's tear,
　Of Love the pure, the sacred gem;
Our souls were equal, and our lot
In that dear moment quite forgot;
　Let Pride alone condemn!

All, all, is dark and cheerless now!
　No smile of Love's deceit
Can warm my veins with wonted glow,
　Can bid Life's pulses beat:
Not e'en the hope of future fame,
Can wake my faint, exhausted frame,
　Or crown with fancied wreaths my head.
Mine is a short inglorious race, —
To humble in the dust my face,
　And mingle with the dead.

Oh Fame! thou goddess of my heart;
　On him who gains thy praise,
Pointless must fall the Spectre's dart,
　Consumed in Glory's blaze;
But me she beckons from the earth,
My name obscure, unmark'd my birth,

* Mary Duff.
** Eddlestono, the Cambridge chorister.

My life a short and vulgar dream:
Lost in the dull, ignoble crowd,
My hopes recline within a shroud,
   My fate is Lethe's stream.

When I repose beneath the sod,
   Unheeded in the clay,
Where once my playful footsteps trod,
   Where now my head must lay;
The meed of Pity will be shed
In dew-drops o'er my narrow bed,
   By nightly skies, and storms alone;
No mortal eye will deign to steep
With tears the dark sepulchral deep
   Which hides a name unknown.

Forget this world, my restless sprite,
   Turn, turn thy thoughts to Heaven:
There must thou soon direct thy flight,
   If errors are forgiven.
To bigots and to sects unknown,
Bow down beneath the Almighty's Throne;
   To Him address thy trembling prayer:
He, who is merciful and just,
Will not reject a child of dust,
   Although his meanest care.

Father of Light! to Thee I call,
   My soul is dark within:
Thou, who canst mark the sparrow's fall,
   Avert the death of sin.
Thou, who canst guide the wandering star,
Who calm'st the elemental war,
   Whose mantle is yon boundless sky,
My thoughts, my words, my crimes forgive;
And, since I soon must cease to live,
   Instruct me how to die.

                1807. [First published 1832.]

### TO A VAIN LADY.

Ah, heedless girl! why thus disclose
   What ne'er was meant for other ears:
Why thus destroy thine own repose,
   And dig the source of future tears?

Oh, thou wilt weep, imprudent maid,
   While lurking envious foes will smile,
For all the follies thou hast said
   Of those who spoke but to beguile.

Vain girl! thy ling'ring woes are nigh,
   If thou believ'st what striplings say:
Oh, from the deep temptation fly,
   Nor fall the specious spoiler's prey.

Dost thou repeat, in childish boast,
   The words man utters to deceive?
Thy peace, thy hope, thy all is lost,
   If thou can'st venture to believe.

While now amongst thy female peers
   Thou tell'st again the soothing tale,
Can'st thou not mark the rising sneers
   Duplicity in vain would veil?

These tales in secret silence hush,
   Nor make thyself the public gaze:
What modest maid without a blush
   Recounts a flattering coxcomb's praise?

Will not the laughing boy despise
   Her who relates each fond conceit —
Who, thinking Heaven is in her eyes,
   Yet cannot see the slight deceit?

For she who takes a soft delight
   These amorous nothings in revealing,
Must credit all we say or write,
   While vanity prevents concealing.

Cease, if you prize your beauty's reign!
　No jealousy bids me reprove:
One, who is thus from nature vain,
　I pity, but I cannot love.

　　　　　January 15. 1807. [First published 1832.]

---

### TO ANNE.

Oh, Anne! your offences to me have been grievous;
　I thought from my wrath no atonement could save you;
But woman is made to command and deceive us —
　I look'd in your face, and I almost forgave you.

I vow'd I could ne'er for a moment respect you,
　Yet thought that a day's separation was long:
When we met, I determin'd again to suspect you —
　Your smile soon convinced me suspicion was wrong.

I swore, in a transport of young indignation,
　With fervent contempt evermore to disdain you:
I saw you — my anger became admiration;
　And now, all my wish, all my hope 's to regain you.

With beauty like yours, oh, how vain the contention!
　Thus lowly I sue for forgiveness before you; —
At once to conclude such a fruitless dissension,
　Be false, my sweet Anne, when I cease to adore you!

　　　　　January 16. 1807. [First published 1832.]

---

### TO THE SAME.

Oh say not, sweet Anne, that the Fates have decreed
　The heart which adores you should wish to dissever;
Such Fates were to me most unkind ones indeed, —
　To bear me from love and from beauty for ever.

Your frowns, lovely girl, are the Fates which alone
  Could bid me from fond admiration refrain;
By these, every hope, every wish were o'erthrown,
  Till smiles should restore me to rapture again.

As the ivy and oak, in the forest entwined,
  The rage of the tempest united must weather,
My love and my life were by nature design'd
  To flourish alike, or to perish together.

Then say not, sweet Anne, that the Fates have decreed,
  Your lover should bid you a lasting adieu;
Till Fate can ordain that his bosom shall bleed,
  His soul, his existence, are centred in you.

1807. [First published 1832.]

---

## TO THE AUTHOR OF A SONNET BEGINNING,

### "'SAD IS MY VERSE,' YOU SAY, 'AND YET NO TEAR.'"

Thy verse is "sad" enough, no doubt:
  A devilish deal more sad than witty!
Why we should weep I can't find out,
  Unless for *thee* we weep in pity.

Yet there is one I pity more;
  And much, alas! I think he needs it:
For he, I'm sure, will suffer sore,
  Who, to his own misfortune, reads it.

Thy rhymes, without the aid of magic,
  May *once* be read — but never after:
Yet their effect's by no means tragic,
  Although by far too dull for laughter.

But would you make our bosoms bleed,
  And of no common pang complain —
If you would make us weep indeed,
  Tell us, you'll read them o'er again.

March 8. 1807. [First published 1832.]

### ON FINDING A FAN.

In one who felt as once he felt,
    This might, perhaps, have fann'd the flame;
But now his heart no more will melt,
    Because that heart is not the same.

As when the ebbing flames are low,
    The aid which once improved their light,
And bade them burn with fiercer glow,
    Now quenches all their blaze in night,

Thus has it been with passion's fires —
    As many a boy and girl remembers —
While every hope of love expires,
    Extinguish'd with the dying embers.

The *first*, though not a spark survive,
    Some careful hand may teach to burn;
The *last*, alas! can ne'er survive;
    No touch can bid its warmth return.

Or, if it chance to wake again,
    Not always doom'd its heat to smother,
It sheds (so wayward fates ordain)
    Its former warmth around another.

                    1807. [First published 1832.]

### FAREWELL TO THE MUSE.

Thou Power! who hast ruled me through infancy's days,
    Young offspring of Fancy, 'tis time we should part;
Then rise on the gale this the last of my lays,
    The coldest effusion which springs from my heart.

This bosom, responsive to rapture no more,
    Shall hush thy wild notes, nor implore thee to sing;
The feelings of childhood, which taught thee to soar,
    Are wafted far distant on Apathy's wing.

Though simple the themes of my rude flowing Lyre,
  Yet even these themes are departed for ever;
No more beam the eyes which my dream could inspire,
  My visions are flown, to return, — alas, never!

When drain'd is the nectar which gladdens the bowl,
  How vain is the effort delight to prolong!
When cold is the beauty which dwelt in my soul,
  What magic of Fancy can lengthen my song?

Can the lips sing of Love in the desert alone,
  Of kisses and smiles which they now must resign?
Or dwell with delight on the hours that are flown?
  Ah, no! for those hours can no longer be mine.

Can they speak of the friends that I lived but to love?
  Ah, surely affection ennobles the strain:
But how can my numbers in sympathy move,
  When I scarcely can hope to behold them again?

Can I sing of the deeds which my Fathers have done,
  And raise my loud harp to the fame of my Sires?
For glories like theirs, oh, how faint is my tone!
  For Heroes' exploits how unequal my fires!

Untouch'd, then, my Lyre shall reply to the blast —
  "Tis hush'd; and my feeble endeavours are o'er;
And those who have heard it will pardon the past,
  When they know that its murmurs shall vibrate no more.

And soon shall its wild erring notes be forgot,
  Since early affection and love is o'ercast:
Oh! blest had my fate been, and happy my lot,
  Had the first strain of love been the dearest, the last.

Farewell, my young Muse! since we now can ne'er meet;
  If our songs have been languid, they surely are few:
Let us hope that the present at least will be sweet —
  The present — which seals our eternal Adieu.

1807. [First published 1832.]

### TO AN OAK AT NEWSTEAD.

Young Oak! when I planted thee deep in the ground,
  I hoped that thy days would be longer than mine;
That thy dark-waving branches would flourish around,
  And ivy thy trunk with its mantle entwine.

Such, such was my hope, when, in infancy's years,
  On the land of my fathers I rear'd thee with pride:
They are past, and I water thy stem with my tears, —
  Thy decay not the weeds that surround thee can hide.

I left thee, my Oak, and, since that fatal hour,
  A stranger has dwelt in the hall of my sire;
Till manhood shall crown me, not mine is the power,
  But his, whose neglect may have bade thee expire.

Oh! hardy thou wert — even now little care
  Might revive thy young head, and thy wounds gently heal:
But thou wert not fated affection to share —
  For who could suppose that a Stranger would feel?

Ah, droop not, my Oak! lift thy head for a while;
  Ere twice round yon Glory this planet shall run,
The hand of thy Master will teach thee to smile,
  When Infancy's years of probation are done.

Oh, live then, my Oak! tow'r aloft from the weeds,
  That clog thy young growth, and assist thy decay,
For still in thy bosom are life's early seeds,
  And still may thy branches their beauty display.

Oh! yet, if maturity's years may be thine,
  Though *I* shall lie low in the cavern of death,
On thy leaves yet the day-beam of ages may shine,
  Uninjured by time, or the rude winter's breath.

For centuries still may thy boughs lightly wave
  O'er the corse of thy lord in thy canopy laid;
While the branches thus gratefully shelter his grave,
  The chief who survives may recline in thy shade.

And as he, with his boys, shall revisit this spot,
  He will tell them in whispers more softly to tread.
Oh! surely, by these I shall ne'er be forgot:
  Remembrance still hallows the dust of the dead.

And here, will they say, when in life's glowing prime,
  Perhaps he has pour'd forth his young simple lay,
And here must he sleep, till the moments of time
  Are lost in the hours of Eternity's day.

1807. [First published 1832.]

## ON REVISITING HARROW.*

Here once engaged the stranger's view
  Young Friendship's record simply traced;
Few were her words, — but yet, though few,
  Resentment's hand the line defaced.

Deeply she cut — but not erased,
  The characters were still so plain,
That Friendship once return'd, and gazed, —
  Till Memory hail'd the words again.

Repentance placed them as before;
  Forgiveness join'd her gentle name;
So fair the inscription seem'd once more,
  That Friendship thought it still the same.

---

* Some years ago, when at Harrow, a friend of the author engraved on a particular spot the names of both, with a few additional words, as a memorial. Afterwards, on receiving some real or imagined injury, the author destroyed the frail record before he left Harrow. On revisiting the place in 1807, he wrote under it these stanzas.

Thus might the Record now have been;
  But, ah, in spite of Hope's endeavour,
Or Friendship's tears, Pride rush'd between,
  And blotted out the line for ever!

*September, 1807.*

---

### EPITAPH ON JOHN ADAMS, OF SOUTHWELL,

#### A CARRIER, WHO DIED OF DRUNKENNESS.

John Adams lies here, of the parish of Southwell,
A *Carrier* who *carried* his can to his mouth well;
He *carried* so much, and he *carried* so fast,
He could *carry* no more — so was *carried* at last;
For, the liquor he drank, being too much for one,
He could not *carry* off, — so he's now *carri-on*.

*September, 1807.*

---

### TO MY SON.

Those flaxen locks, those eyes of blue,
Bright as thy mother's in their hue;
Those rosy lips, whose dimples play
And smile to steal the heart away,
Recall a scene of former joy,
And touch thy father's heart, my Boy!

And thou canst lisp a father's name —
Ah, William, were thine own the same, —
No self-reproach — but, let me cease —
My care for thee shall purchase peace;
Thy mother's shade shall smile in joy,
And pardon all the past, my Boy!

Her lowly grave the turf has prest,
And thou hast known a stranger's breast.

Derision sneers upon thy birth,
And yields thee scarce a name on earth;
Yet shall not these one hope destroy, —
A Father's heart is thine, my Boy!

Why, let the world unfeeling frown,
Must I fond Nature's claim disown?
Ah, no — though moralists reprove,
I hail thee, dearest child of love,
Fair cherub, pledge of youth and joy —
A Father guards thy birth, my Boy!

Oh, 'twill be sweet in thee to trace,
Ere age has wrinkled o'er my face,
Ere half my glass of life is run,
At once a brother and a son;
And all my wane of years employ
In justice done to thee, my Boy!

Although so young thy heedless sire,
Youth will not damp parental fire;
And, wert thou still less dear to me,
While Helen's form revives in thee,
The breast, which beat to former joy,
Will ne'er desert its pledge, my Boy!

1807.

---

FAREWELL! IF EVER FONDEST PRAYER.

Farewell! if ever fondest prayer
  For other's weal avail'd on high,
Mine will not all be lost in air,
  But waft thy name beyond the sky.
'Twere vain to speak, to weep, to sigh:
  Oh! more than tears of blood can tell,
When wrung from guilt's expiring eye,
  Are in that word — Farewell! — Farewell!

These lips are mute, these eyes are dry;
  But in my breast and in my brain,
Awake the pangs that pass not by,
  The thought that ne'er shall sleep again.
My soul nor deigns nor dares complain,
  Though grief and passion there rebel:
I only know we loved in vain —
  I only feel — Farewell! — Farewell!

1808.

---

### BRIGHT BE THE PLACE OF THY SOUL.

Bright be the place of thy soul!
  No lovelier spirit than thine
E'er burst from its mortal control,
  In the orbs of the blessed to shine.

On earth thou wert all but divine,
  As thy soul shall immortally be;
And our sorrow may cease to repine,
  When we know that thy God is with thee.

Light be the turf of thy tomb!
  May its verdure like emeralds be:
There should not be the shadow of gloom
  In aught that reminds us of thee.

Young flowers and an evergreen tree
  May spring from the spot of thy rest:
But nor cypress nor yew let us see;
  For why should we mourn for the blest?

1808.

---

### WHEN WE TWO PARTED.

When we two parted
  In silence and tears,
Half broken-hearted
  To sever for years,

Pale grew thy cheek and cold,
  Colder thy kiss;
Truly that hour foretold
  Sorrow to this.

The dew of the morning
  Sunk chill on my brow —
It felt like the warning
  Of what I feel now.
Thy vows are all broken,
  And light is thy fame;
I hear thy name spoken,
  And share in its shame.

They name thee before me,
  A knell to mine ear;
A shudder comes o'er me —
  Why wert thou so dear?
They know not I knew thee,
  Who knew thee too well: —
Long, long shall I rue thee,
  Too deeply to tell.

In secret we met —
  In silence I grieve,
That thy heart could forget,
  Thy spirit deceive.
If I should meet thee
  After long years,
How should I greet thee? —
  With silence and tears.

1808.

## TO A YOUTHFUL FRIEND.

Few years have pass'd since thou and I
  Were firmest friends, at least in name,
And childhood's gay sincerity
  Preserved our feelings long the same.

But now, like me, too well thou know'st
    What trifles oft the heart recall;
And those who once have loved the most
    Too soon forget they loved at all.

And such the change the heart displays,
    So frail is early friendship's reign,
A month's brief lapse, perhaps a day's,
    Will view thy mind estranged again.

If so, it never shall be mine
    To mourn the loss of such a heart;
The fault was Nature's fault, not thine,
    Which made thee fickle as thou art.

As rolls the ocean's changing tide,
    So human feelings ebb and flow;
And who would in a breast confide,
    Where stormy passions ever glow?

It boots not that, together bred,
    Our childish days were days of joy:
My spring of life has quickly fled;
    Thou, too, hast ceased to be a boy.

And when we bid adieu to youth,
    Slaves to the specious world's control,
We sigh a long farewell to truth;
    That world corrupts the noblest soul.

Ah, joyous season! when the mind
    Dares all things boldly but to lie;
When thought ere spoke is unconfined,
    And sparkles in the placid eye.

Not so in Man's maturer years,
    When Man himself is but a tool;
When interest sways our hopes and fears,
    And all must love and hate by rule.

With fools in kindred vice the same,
  We learn at length our faults to blend;
And those, and those alone, may claim
  The prostituted name of friend.

Such is the common lot of man:
  Can we then 'scape from folly free?
Can we reverse the general plan,
  Nor be what all in turn must be?

No; for myself, so dark my fate
  Through every turn of life hath been;
Man and the world so much I hate,
  I care not when I quit the scene.

But thou, with spirit frail and light,
  Wilt shine awhile, and pass away;
As glow-worms sparkle through the night,
  But dare not stand the test of day.

Alas! whenever folly calls
  Where parasites and princes meet,
(For cherish'd first in royal halls,
  The welcome vices kindly greet)

Ev'n now thou'rt nightly seen to add
  One insect to the fluttering crowd;
And still thy trifling heart is glad
  To join the vain, and court the proud.

There dost thou glide from fair to fair,
  Still simpering on with eager haste,
As flies along the gay parterre,
  That taint the flowers they scarcely taste.

But say, what nymph will prize the flame
  Which seems, as marshy vapours move,
To flit along from dame to dame,
  An ignis-fatuus gleam of love?

What friend for thee, howe'er inclined,
  Will deign to own a kindred care?
Who will debase his manly mind,
  For friendship every fool may share!

In time forbear; amidst the throng
  No more so base a thing be seen;
No more so idly pass along:
  Be something, any thing, but — mean.

1808.

## LINES INSCRIBED UPON A CUP FORMED FROM A SKULL.

Start not — nor deem my spirit fled:
  In me behold the only skull,
From which, unlike a living head,
  Whatever flows is never dull.

I lived, I loved, I quaff'd, like thee;
  I died: let earth my bones resign:
Fill up — thou canst not injure me;
  The worm hath fouler lips than thine.

Better to hold the sparkling grape,
  Than nurse the earth-worm's slimy brood;
And circle in the goblet's shape
  The drink of Gods, than reptile's food.

Where once my wit, perchance, hath shone,
  In aid of others' let me shine;
And when, alas! our brains are gone,
  What nobler substitute than wine?

Quaff while thou canst: another race,
  When thou and thine like me are sped,
May rescue thee from earth's embrace,
  And rhyme and revel with the dead.

Why not? since through life's little day
  Our heads such sad effects produce;
Redeem'd from worms and wasting clay,
  This chance is theirs, to be of use.

Newstead Abbey, 1808.

## WRITTEN IN 1809—10.

### WELL! THOU ART HAPPY.

Well! thou art happy, and I feel
  That I should thus be happy too;
For still my heart regards thy weal
  Warmly, as it was wont to do.

Thy husband's blest — and 'twill impart
  Some pangs to view his happier lot:
But let them pass — Oh! how my heart
  Would hate him, if he loved thee not!

When late I saw thy favourite child,
  I thought my jealous heart would break;
But when the unconscious infant smiled,
  I kiss'd it for its mother's sake.

I kiss'd it, — and repress'd my sighs,
  Its father in its face to see;
But then it had its mother's eyes,
  And they were all to love and me.

Mary, adieu! I must away:
  While thou art blest I'll not repine;
But near thee I can never stay;
  My heart would soon again be thine.

I deem'd that time, I deem'd that pride
  Had quench'd at length my boyish flame;
Nor knew, till seated by thy side,
  My heart in all, — save hope, — the same.

Yet was I calm: I knew the time
  My breast would thrill before thy look;
But now to tremble were a crime —
  We met, — and not a nerve was shook.

I saw thee gaze upon my face,
  Yet meet with no confusion there:
One only feeling could'st thou trace;
  The sullen calmness of despair.

Away! away! my early dream
  Remembrance never must awake:
Oh! where is Lethe's fabled stream?
  My foolish heart be still, or break.

November 2. 1808.

### INSCRIPTION ON THE MONUMENT OF A NEWFOUNDLAND DOG.*

When some proud son of man returns to earth,
Unknown to glory, but upheld by birth,

---

\* This monument is still a conspicuous ornament in the garden of Newstead. The following is the inscription by which the verses are preceded: —

> "Near this spot
> Are deposited the Remains of one
> Who possessed Beauty without Vanity,
> Strength without Insolence,
> Courage without Ferocity,
> And all the Virtues of Man without his Vices.
> This Praise, which would be unmeaning Flattery
> If inscribed over human ashes,
> Is but a just tribute to the Memory of
> BOATSWAIN, a Dog,
> Who was born at Newfoundland, May, 1803,
> And died at Newstead Abbey, Nov. 18. 1808."

Lord Byron thus announced the death of his favourite to Mr. Hodgson: — "Boatswain is dead! — he expired in a state of madness, on the 18th, after suffering much, yet retaining all the gentleness of his nature to the last; never attempting to do the least injury to any one near him. I have now lost every 'thing except old Murray." By the will which he executed in 1811, he directed that his own body should be buried in a vault in the garden, near his faithful dog. — E.

The sculptor's art exhausts the pomp of woe,
And storied urns record who rests below;
When all is done, upon the tomb is seen,
Not what he was, but what he should have been:
But the poor dog, in life the firmest friend,
The first to welcome, foremost to defend,
Whose honest heart is still his master's own,
Who labours, fights, lives, breathes for him alone,
Unhonour'd falls, unnoticed all his worth,
Denied in heaven the soul he held on earth:
While man, vain insect! hopes to be forgiven,
And claims himself a sole exclusive heaven.
Oh man! thou feeble tenant of an hour,
Debased by slavery, or corrupt by power,
Who knows thee well must quit thee with disgust,
Degraded mass of animated dust!
Thy love is lust, thy friendship all a cheat,
Thy smiles hypocrisy, thy words deceit!
By nature vile, ennobled but by name,
Each kindred brute might bid thee blush for shame.
Ye! who perchance behold this simple urn,
Pass on — it honours none you wish to mourn:
To mark a friend's remains these stones arise;
I never knew but one, — and here he lies.
Newstead Abbey, November 30. 1808.

## TO A LADY, ON BEING ASKED MY REASON FOR QUITTING ENGLAND IN THE SPRING.

When Man, expell'd from Eden's bowers,
 A moment linger'd near the gate,
Each scene recall'd the vanish'd hours,
 And bade him curse his future fate.

But, wandering on through distant climes,
 He learnt to bear his load of grief;
Just gave a sigh to other times,
 And found in busier scenes relief.

Thus, lady! will it be with me,
  And I must view thy charms no more;
For, while I linger near to thee,
  I sigh for all I knew before.

In flight I shall be surely wise,
  Escaping from temptation's snare;
I cannot view my paradise
  Without the wish of dwelling there.

December 2. 1808.

### REMIND ME NOT, REMIND ME NOT.

Remind me not, remind me not,
  Of those beloved, those vanish'd hours
    When all my soul was given to thee;
Hours that may never be forgot,
  Till time unnerves our vital powers,
    And thou and I shall cease to be.

Can I forget — canst thou forget,
  When playing with thy golden hair,
    How quick thy fluttering heart did move?
Oh! by my soul, I see thee yet,
  With eyes so languid, breast so fair,
    And lips, though silent, breathing love.

When thus reclining on my breast,
  Those eyes threw back a glance so sweet,
    As half reproach'd yet raised desire,
And still we near and nearer prest,
  And still our glowing lips would meet,
    As if in kisses to expire.

And then those pensive eyes would close,
  And bid their lids each other seek,
    Veiling the azure orbs below;
While their long lashes' darken'd gloss
  Seem'd stealing o'er thy brilliant cheek,
    Like raven's plumage smooth'd on snow.

I dreamt last night our love return'd,
  And, sooth to say, that very dream
    Was sweeter in its phantasy,
Than if for other hearts I burn'd,
  For eyes that ne'er like thine could beam
    In rapture's wild reality.

Then tell me not, remind me not,
  Of hours which, though for ever gone,
    Can still a pleasing dream restore,
Till thou and I shall be forgot,
  And senseless as the mouldering stone
    Which tells that we shall be no more.

---

### THERE WAS A TIME, I NEED NOT NAME.

There was a time, I need not name,
  Since it will ne'er forgotten be,
When all our feelings were the same
  As still my soul hath been to thee.

And from that hour when first thy tongue
  Confess'd a love which equall'd mine,
Though many a grief my heart hath wrung,
  Unknown and thus unfelt by thine,

None, none hath sunk so deep as this —
  To think how all that love hath flown;
Transient as every faithless kiss,
  But transient in thy breast alone.

And yet my heart some solace knew,
  When late I heard thy lips declare,
In accents once imagined true,
  Remembrance of the days that were.

Yes! my adored, yet most unkind!
  Though thou wilt never love again,
To me 'tis doubly sweet to find
  Remembrance of that love remain.

Yes! 'tis a glorious thought to me,
  Nor longer shall my soul repine,
Whate'er thou art or e'er shalt be,
  Thou hast been dearly, solely mine.

## AND WILT THOU WEEP WHEN I AM LOW?

And wilt thou weep when I am low?
  Sweet lady! speak those words again:
Yet if they grieve thee, say not so —
  I would not give that bosom pain.

My heart is sad, my hopes are gone,
  My blood runs coldly through my breast;
And when I perish, thou alone
  Wilt sigh above my place of rest.

And yet, methinks, a gleam of peace
  Doth through my cloud of anguish shine;
And for awhile my sorrows cease,
  To know thy heart hath felt for mine.

Oh lady! blessed be that tear —
  It falls for one who cannot weep:
Such precious drops are doubly dear
  To those whose eyes no tear may steep.

Sweet lady! once my heart was warm
  With every feeling soft as thine;
But beauty's self hath ceased to charm
  A wretch created to repine

Yet wilt thou weep when I am low?
  Sweet lady! speak those words again;
Yet if they grieve thee, say not so —
  I would not give that bosom pain.

## FILL THE GOBLET AGAIN.

### A SONG.

Fill the goblet again! for I never before
Felt the glow which now gladdens my heart to its core;
Let us drink! — who would not? — since, through life's varied
   round,
In the goblet alone no deception is found.

I have tried in its turn all that life can supply;
I have bask'd in the beam of a dark rolling eye;
I have loved! — who has not? — but what heart can declare,
That pleasure existed while passion was there?

In the days of my youth, when the heart's in its spring,
And dreams that affection can never take wing,
I had friends! — who has not? — but what tongue will avow,
That friends, rosy wine! are so faithful as thou?

The heart of a mistress some boy may estrange,
Friendship shifts with the sunbeam — thou never cans
   change:
Thou grow'st old — who does not? — but on earth what
   appears,
Whose virtues, like thine, still increase with its years?

Yet if blest to the utmost that love can bestow,
Should a rival bow down to our idol below,
We are jealous! — who's not? — thou hast no such alloy;
For the more that enjoy thee, the more we enjoy.

Then the season of youth and its vanities past,
For refuge we fly to the goblet at last;
There we find — do we not? — in the flow of the soul,
That truth, as of yore, is confined to the bowl.

When the box of Pandora was open'd on earth,
And Misery's triumph commenced over Mirth,
Hope was left, — was she not? — but the goblet we kiss,
And care not for Hope, who are certain of bliss.

Long life to the grape! for when summer is flown,
The age of our nectar shall gladden our own:
We must die — who shall not? — May our sins be forgiven,
And Hebe shall never be idle in heaven.

### STANZAS TO A LADY*, ON LEAVING ENGLAND.

'Tis done — and shivering in the gale
The bark unfurls her snowy sail;
And whistling o'er the bending mast,
Loud sings on high the fresh'ning blast;
And I must from this land be gone,
Because I cannot love but one.

But could I be what I have been,
And could I see what I have seen —
Could I repose upon the breast
Which once my warmest wishes blest —
I should not seek another zone,
Because I cannot love but one.

'Tis long since I beheld that eye
Which gave me bliss or misery;
And I have striven, but in vain,
Never to think of it again:
For though I fly from Albion,
I still can only love but one.

As some lone bird, without a mate,
My weary heart is desolate;
I look around, and cannot trace
One friendly smile or welcome face,
And ev'n in crowds am still alone,
Because I cannot love but one.

And I will cross the whitening foam,
And I will seek a foreign home;

* Mrs. Musters.

Till I forget a false fair face,
I ne'er shall find a resting-place;
My own dark thoughts I cannot shun,
But ever love, and love but one.

The poorest, veriest wretch on earth
Still finds some hospitable hearth,
Where friendship's or love's softer glow
May smile in joy or soothe in woe;
But friend or leman I have none,
Because I cannot love but one.

I go — but wheresoe'er I flee,
There's not an eye will weep for me;
There's not a kind congenial heart,
Where I can claim the meanest part;
Nor thou, who hast my hopes undone,
Wilt sigh, although I love but one.

To think of every early scene,
Of what we are, and what we 've been,
Would whelm some softer hearts with woe —
But mine, alas! has stood the blow;
Yet still beats on as it begun,
And never truly loves but one.

And who that dear loved one may be
Is not for vulgar eyes to see,
And why that early love was crost,
Thou know'st the best, I feel the most;
But few that dwell beneath the sun
Have loved so long, and loved but one.

I 've tried another's fetters too,
With charms perchance as fair to view;
And I would fain have loved as well,
But some unconquerable spell
Forbade my bleeding breast to own
A kindred care for aught but one.

'Twould soothe to take one lingering view,
And bless thee in my last adieu;
Yet wish I not those eyes to weep
For him that wanders o'er the deep;
His home, his hope, his youth are gone,
Yet still he loves, and loves but one.

1809.

### LINES TO MR. HODGSON.
#### WRITTEN ON BOARD THE LISBON PACKET.

Huzza! Hodgson, we are going,
  Our embargo's off at last;
Favourable breezes blowing
  Bend the canvas o'er the mast.
From aloft the signal's streaming,
  Hark! the farewell gun is fired;
Women screeching, tars blaspheming,
  Tell us that our time's expired.
      Here's a rascal
      Come to task all,
Prying from the custom-house;
      Trunks unpacking,
      Cases cracking,
Not a corner for a mouse
'Scapes unsearch'd amid the racket,
Ere we sail on board the Packet.

Now our boatmen quit their mooring,
  And all hands must ply the oar;
Baggage from the quay is lowering,
  We're impatient — push from shore.
"Have a care! that case holds liquor —
  Stop the boat — I'm sick — oh Lord!"
"Sick, ma'am, damme, you'll be sicker,
  Ere you've been an hour on board."
      Thus are screaming
      Men and women,

Gemmen, ladies, servants, Jacks;
  Here entangling,
  All are wrangling,
Stuck together close as wax. —
Such the general noise and racket,
Ere we reach the Lisbon Packet.

Now we've reach'd her, lo! the captain,
  Gallant Kidd, commands the crew;
Passengers their births are clapt in,
  Some to grumble, some to spew.
"Hey day! call you that a cabin?
Why 'tis hardly three feet square;
Not enough to stow Queen Mab in —
  Who the deuce can harbour there?"
    "Who, sir? plenty —
    Nobles twenty
Did at once my vessel fill."
    "Did they? Jesus,
    How you squeeze us!
Would to God they did so still:
Then I'd scape the heat and racket
Of the good ship, Lisbon Packet."

Fletcher! Murray! Bob! where are you?
  Stretch'd along the deck like logs —
Bear a hand, you jolly tar, you!
  Here's a rope's end for the dogs.
Hobhouse muttering fearful curses,
  As the hatchway down he rolls,
Now his breakfast, now his verses,
  Vomits forth — and damns our souls.
    "Here's a stanza
    On Braganza —
Help!" — "A couplet?" — "No, a cup
    Of warm water —"
    "What's the matter?"
"Zounds! my liver's coming up;

I shall not survive the racket
Of this brutal Lisbon Packet."

Now at length we're off for Turkey,
  Lord knows when we shall come back!
Breezes foul and tempests murky
  May unship us in a crack.
But, since life at most a jest is,
  As philosophers allow,
Still to laugh by far the best is,
  Then laugh on — as I do now.
    Laugh at all things,
    Great and small things,
  Sick or well, at sea or shore;
    While we're quaffing,
    Let's have laughing —
Who the devil cares for more? —
Some good wine! and who would lack it,
Ev'n on board the Lisbon Packet?
Falmouth Roads, June 30. 1809.

### LINES WRITTEN IN AN ALBUM, AT MALTA.

As o'er the cold sepulchral stone
  Some name arrests the passer-by;
Thus, when thou view'st this page alone,
  May mine attract thy pensive eye!

And when by thee that name is read,
  Perchance in some succeeding year,
Reflect on me as on the dead,
  And think my heart is buried here.
September 14. 1809.

### TO FLORENCE.

Oh Lady! when I left the shore,
  The distant shore which gave me birth,
I hardly thought to grieve once more,
  To quit another spot on earth:

Yet here, amidst this barren isle,
  Where panting Nature droops the head,
Where only thou art seen to smile,
  I view my parting hour with dread.

Though far from Albion's craggy shore,
  Divided by the dark-blue main;
A few, brief rolling seasons o'er,
  Perchance I view her cliffs again:

But wheresoe'er I now may roam,
  Through scorching clime, and varied sea,
Though Time restore me to my home,
  I ne'er shall bend mine eyes on thee:

On thee, in whom at once conspire
  All charms which heedless hearts can move,
Whom but to see is to admire,
  And, oh! forgive the word — to love.

Forgive the word, in one who ne'er
  With such a word can more offend;
And since thy heart I cannot share,
  Believe me, what I am, thy friend.

And who so cold as look on thee,
  Thou lovely wand'rer, and be less?
Nor be, what man should ever be,
  The friend of Beauty in distress?

Ah! who would think that form had past
  Through Danger's most destructive path,
Had braved the death-wing'd tempest's blast,
  And 'scaped a tyrant's fiercer wrath?

Lady! when I shall view the walls
  Where free Byzantium once arose,
And Stamboul's Oriental halls
  The Turkish tyrants now enclose;

Though mightiest in the lists of fame,
  That glorious city still shall be;
On me 'twill hold a dearer claim,
  As spot of thy nativity!

And though I bid thee now farewell,
  When I behold that wond'rous scene,
Since where thou art I may not dwell,
  'Twill soothe to be, where thou hast been.
                                September, 1809.

## STANZAS

#### COMPOSED DURING A THUNDERSTORM.

Chill and mirk is the nightly blast,
  Where Pindus' mountains rise,
And angry clouds are pouring fast
  The vengeance of the skies.

Our guides are gone, our hope is lost,
  And lightnings, as they play,
But show where rocks our path have crost,
  Or gild the torrent's spray.

Is yon a cot I saw, though low?
  When lightning broke the gloom —
How welcome were its shade! — ah, no!
  'Tis but a Turkish tomb.

Through sounds of foaming waterfalls,
  I hear a voice exclaim —
My way-worn countryman, who calls
  On distant England's name.

A shot is fired — by foe or friend?
  Another — 'tis to tell
The mountain-peasants to descend,
  And lead us where they dwell.

Oh! who in such a night will dare
  To tempt the wilderness?
And who 'mid thunder peals can hear
  Our signal of distress?

And who that heard our shouts would rise
  To try the dubious road?
Nor rather deem from nightly cries
  That outlaws were abroad.

Clouds burst, skies flash, oh, dreadful hour!
  More fiercely pours the storm!
Yet here one thought has still the power
  To keep my bosom warm.

While wand'ring through each broken path,
  O'er brake and craggy brow;
While elements exhaust their wrath,
  Sweet Florence, where art thou?

Not on the sea, not on the sea,
  Thy bark hath long been gone:
Oh, may the storm that pours on me,
  Bow down my head alone!

Full swiftly blew the swift Siroc,
  When last I press'd thy lip;
And long ere now, with foaming shock,
  Impell'd thy gallant ship.

Now thou art safe; nay, long ere now
  Hast trod the shore of Spain;
'Twere hard if aught so fair as thou
  Should linger on the main.

And since I now remember thee
  In darkness and in dread,
As in those hours of revelry
  Which mirth and music sped;

Do thou, amid the fair white walls,
  If Cadiz yet be free,
At times from out her latticed halls
  Look o'er the dark blue sea;

Then think upon Calypso's isles,
  Endear'd by days gone by;
To others give a thousand smiles,
  To me a single sigh.

And when the admiring circle mark
  The paleness of thy face,
A half-form'd tear, a transient spark
  Of melancholy grace,

Again thou'lt smile, and blushing shun
  Some coxcomb's raillery;
Nor own for once thou thought'st of one,
  Who ever thinks on thee.

Though smile and sigh alike are vain,
  When sever'd hearts repine,
My spirit flies o'er mount and main,
  And mourns in search of thine.

### STANZAS

#### WRITTEN IN PASSING THE AMBRACIAN GULF.

Through cloudless skies, in silvery sheen,
  Full beams the moon on Actium's coast:
And on these waves, for Egypt's queen,
  The ancient world was won and lost.

And now upon the scene I look,
  The azure grave of many a Roman;
Where stern Ambition once forsook
  His wavering crown to follow woman.

Florence! whom I will love as well
  As ever yet was said or sung,
(Since Orpheus sang his spouse from hell)
  Whilst thou art fair and I am young;

Sweet Florence! those were pleasant times,
  When worlds were staked for ladies' eyes:
Had bards as many realms as rhymes,
  Thy charms might raise new Antonies.

Though Fate forbids such things to be:
  Yet, by thine eyes and ringlets curl'd!
I cannot lose a world for thee,
  But would not lose thee for a world.
November 14. 1809.

---

### THE SPELL IS BROKE, THE CHARM IS FLOWN!

#### WRITTEN AT ATHENS, JANUARY 16. 1810.

The spell is broke, the charm is flown!
  Thus is it with life's fitful fever:
We madly smile when we should groan;
  Delirium is our best deceiver.

Each lucid interval of thought
  Recalls the woes of Nature's charter,
And he that acts as wise men ought,
  But lives, as saints have died, a martyr.

## WRITTEN AFTER SWIMMING FROM SESTOS TO ABYDOS.*

If, in the month of dark December,
  Leander, who was nightly wont
(What maid will not the tale remember?)
  To cross thy stream, broad Hellespont!

If, when the wintry tempest roar'd,
  He sped to Hero, nothing loth,
And thus of old thy current pour'd,
  Fair Venus! how I pity both!

For *me*, degenerate modern wretch,
  Though in the genial month of May,
My dripping limbs I faintly stretch,
  And think I've done a feat to-day.

---

* On the 3d of May, 1810, while the Salsette (Captain Bathurst) was lying in the Dardanelles, Lieutenant Ekenhead, of that frigate and the writer of these rhymes swam from the European shore to the Asiatic — by the by, from Abydos to Sestos would have been more correct. The whole distance, from the place whence we started to our landing on the other side, including the length we were carried by the current, was computed by those on board the frigate at upwards of four English miles; though the actual breadth is barely one. The rapidity of the current is such that no boat can row directly across, and it may, in some measure, be estimated from the circumstance of the whole distance being accomplished by one of the parties in an hour and five, and by the other in an hour and ten, minutes. The water was extremely cold, from the melting of the mountain snows. About three weeks before, in April, we had made an attempt; but, having ridden all the way from the Troad the same morning, and the water being of an icy chiliness, we found it necessary to postpone the completion till the frigate anchored below the castles, when we swam the straits, as just stated; entering a considerable way above the European, and landing below the Asiatic, fort. Chevalier says that a young Jew swam the same distance for his mistress; and Oliver mentions its having been done by a Neapolitan; but our consul, Tarragona, remembered neither of those circumstances, and tried to dissuade us from the attempt. A number of the Salsette's crew were known to have accomplished a greater distance; and the only thing that surprised me was, that, as doubts had been entertained of the truth of Leander's story, no traveller had ever endeavoured to ascertain its practicability.

But since he cross'd the rapid tide,
  According to the doubtful story,
To woo, — and — Lord knows what beside,
  And swam for Love, as I for Glory;

'Twere hard to say who fared the best:
  Sad mortals! thus the Gods still plague you!
He lost his labour, I my jest:
  For he was drown'd, and I've the ague.

May 9. 1810.

---

## MAID OF ATHENS, ERE WE PART.

*Ζώη μοῦ, σᾶς ἀγαπῶ.*

Maid of Athens, ere we part,
Give, oh, give me back my heart!
Or, since that has left my breast,
Keep it now, and take the rest!
Hear my vow before I go,
*Ζώη μοῦ, σᾶς ἀγαπῶ.*\*

By those tresses unconfined,
Woo'd by each Ægean wind;
By those lids whose jetty fringe
Kiss thy soft cheeks' blooming tinge;
By those wild eyes like the roe,
*Ζώη μοῦ, σᾶς ἀγαπῶ.*

---

\* Romaic expression of tenderness: If I translate it, I shall affront the gentlemen, as it may seem that I supposed they could not; and if I do not, I may affront the ladies. For fear of any misconstruction on the part of the latter, I shall do so, begging pardon of the learned. It means, "My life, I love you!" which sounds very prettily in all languages, and is as much in fashion in Greece at this day as, Juvenal tells us, the two first words were amongst the Roman ladies, whose erotic expressions were all Hellenised.

By that lip I long to taste;
By that zone-encircled waist;
By all the token-flowers* that tell
What words can never speak so well;
By love's alternate joy and woe,
Ζωή μοῦ, σᾶς ἀγαπῶ.

Maid of Athens! I am gone:
Think of me, sweet! when alone.
Though I fly to Istambol,**
Athens holds my heart and soul:
Can I cease to love thee? No!
Ζωή μοῦ, σᾶς ἀγαπῶ.

Athens, 1810.

* In the East (where ladies are not taught to write, lest they should scribble assignations) flowers, cinders, pebbles, &c. convey the sentiments of the parties by that universal deputy of Mercury — an old woman. A cinder says, "I burn for thee;" a bunch of flowers tied with hair, "Take me and fly;" but a pebble declares — what nothing else can.

** Constantinople.

## WRITTEN IN 1811—1813.

### LINES WRITTEN BENEATH A PICTURE.

Dear object of defeated care!
  Though now of Love and thee bereft,
To reconcile me with despair,
  Thine image and my tears are left.

'Tis said with Sorrow Time can cope;
  But this I feel can ne'er be true:
For by the death-blow of my Hope
  My Memory immortal grew.

Athens, January, 1811.

### SUBSTITUTE FOR AN EPITAPH.

Kind Reader! take your choice to cry or laugh;
Here Harold lies — but where's his Epitaph?
If such you seek, try Westminster, and view
Ten thousand just as fit for him as you.

Athens.

### TRANSLATION OF THE FAMOUS GREEK WAR SONG,

"Δεῦτε παῖδες τῶν Ἑλλήνων."*

Sons of the Greeks, arise!
  The glorious hour's gone forth,
And, worthy of such ties,
  Display who gave us birth.

#### CHORUS.

Sons of Greeks! let us go
  In arms against the foe,
'Till their hated blood shall flow
  In a river past our feet.

* The song Δεῦτε παῖδες, &c., was written by Riga, who perished in the attempt to revolutionise Greece. This translation is as literal as the author could make it in verse. It is of the same measure as that of the original.

Then manfully despising
  The Turkish tyrant's yoke,
Let your country see you rising,
  And all her chains are broke.
Brave shades of chiefs and sages,
  Behold the coming strife!
Hellénes of past ages,
  Oh, start again to life!
At the sound of my trumpet, breaking
  Your sleep, oh, join with me!
And the seven-hill'd \* city seeking,
  Fight, conquer, till we're free.
                    Sons of Greeks, &c.

Sparta, Sparta, why in slumbers
  Lethargic dost thou lie?
Awake, and join thy numbers
  With Athens, old ally!
Leonidas recalling,
  That chief of ancient song,
Who saved ye once from falling,
  The terrible! the strong!
Who made that bold diversion
  In old Thermopylæ,
And warring with the Persian
  To keep his country free;
With his three hundred waging
  The battle, long he stood,
And like a lion raging,
  Expired in seas of blood.
                    Sons of Greeks, &c.

  \* Constantinople. "Ἑπτάλοφος."

## TRANSLATION OF THE ROMAIC SONG,

"*Μπενω μες 'το' περιβόλι*
*'Ωραιότατη Χάηδή,*" &c.*

I enter thy garden of roses,
  Beloved and fair Haidée,
Each morning where Flora reposes,
  For surely I see her in thee.
Oh, Lovely! thus low I implore thee,
  Receive this fond truth from my tongue,
Which utters its song to adore thee,
  Yet trembles for what it has sung;
As the branch, at the bidding of Nature,
  Adds fragrance and fruit to the tree,
Through her eyes, through her every feature,
  Shines the soul of the young Haidée.

But the loveliest garden grows hateful
  When Love has abandon'd the bowers;
Bring me hemlock — since mine is ungrateful,
  That herb is more fragrant than flowers.
The poison, when pour'd from the chalice,
  Will deeply embitter the bowl;
But when drunk to escape from thy malice,
  The draught shall be sweet to my soul.
Too cruel! in vain I implore thee
  My heart from these horrors to save:
Will nought to my bosom restore thee?
  Then open the gates of the grave.

As the chief who to combat advances,
  Secure of his conquest before,
Thus thou, with those eyes for thy lances,
  Hast pierced through my heart to its core.

---

* The song from which this is taken is a great favourite with the young girls of Athens of all classes. Their manner of singing it is by verses in rotation, the whole number present joining in the chorus. I have heard it frequently at our "χόροι," in the winter of 1810-11. The air is plaintive and pretty.

Ah, tell me, my soul! must I perish
  By pangs which a smile would dispel?
Would the hope, which thou once bad'st me cherish,
  For torture repay me too well?
Now sad is the garden of roses,
  Beloved but false Haidée!
There Flora all wither'd reposes,
  And mourns o'er thine absence with me.

---

## LINES IN THE TRAVELLERS' BOOK AT ORCHOMENUS.

### IN THIS BOOK A TRAVELLER HAD WRITTEN:—

"Fair Albion, smiling, sees her son depart
To trace the birth and nursery of art:
Noble his object, glorious is his aim;
He comes to Athens, and he writes his name."

### BENEATH WHICH LORD BYRON INSERTED THE FOLLOWING:—

The modest bard, like many a bard unknown,
Rhymes on our names, but wisely hides his own;
But yet, whoe'er he be, to say no worse,
His name would bring more credit than his verse.

---

## ON PARTING.

The kiss, dear maid! thy lip has left
  Shall never part from mine,
Till happier hours restore the gift
  Untainted back to thine.

Thy parting glance, which fondly beams,
  An equal love may see:
The tear that from thine eyelid streams
  Can weep no change in me.

I ask no pledge to make me blest
  In gazing when alone;
Nor one memorial for a breast,
  Whose thoughts are all thine own.

Nor need I write — to tell the tale
  My pen were doubly weak:
Oh! what can idle words avail,
  Unless the heart could speak?

By day or night, in weal or woe,
  That heart, no longer free,
Must bear the love it cannot show
  And silent ache for thee.

March, 1811.

### EPITAPH FOR JOSEPH BLACKETT, LATE POET AND SHOEMAKER.

STRANGER! behold, interr'd together,
The *souls* of learning and of leather.
Poor Joe is gone, but left his *all:*
You'll find his relics in a *stall.*
His works were neat, and often found
Well stitch'd, and with *morocco* bound.
'Tread lightly — where the bard is laid
He cannot mend the shoe he made;
Yet is he happy in his hole,
With verse immortal as his *sole.*
But still to business he held fast,
And stuck to Phœbus to the last.
Then who shall say so good a fellow
Was only "leather and prunella?"
For character — he did not lack it;
And if he did, 'twere shame to "Black-it."

Malta, May 16. 1811.

## ON MOORE'S LAST OPERATIC FARCE, OR FARCICAL OPERA.

Good plays are scarce,
So Moore writes farce:
The poet's fame grows brittle —
We knew before
That *Little*'s Moore,
But now 'tis *Moore* that's *little*.

September 14. 1811.

## EPISTLE TO A FRIEND,

### IN ANSWER TO SOME LINES EXHORTING THE AUTHOR TO BE CHEERFUL, AND TO "BANISH CARE."

"Oh! banish care" — such ever be
The motto of *thy* revelry!
Perchance of *mine*, when wassail nights
Renew those riotous delights,
Wherewith the children of Despair
Lull the lone heart, and "banish care."
But not in morn's reflecting hour,
When present, past, and future lower,
When all I loved is changed or gone,
Mock with such taunts the woes of one,
Whose every thought — but let them pass —
Thou know'st I am not what I was.
But, above all, if thou wouldst hold
Place in a heart that ne'er was cold,
By all the powers that men revere,
By all unto thy bosom dear,
Thy joys below, thy hopes above,
Speak — speak of any thing but love.

'Twere long to tell, and vain to hear,
The tale of one who scorns a tear;
And there is little in that tale
Which better bosoms would bewail.

But mine has suffer'd more than well
"I" would suit philosophy to tell.
I've seen my bride another's bride, —
Have seen her seated by his side, —
Have seen the infant, which she bore,
Wear the sweet smile the mother wore,
When she and I in youth have smiled,
As fond and faultless as her child; —
Have seen her eyes, in cold disdain,
Ask if I felt no secret pain;
And *I* have acted well my part,
And made my cheek belie my heart,
Return'd the freezing glance she gave,
Yet felt the while *that* woman's slave; —
Have kiss'd, as if without design,
The babe which ought to have been mine,
And show'd, alas! in each caress
Time had not made me love the less.

But let this pass — I'll whine no more,
Nor seek again an eastern shore;
The world befits a busy brain, —
I'll hie me to its haunts again.
But if, in some succeeding year,
When Britain's "May is in the sere,"
Thou hear'st of one, whose deepening crimes
Suit with the sablest of the times,
Of one, whom love nor pity sways,
Nor hope of fame, nor good men's praise;
One, who in stern ambition's pride,
Perchance not blood shall turn aside,
One rank'd in some recording page
With the worst anarchs of the age,
Him wilt thou *know* — and *knowing* pause,
Nor with the *effect* forget the cause.
Newstead Abbey, Oct. 11. 1811.

## TO THYRZA.

Without a stone to mark the spot,
  And say, what Truth might well have said,
By all, save one, perchance forgot,
  Ah! wherefore art thou lowly laid?

By many a shore and many a sea
  Divided, yet beloved in vain;
The past, the future fled to thee
  To bid us meet — no — ne'er again!

Could this have been — a word, a look
  That softly said, "We part in peace,"
Had taught my bosom how to brook,
  With fainter sighs, thy soul's release.

And didst thou not, since Death for thee
  Prepared a light and pangless dart,
Once long for him thou ne'er shalt see,
  Who held, and holds thee in his heart?

Oh! who like him had watch'd thee here?
  Or sadly mark'd thy glazing eye,
In that dread hour ere death appear,
  When silent sorrow fears to sigh,

Till all was past? But when no more
  'Twas thine to reck of human woe,
Affection's heart-drops, gushing o'er,
  Had flow'd as fast — as now they flow.

Shall they not flow, when many a day
  In these, to me, deserted towers,
Ere call'd but for a time away,
  Affection's mingling tears were ours?

Ours too the glance none saw beside;
  The smile none else might understand;
The whisper'd thought of hearts allied,
  The pressure of the thrilling hand;

The kiss, so guiltless and refined
   That Love each warmer wish forbore;
Those eyes proclaim'd so pure a mind,
   Even passion blush'd to plead for more.

The tone, that taught me to rejoice,
   When prone, unlike thee, to repine;
The song, celestial from thy voice,
   But sweet to me from none but thine;

The pledge we wore — I wear it still,
   But where is thine? — Ah! where art thou?
Oft have I borne the weight of ill,
   But never bent beneath till now!

Well hast thou left in life's best bloom
   The cup of woe for me to drain.
If rest alone be in the tomb,
   I would not wish thee here again;

But if in worlds more blest than this
   Thy virtues seek a fitter sphere,
Impart some portion of thy bliss,
   To wean me from mine anguish here.

Teach me — too early taught by thee!
   To bear, forgiving and forgiven:
On earth thy love was such to me;
   It fain would form my hope in heaven!
                              October 11. 1811.

## STANZAS.
### ["AWAY, AWAY," &c.]

Away, away, ye notes of woe!
   Be silent, thou once soothing strain,
Or I must flee from hence — for, oh!
   I dare not trust those sounds again.

To me they speak of brighter days —
   But lull the chords, for now, alas!
I must not think, I may not gaze
   On what I am — on what I was.

The voice that made those sounds more sweet
   Is hush'd, and all their charms are fled;
And now their softest notes repeat
   A dirge, an anthem o'er the dead!
Yes, Thyrza! yes, they breathe of thee,
   Beloved dust! since dust thou art;
And all that once was harmony
   Is worse than discord to my heart!

'Tis silent all! — but on my ear
   The well remember'd echoes thrill;
I hear a voice I would not hear,
   A voice that now might well be still:
Yet oft my doubting soul 'twill shake;
   Even slumber owns its gentle tone,
Till consciousness will vainly wake
   To listen, though the dream be flown.

Sweet Thyrza! waking as in sleep,
   Thou art but now a lovely dream;
A star that trembled o'er the deep,
   Then turn'd from earth its tender beam.
But he who through life's dreary way
   Must pass, when heaven is veil'd in wrath,
Will long lament the vanish'd ray
   That scatter'd gladness o'er his path.

December 6. 1811.

### STANZAS.

["ONE STRUGGLE MORE," &c.]

One struggle more, and I am free
   From pangs that rend my heart in twain;
One last long sigh to love and thee,
   Then back to busy life again.

## OCCASIONAL PIECES.

It suits me well to mingle now
  With things that never pleased before:
Though every joy is fled below,
  What future grief can touch me more?

Then bring me wine, the banquet bring;
  Man was not form'd to live alone:
I'll be that light, unmeaning thing
  That smiles with all, and weeps with none.
It was not thus in days more dear,
  It never would have been, but thou
Hast fled, and left me lonely here;
  Thou 'rt nothing,—all are nothing now.

In vain my lyre would lightly breathe!
  The smile that sorrow fain would wear
But mocks the woe that lurks beneath,
  Like roses o'er a sepulchre.
Though gay companions o'er the bowl
  Dispel awhile the sense of ill;
Though pleasure fires the maddening soul,
  The heart — the heart is lonely still!

On many a lone and lovely night
  It sooth'd to gaze upon the sky;
For then I deem'd the heavenly light
  Shone sweetly on thy pensive eye:
And oft I thought at Cynthia's noon,
  When sailing o'er the Ægean wave,
"Now Thyrza gazes on that moon —"
  Alas, it gleam'd upon her grave!

When stretch'd on fever's sleepless bed,
  And sickness shrunk my throbbing veins,
"'Tis comfort still," I faintly said,
  "That Thyrza cannot know my pains:"
Like freedom to the time-worn slave,
  A boon 'tis idle then to give,
Relenting Nature vainly gave
  My life, when Thyrza ceased to live!

My Thyrza's pledge in better days,
  When love and life alike were new!
How different now thou meet'st my gaze!
  How tinged by time with sorrow's hue!
The heart that gave itself with thee
  Is silent — ah, were mine as still!
Though cold as e'en the dead can be,
  It feels, it sickens with the chill.

Thou bitter pledge! thou mournful token!
  Though painful, welcome to my breast!
Still, still, preserve that love unbroken,
  Or break the heart to which thou 'rt press'd!
Time tempers love, but not removes,
  More hallow'd when its hope is fled:
Oh! what are thousand living loves
  To that which cannot quit the dead?

### EUTHANASIA.

When Time, or soon or late, shall bring
  The dreamless sleep that lulls the dead,
Oblivion! may thy languid wing
  Wave gently o'er my dying bed!

No band of friends or heirs be there,
  To weep, or wish, the coming blow:
No maiden, with dishevell'd hair,
  To feel, or feign, decorous woe.

But silent let me sink to earth,
  With no officious mourners near:
I would not mar one hour of mirth,
  Nor startle friendship with a fear.

Yet Love, if Love in such an hour
  Could nobly check its useless sighs,
Might then exert its latest power
  In her who lives and him who dies.

'Twere sweet, my Psyche! to the last
  Thy features still serene to see:
Forgetful of its struggles past,
  E'en Pain itself should smile on thee.

But vain the wish — for Beauty still
  Will shrink, as shrinks the ebbing breath;
And woman's tears, produced at will,
  Deceive in life, unman in death.

Then lonely be my latest hour,
  Without regret, without a groan;
For thousands Death hath ceased to lower,
  And pain been transient or unknown.

"Ay, but to die, and go," alas!
  Where all have gone, and all must go!
To be the nothing that I was
  Ere born to life and living woe!

Count o'er the joys thine hours have seen,
  Count o'er thy days from anguish free,
And know, whatever thou hast been,
  'Tis something better not to be.

---

### STANZAS.

["AND THOU ART DEAD," &c.]

"Heu, quanto minus est cum reliquis versari quam tui meminisse!"

AND thou art dead, as young and fair
  As aught of mortal birth;
And form so soft, and charms so rare,
  Too soon return'd to Earth!
Though Earth received them in her bed,
And o'er the spot the crowd may tread
  In carelessness or mirth,
There is an eye which could not brook
A moment on that grave to look.

I will not ask where thou liest low,
   Nor gaze upon the spot;
There flowers or weeds at will may grow,
   So I behold them not:
It is enough for me to prove
That what I loved, and long must love,
   Like common earth can rot;
To me there needs no stone to tell,
'Tis Nothing that I loved so well.

Yet did I love thee to the last
   As fervently as thou,
Who didst not change through all the past,
   And canst not alter now.
The love where Death has set his seal,
Nor age can chill, nor rival steal,
   Nor falsehood disavow:
And, what were worse, thou canst not see
Or wrong, or change, or fault in me.

The better days of life were ours;
   The worst can be but mine:
The sun that cheers, the storm that lowers,
   Shall never more be thine.
The silence of that dreamless sleep
I envy now too much to weep;
   Nor need I to repine
That all those charms have pass'd away;
I might have watch'd through long decay.

The flower in ripen'd bloom unmatch'd
   Must fall the earliest prey;
Though by no hand untimely snatch'd,
   The leaves must drop away:
And yet it were a greater grief
To watch it withering, leaf by leaf,
   Than see it pluck'd to-day;
Since earthly eye but ill can bear
To trace the change to foul from fair.

I know not if I could have borne
  To see thy beauties fade;
The night that follow'd such a morn
  Had worn a deeper shade:
Thy day without a cloud hath pass'd,
And thou wert lovely to the last;
  Extinguish'd, not decay'd;
As stars that shoot along the sky
Shine brightest as they fall from high.

As once I wept, if I could weep,
  My tears might well be shed,
To think I was not near to keep
  One vigil o'er thy bed;
To gaze, how fondly! on thy face,
To fold thee in a faint embrace,
  Uphold thy drooping head;
And show that love, however vain,
Nor thou nor I can feel again.

Yet how much less it were to gain,
  Though thou hast left me free,
The loveliest things that still remain,
  Than thus remember thee!
The all of thine that cannot die
Through dark and dread Eternity
  Returns again to me,
And more thy buried love endears
Than aught, except its living years.
February, 1812.

---

## STANZAS.

["IF SOMETIMES," &c.]

IF sometimes in the haunts of men
  Thine image from my breast may fade,
The lonely hour presents again
  The semblance of thy gentle shade:

And now that sad and silent hour
  Thus much of thee can still restore,
And sorrow unobserved may pour
  The plaint she dare not speak before.

Oh, pardon that in crowds awhile
  I waste one thought I owe to thee,
And, self-condemn'd, appear to smile,
  Unfaithful to thy Memory!
Nor deem that memory less dear,
  That then I seem not to repine;
I would not fools should overhear
  One sigh that should be wholly *thine*.

If not the goblet pass unquaff'd,
  It is not drain'd to banish care;
The cup must hold a deadlier draught,
  That brings a Lethe for despair.
And could Oblivion set my soul
  From all her troubled visions free,
I'd dash to earth the sweetest bowl
  That drown'd a single thought of thee.

For wert thou vanish'd from my mind,
  Where could my vacant bosom turn?
And who would then remain behind
  To honour thine abandon'd Urn?
No, no — it is my sorrow's pride
  That last dear duty to fulfil;
Though all the world forget beside,
  'Tis meet that I remember still.

For well I know, that such had been
  Thy gentle care for him, who now
Unmourn'd shall quit this mortal scene,
  Where none regarded him, but thou:
And, oh! I feel in *that* was given
  A blessing never meant for me;
Thou wert too like a dream of Heaven,
  For earthly Love to merit thee.    March 14. 1812.

### ON A CORNELIAN HEART WHICH WAS BROKEN.

Ill-fated Heart! and can it be
    That thou shouldst thus be rent in twain?
Have years of care for thine and thee
    Alike been all employ'd in vain?

Yet precious seems each shatter'd part,
    And every fragment dearer grown,
Since he who wears thee feels thou art
    A fitter emblem of *his own*.
March 16. 1812.

---

### LINES TO A LADY WEEPING.

Weep, daughter of a royal line,
    A Sire's disgrace, a realm's decay;
Ah! happy if each tear of thine
    Could wash a father's fault away!

Weep — for thy tears are Virtue's tears —
    Auspicious to these suffering isles;
And be each drop in future years
    Repaid thee by thy people's smiles!
March, 1812.

---

### THE CHAIN I GAVE.
*(From the Turkish.)*

The chain I gave was fair to view,
    The lute I added sweet in sound;
The heart that offer'd both was true,
    And ill deserved the fate it found.

These gifts were charm'd by secret spell,
    Thy truth in absence to divine;
And they have done their duty well, —
    Alas! they could not teach thee thine.

That chain was firm in every link,
　But not to bear a stranger's touch;
That lute was sweet — till thou could'st think
　In other hands its notes were such.

Let him, who from thy neck unbound
　The chain which shiver'd in his grasp,
Who saw that lute refuse to sound,
　Restring the chords, renew the clasp.

When thou wert changed, they alter'd too;
　The chain is broke, the music mute.
'Tis past — to them and thee adieu —
　False heart, frail chain, and silent lute.

---

**LINES WRITTEN ON A BLANK LEAF OF THE
"PLEASURES OF MEMORY."**

ABSENT or present, still to thee,
　My friend, what magic spells belong!
As all can tell, who share, like me,
　In turn thy converse, and thy song.

But when the dreaded hour shall come
　By Friendship ever deem'd too nigh,
And "MEMORY" o'er her Druid's tomb
　Shall weep that aught of thee can die,

How fondly will she then repay
　Thy homage offer'd at her shrine,
And blend, while ages roll away,
　*Her* name immortally with *thine!*
　　　　　　　　　April 19. 1812.

---

### ADDRESS,

**SPOKEN AT THE OPENING OF DRURY-LANE THEATRE, SATURDAY, OCTOBER 10. 1812.**

In one dread night our city saw, and sigh'd,
Bow'd to the dust, the Drama's tower of pride;
In one short hour beheld the blazing fane,
Apollo sink, and Shakspeare cease to reign.

Ye who beheld, (oh! sight admired and mourn'd,
Whose radiance mock'd the ruin it adorn'd!)
Through clouds of fire the massy fragments riven,
Like Israel's pillar, chase the night from heaven;
Saw the long column of revolving flames
Shake its red shadow o'er the startled Thames,
While thousands, throng'd around the burning dome,
Shrank back appall'd, and trembled for their home,
As glared the volumed blaze, and ghastly shone
The skies, with lightnings awful as their own,
Till blackening ashes and the lonely wall
Usurp'd the Muse's realm, and mark'd her fall;
Say — shall this new, nor less aspiring pile,
Rear'd where once rose the mightiest in our isle,
Know the same favour which the former knew,
A shrine for Shakspeare — worthy him and *you?*

Yes — it shall be — the magic of that name
Defies the scythe of time, the torch of flame;
On the same spot still consecrates the scene,
And bids the Drama *be* where she hath *been:*
This fabric's birth attests the potent spell —
Indulge our honest pride, and say, *How well!*

As soars this fane to emulate the last,
Oh! might we draw our omens from the past,
Some hour propitious to our prayers may boast
Names such as hallow still the dome we lost.

On Drury first your Siddons' thrilling art
O'erwhelm'd the gentlest, storm'd the sternest heart.
On Drury, Garrick's latest laurels grew;
Here your last tears retiring Roscius drew,
Sigh'd his last thanks, and wept his last adieu:
But still for living wit the wreaths may bloom
That only waste their odours o'er the tomb.
Such Drury claim'd and claims — nor you refuse
One tribute to revive his slumbering muse;
With garlands deck your own Menander's head!
Nor hoard your honours idly for the dead!

Dear are the days which made our annals bright,
Ere Garrick fled, or Brinsley ceased to write.
Heirs to their labours, like all high-born heirs,
Vain of *our* ancestry as they of *theirs;*
While thus Remembrance borrows Banquo's glass
To claim the sceptred shadows as they pass,
And we the mirror hold, where imaged shine
Immortal names, emblazon'd on our line,
Pause — ere their feebler offspring you condemn,
Reflect how hard the task to rival them!

Friends of the stage! to whom both Players and Plays
Must sue alike for pardon or for praise,
Whose judging voice and eye alone direct
The boundless power to cherish or reject;
If e'er frivolity has led to fame,
And made us blush that you forbore to blame;
If e'er the sinking stage could condescend
To soothe the sickly taste it dare not mend,
All past reproach may present scenes refute,
And censure, wisely loud, be justly mute!
Oh! since your fiat stamps the Drama's laws,
Forbear to mock us with misplaced applause;
So pride shall doubly nerve the actor's powers,
And reason's voice be echo'd back by ours!

## OCCASIONAL PIECES.

This greeting o'er, the ancient rule obey'd,
The Drama's homage by her herald paid,
Receive *our* welcome too, whose every tone
Springs from our hearts, and fain would win your own.
The curtain rises — may our stage unfold
Scenes not unworthy Drury's days of old!
Britons our judges, Nature for our guide,
Still may *we* please — long, long may *you* preside!

---

### TO TIME.

Time! on whose arbitrary wing
   The varying hours must flag or fly,
Whose tardy winter, fleeting spring,
   But drag or drive us on to die —

Hail thou! who on my birth bestow'd
   Those boons to all that know thee known;
Yet better I sustain thy load,
   For now I bear the weight alone.

I would not one fond heart should share
   The bitter moments thou hast given;
And pardon thee, since thou could'st spare
   All that I loved, to peace or heaven.

To them be joy or rest, on me
   Thy future ills shall press in vain;
I nothing owe but years to thee,
   A debt already paid in pain.

Yet even that pain was some relief;
   It felt, but still forgot thy power:
The active agony of grief
   Retards, but never counts the hour.

In joy I've sigh'd to think thy flight
   Would soon subside from swift to slow;
Thy cloud could overcast the light,
   But could not add a night to woe;

For them, however drear and dark,
  My soul was suited to thy sky;
One star alone shot forth a spark
  To prove thee — not Eternity.

That beam hath sunk, and now thou art
  A blank; a thing to count and curse
Through each dull tedious trifling part,
  Which all regret, yet all rehearse.

One scene even thou canst not deform;
  The limit of thy sloth or speed
When future wanderers bear the storm
  Which we shall sleep too sound to heed:

And I can smile to think how weak
  Thine efforts shortly shall be shown,
When all the vengeance thou canst wreak
  Must fall upon — a nameless stone.

### TRANSLATION OF A ROMAIC LOVE SONG.

Ah! Love was never yet without
The pang, the agony, the doubt,
Which rends my heart with ceaseless sigh,
While day and night roll darkling by.

Without one friend to hear my woe,
I faint, I die beneath the blow.
That Love had arrows, well I knew;
Alas! I find them poison'd too.

Birds, yet in freedom, shun the net
Which Love around your haunts hath set;
Or, circled by his fatal fire,
Your hearts shall burn, your hopes expire.

A bird of free and careless wing
Was I, through many a smiling spring;
But caught within the subtle snare,
I burn, and feebly flutter there.

Who ne'er have loved, and loved in vain,
Can neither feel nor pity pain,
The cold repulse, the look askance,
The lightning of Love's angry glance.

In flattering dreams I deem'd thee mine;
Now hope, and he who hoped, decline;
Like melting wax, or withering flower,
I feel my passion, and thy power.

My light of life! ah, tell me why
That pouting lip, and alter'd eye?
My bird of love! my beauteous mate!
And art thou changed, and canst thou hate?

Mine eyes like wintry streams o'erflow:
What wretch with me would barter woe?
My bird! relent: one note could give
A charm, to bid thy lover live.

My curdling blood, my madd'ning brain,
In silent anguish I sustain;
And still thy heart, without partaking
One pang, exults — while mine is breaking.

Pour me the poison; fear not thou!
Thou canst not murder more than now:
I've lived to curse my natal day,
And Love, that thus can lingering slay.

My wounded soul, my bleeding breast,
Can patience preach thee into rest?
Alas! too late, I dearly know
That joy is harbinger of woe.

## STANZAS.

### ["THOU ART NOT FALSE."]

Thou art not false, but thou art fickle,
    To those thyself so fondly sought;
The tears that thou hast forced to trickle
    Are doubly bitter from that thought:
'Tis this which breaks the heart thou grievest,
Too well thou lov'st — too soon thou leavest.

The wholly false the heart despises,
    And spurns decciver and deceit;
But she who not a thought disguises,
    Whose love is as sincere as sweet, —
When she can change who loved so truly,
It feels what mine has felt so newly.

To dream of joy and wake to sorrow
    Is doom'd to all who love or live;
And if, when conscious on the morrow,
    We scarce our fancy can forgive,
That cheated us in slumber only,
To leave the waking soul more lonely,

What must they feel whom no false vision,
    But truest, tenderest passion warm'd?
Sincere, but swift in sad transition;
    As if a dream alone had charm'd?
Ah! sure such grief is fancy's scheming,
And all thy change can be but dreaming!

---

### ON BEING ASKED WHAT WAS THE
### "ORIGIN OF LOVE."

The "Origin of Love!" — Ah, why
    That cruel question ask of me,
When thou mayst read in many an eye
    He starts to life on seeing thee?

And shouldst thou seek his *end* to know:
My heart forebodes, my fears foresee,
He'll linger long in silent woe;
But live — until I cease to be.

---

### STANZAS.

["REMEMBER HIM," &c.]

REMEMBER him, whom passion's power
  Severely, deeply, vainly proved:
Remember thou that dangerous hour
  When neither fell, though both were loved.

That yielding breast, that melting eye,
  Too much invited to be bless'd:
That gentle prayer, that pleading sigh,
  The wilder wish reproved, repress'd.

Oh! let me feel that all I lost
  But saved thee all that conscience fears;
And blush for every pang it cost
  To spare the vain remorse of years.

Yet think of this when many a tongue,
  Whose busy accents whisper blame,
Would do the heart that loved thee wrong,
  And brand a nearly blighted name.

Think that, whate'er to others, thou
  Hast seen each selfish thought subdued:
I bless thy purer soul even now,
  Even now, in midnight solitude.

Oh, God! that we had met in time,
  Our hearts as fond, thy hand more free;
When thou hadst loved without a crime,
  And I been less unworthy thee!

Far may thy days, as heretofore,
  From this our gaudy world be past!
And that too bitter moment o'er,
  Oh! may such trial be thy last!

This heart, alas! perverted long,
  Itself destroy'd might there destroy;
To meet thee in the glittering throng,
  Would wake Presumption's hope of joy.

Then to the things whose bliss or woe,
  Like mine, is wild and worthless all,
That world resign — such scenes forego,
  Where those who feel must surely fall.

Thy youth, thy charms, thy tenderness,
  Thy soul from long seclusion pure;
From what even here hath pass'd, may guess
  What there thy bosom must endure.

Oh! pardon that imploring tear,
  Since not by Virtue shed in vain,
My frenzy drew from eyes so dear;
  For me they shall not weep again.

Though long and mournful must it be,
  The thought that we no more may meet;
Yet I deserve the stern decree,
  And almost deem the sentence sweet.

Still, had I loved thee less, my heart
  Had then less sacrificed to thine;
It felt not half so much to part,
  As if its guilt had made thee mine.

# OCCASIONAL PIECES.

## ON LORD THURLOW'S POEMS.

When Thurlow this damn'd nonsense sent,
(I hope I am not violent)
Nor men nor gods knew what he meant.

And since not ev'n our Rogers' praise
To common sense his thoughts could raise —
Why *would* they let him print his lays?

\* \* \* \* \*

\* \* \* \* \*

To me, divine Apollo, grant — O!
Hermilda's first and second canto,
I'm fitting up a new portmanteau;

And thus to furnish decent lining,
My own and others' bays I'm twining —
So, gentle Thurlow, throw me thine in.

---

## TO LORD THURLOW.

"I lay my branch of laurel down,
  Then thus to form Apollo's crown
  Let every other bring his own."
          *Lord Thurlow's lines to Mr. Rogers.*

"*I lay my branch of laurel down.*"
Thou "lay thy branch of *laurel* down!"
  Why, what thou'st stole is not enow;
And, were it lawfully thine own,
  Does Rogers want it most, or thou?
Keep to thyself thy wither'd bough,
  Or send it back to Doctor Donne:
Were justice done to both, I trow,
  He'd have but little, and thou — none.

"*Then thus to form Apollo's crown.*"
A crown! why, twist it how you will,
    Thy chaplet must be foolscap still.
When next you visit Delphi's town,
    Enquire amongst your fellow-lodgers,
They'll tell you Phœbus gave his crown,
    Some years before your birth, to Rogers.

"*Let every other bring his own.*"
When coals to Newcastle are carried,
    And owls sent to Athens, as wonders,
From his spouse when the Regent's unmarried,
    Or Liverpool weeps o'er his blunders;
When Tories and Whigs cease to quarrel,
    When Castlereagh's wife has an heir,
Then Rogers shall ask us for laurel,
    And thou shalt have plenty to spare.

---

### TO THOMAS MOORE.

WRITTEN THE EVENING BEFORE HIS VISIT TO MR. LEIGH HUNT IN COLD BATH FIELDS PRISON, MAY 19. 1813.

Oh you, who in all names can tickle the town,
Anacreon, Tom Little, Tom Moore, or Tom Brown, —
For hang me if I know of which you may most brag,
Your Quarto two-pounds, or your Two-penny Post Bag;
    \*   \*   \*   \*   \*
But now to my letter — to *yours* 'tis an answer —
To-morrow be with me, as soon as you can, sir,
All ready and dress'd for proceeding to spunge on
(According to compact) the wit in the dungeon —
Pray Phœbus at length our political malice
May not get us lodgings within the same palace!
I suppose that to-night you're engaged with some codgers,
And for Sotheby's Blues have deserted Sam Rogers;

And I, though with cold I have nearly my death got,
Must put on my breeches, and wait on the Heath-cote,
But to-morrow, at four, we will both play the *Scurra*,
And you'll be Catullus, the Regent Mamurra.

---

### IMPROMPTU, IN REPLY TO A FRIEND.

When, from the heart where Sorrow sits,
　Her dusky shadow mounts too high,
And o'er the changing aspect flits,
　And clouds the brow, or fills the eye;
Heed not that gloom, which soon shall sink:
　My thoughts their dungeon know too well;
Back to my breast the wanderers shrink,
　And droop within their silent cell.

September, 1813.

---

### SONNET, TO GENEVRA.

Thine eyes' blue tenderness, thy long fair hair,
　And the wan lustre of thy features — caught
　From contemplation — where serenely wrought,
Seems Sorrow's softness charm'd from its despair —
Have thrown such speaking sadness in thine air,
　That — but I know thy blessed bosom fraught
　With mines of unalloy'd and stainless thought —
I should have deem'd thee doom'd to earthly care.
With such an aspect, by his colours blent,
　When from his beauty-breathing pencil born,
(Except that *thou* hast nothing to repent)
　The Magdalen of Guido saw the morn —
Such seem'st thou — but how much more excellent!
　With nought Remorse can claim — nor Virtue scorn.

December 17. 1813.

### SONNET, TO THE SAME.

Thy cheek is pale with thought, but not from woe,
   And yet so lovely, that if Mirth could flush
   Its rose of whiteness with the brightest blush,
My heart would wish away that ruder glow:
And dazzle not thy deep-blue eyes — but, oh!
   While gazing on them sterner eyes will gush,
   And into mine my mother's weakness rush,
Soft as the last drops round heaven's airy bow.
For, through thy long dark lashes low depending,
   The soul of melancholy Gentleness
Gleams like a seraph from the sky descending,
   Above all pain, yet pitying all distress;
At once such majesty with sweetness blending,
   I worship more, but cannot love thee less.
December 17. 1813.

---

### FROM THE PORTUGUESE.
#### "TU MI CHAMAS."

In moments to delight devoted,
   "My life!" with tenderest tone, you cry;
Dear words! on which my heart had doted,
   If youth could neither fade nor die.

To death even hours like these must roll,
   Ah! then repeat those accents never;
Or change "my life!" into "my soul!"
   Which, like my love, exists for ever.

#### ANOTHER VERSION.

You call me still your *life*.— Oh! change the word —
   Life is as transient as the inconstant sigh:
Say rather I'm your soul; more just that name,
   For, like the soul, my love can never die.

## 1814—1816.

### THE DEVIL'S DRIVE;
#### AN UNFINISHED RHAPSODY.

THE Devil return'd to hell by two,
  And he stay'd at home till five;
When he dined on some homicides done in *ragoût*,
  And a rebel or so in an *Irish* stew,
And sausages made of a self-slain Jew —
And bethought himself what next to do,
  "And," quoth he, "I'll take a drive.
I walk'd in the morning, I'll ride to-night;
In darkness my children take most delight,
  And I'll see how my favourites thrive.

"And what shall I ride in?" quoth Lucifer then —
  "If I follow'd my taste, indeed,
I should mount in a waggon of wounded men,
  And smile to see them bleed.
But these will be furnish'd again and again,
  And at present my purpose is speed;
To see my manor as much as I may,
And watch that no souls shall be poach'd away.

"I have a state-coach at Carlton House,
  A chariot in Seymour Place;
But they're lent to two friends, who make me amends
  By driving my favourite pace:
And they handle their reins with such a grace,
I have something for both at the end of their race.

"So now for the earth to take my chance."
  Then up to the earth sprung he;
And making a jump from Moscow to France,
  He stepp'd across the sea,
And rested his hoof on a turnpike road,
No very great way from a bishop's abode.

But first as he flew, I forgot to say,
That he hover'd a moment upon his way
    To look upon Leipsic plain;
And so sweet to his eye was its sulphury glare,
And so soft to his ear was the cry of despair,
    That he perch'd on a mountain of slain;
And he gazed with delight from its growing height,
Nor often on earth had he seen such a sight,
    Nor his work done half as well:
For the field ran so red with the blood of the dead,
    That it blush'd like the waves of hell!
Then loudly, and wildly, and long laugh'd he:
"Methinks they have here little need of *me!*"
  *  *  *  *  *

But the softest note that soothed his ear
    Was the sound of a widow sighing;
And the sweetest sight was the icy tear,
Which horror froze in the blue eye clear
    Of a maid by her lover lying —
As round her fell her long fair hair;
And she look'd to heaven with that frenzied air,
    Which seem'd to ask if a God were there!
And, stretch'd by the wall of a ruin'd hut,
With its hollow cheek, and eyes half shut,
    A child of famine dying:
And the carnage begun, when resistance is done
    And the fall of the vainly flying!
  *  .*  *  *  *

But the Devil has reach'd our cliffs so white,
    And what did he there, I pray?
If his eyes were good, he but saw by night
    What we see every day:
But he made a tour, and kept a journal
Of all the wondrous sights nocturnal,
And he sold it in shares to the *Men* of the *Row*,
Who bid pretty well — but they *cheated* him, though!

The Devil first saw, as he thought, the *Mail*,
    Its coachman and his coat;
So instead of a pistol he cock'd his tail,
    And seized him by the throat:
"Aha!" quoth he, "what have we here?
'Tis a new barouche, and an ancient peer!"

So he sat him on his box again,
    And bade him have no fear,
But be true to his club, and stanch to his rein,
    His brothel, and his beer;
"Next to seeing a lord at the council board,
    I would rather see him here."

   \*      \*      \*      \*      \*

The Devil gat next to Westminster,
    And he turn'd to "the room" of the Commons;
But he heard, as he purposed to enter in there,
    That "the Lords" had received a summons;
And he thought, as a "*quondam* aristocrat,"
He might peep at the peers, though to *hear* them were flat;
And he walk'd up the house so like one of our own,
That they say that he stood pretty near the throne.

He saw the Lord Liverpool seemingly wise,
    The Lord Westmoreland certainly silly,
And Johnny of Norfolk — a man of some size —
    And Chatham, so like his friend Billy;
And he saw the tears in Lord Eldon's eyes,
    Because the Catholics would *not* rise,
    In spite of his prayers and his prophecies;
And he heard — which set Satan himself a staring —
A certain Chief Justice say something like *swearing*.
And the Devil was shock'd — and quoth he, "I must go,
For I find we have much better manners below:
If thus he harangues when he passes my border,
I shall hint to friend Moloch to call him to order."

### WINDSOR POETICS.

Lines composed on the occasion of His Royal Highness the Prince Regent being seen standing between the coffins of Henry VIII. and Charles I., in the royal vault at Windsor.

Famed for contemptuous breach of sacred ties,
By headless Charles see heartless Henry lies;
Between them stands another sceptred thing —
It moves, it reigns — in all but name, a king:

Charles to his people, Henry to his wife,
— In him the double tyrant starts to life:
Justice and death have mix'd their dust in vain,
Each royal vampire wakes to life again.
Ah, what can tombs avail! — since these disgorge
The blood and dust of both — to mould a George.

---

### STANZAS FOR MUSIC.

["I SPEAK NOT, I TRACE NOT," &c.]

I speak not, I trace not, I breathe not thy name,
There is grief in the sound, there is guilt in the fame:
But the tear which now burns on my cheek may impart
The deep thoughts that dwell in that silence of heart.

Too brief for our passion, too long for our peace
Were those hours — can their joy or their bitterness cease?
We repent — we abjure — we will break from our chain, —
We will part, — we will fly to — unite it again!

Oh! thine be the gladness, and mine be the guilt!
Forgive me, adored one! — forsake, if thou wilt; —
But the heart which is thine shall expire undebased,
And man shall not break it — whatever *thou* mayst.

And stern to the haughty, but humble to thee,
This soul, in its bitterest blackness, shall be;
And our days seem as swift, and our moments more sweet,
With thee by my side, than with worlds at our feet.

One sigh of thy sorrow, one look of thy love,
Shall turn me or fix, shall reward or reprove;
And the heartless may wonder at all I resign —
Thy lip shall reply, not to them, but to *mine*.

May, 1814.

## ADDRESS INTENDED TO BE RECITED AT THE CALEDONIAN MEETING.

Who hath not glow'd above the page where fame
Hath fix'd high Caledon's unconquer'd name;
The mountain-land which spurn'd the Roman chain,
And baffled back the fiery-crested Dane,
Whose bright claymore and hardihood of hand
No foe could tame — no tyrant could command?
That race is gone — but still their children breathe,
And glory crowns them with redoubled wreath:
O'er Gael and Saxon mingling banners shine,
And, England! add their stubborn strength to thine.
The blood which flow'd with Wallace flows as free,
But now 'tis only shed for fame and thee!
Oh! pass not by the northern veteran's claim,
But give support — the world hath given him fame!

The humbler ranks, the lowly brave, who bled
While cheerly following where the mighty led —
Who sleep beneath the undistinguish'd sod
Where happier comrades in their triumph trod,
To us bequeath — 'tis all their fate allows —
The sireless offspring and the lonely spouse:
She on high Albyn's dusky hills may raise
The tearful eye in melancholy gaze,
Or view, while shadowy auguries disclose
The Highland seer's anticipated woes,
The bleeding phantom of each martial form
Dim in the cloud, or darkling in the storm;
While sad, she chants the solitary song,
The soft lament for him who tarries long —

For him, whose distant relics vainly crave
The Coronach's wild requiem to the brave!

'Tis Heaven — not man — must charm away the woe
Which bursts when Nature's feelings newly flow;
Yet tenderness and time may rob the tear
Of half its bitterness for one so dear;
A nation's gratitude perchance may spread
A thornless pillow for the widow'd head;
May lighten well her heart's maternal care,
And wean from penury the soldier's heir.

May, 1814.

### FRAGMENT OF AN EPISTLE TO THOMAS MOORE.

"WHAT say I?" — not a syllable further in prose;
I'm your man "of all measures," dear Tom, — so, here goes!
Here goes, for a swim on the stream of old Time,
On those buoyant supporters, the bladders of rhyme.
If our weight breaks them down, and we sink in the flood,
We are smother'd, at least, in respectable mud,
Where the Divers of Bathos lie drown'd in a heap,
And Southey's last Pæan has pillow'd his sleep; —
That "Felo de se" who, half drunk with his malmsey,
Walk'd out of his depth and was lost in a calm sea,
Singing "Glory to God" in a spick and span stanza,
The like (since Tom Sternhold was choked) never man saw.

The papers have told you, no doubt, of the fusses,
The fêtes, and the gapings to get at these Russes, —
Of his Majesty's suite, up from coachman to Hetman, —
And what dignity decks the flat face of the great man.
I saw him, last week, at two balls and a party, —
For a prince, his demeanour was rather too hearty.
You know, *we* are used to quite different graces,
* * * * *

The Czar's look, I own, was much brighter and brisker,
But then he is sadly deficient in whisker;

And wore but a starless blue coat, and in kersey-
mere breeches whisk'd round, in a waltz with the Jersey,
Who, lovely as ever, seem'd just as delighted
With majesty's presence as those she invited.
   &ast;  &ast;  &ast;  &ast;  &ast;
   &ast;  &ast;  &ast;  &ast;  &ast;
June, 1814.

## CONDOLATORY ADDRESS TO SARAH, COUNTESS OF JERSEY, ON THE PRINCE REGENT'S RETURNING HER PICTURE TO MRS. MEE.

When the vain triumph of the imperial lord,
Whom servile Rome obey'd, and yet abhorr'd,
Gave to the vulgar gaze each glorious bust,
That left a likeness of the brave, or just;
What most admired each scrutinising eye
Of all that deck'd that passing pageantry?
What spread from face to face that wondering air?
The thought of Brutus — for his was not there!
That absence proved his worth, — that absence fix'd
His memory on the longing mind, unmix'd;
And more decreed his glory to endure,
Than all a gold Colossus could secure.
 If thus, fair Jersey, our desiring gaze
Search for thy form, in vain and mute amaze,
Amidst those pictured charms, whose loveliness,
Bright though they be, thine own had render'd less;
If he, that vain old man, whom truth admits
Heir of his father's crown, and of his wits,
If his corrupted eye, and wither'd heart,
Could with thy gentle image bear depart;
That tasteless shame be *his*, and ours the grief,
To gaze on Beauty's band without its chief:
Yet comfort still one selfish thought imparts,
We lose the portrait, but preserve our hearts
 What can his vaulted gallery now disclose?
A garden with all flowers — except the rose; —

A fount that only wants its living stream;
A night, with every star, save Dian's beam.
Lost to our eyes the present forms shall be,
That turn from tracing them to dream of thee;
And more on that recall'd resemblance pause,
'Than all he *shall* not force on our applause.

Long may thy yet meridian lustre shine,
With all that Virtue asks of Homage thine:
The symmetry of youth — the grace of mien —
The eye that gladdens — and the brow serene;
The glossy darkness of that clustering hair,
Which shades, yet shows that forehead more than fair!
Each glance that wins us, and the life that throws
A spell which will not let our looks repose,
But turn to gaze again, and find anew
Some charm that well rewards another view.
These are not lessen'd, these are still as bright,
Albeit too dazzling for a dotard's sight;
And those must wait till ev'ry charm is gone,
To please the paltry heart that pleases none; —
That dull cold sensualist, whose sickly eye
In envious dimness pass'd thy portrait by;
Who rack'd his little spirit to combine
Its hate of *Freedom's* loveliness, and *thine.*

August, 1814.

---

### TO BELSHAZZAR.

BELSHAZZAR! from the banquet turn,
    Nor in thy sensual fulness fall;
Behold! while yet before thee burn
    The graven words, the glowing wall.
Many a despot men miscall
    Crown'd and anointed from on high;
But thou, the weakest, worst of all —
    Is it not written, thou must die?

Go! dash the roses from thy brow —
  Grey hairs but poorly wreathe with them;
Youth's garlands misbecome thee now,
  More than thy very diadem,
Where thou hast tarnish'd every gem: —
  Then throw the worthless bauble by,
Which, worn by thee, ev'n slaves contemn;
  And learn like better men to die!

Oh! early in the balance weigh'd,
  And ever light of word and worth,
Whose soul expired ere youth decay'd,
  And left thee but a mass of earth.
To see thee moves the scorner's mirth:
  But tears in Hope's averted eye
Lament that even thou hadst birth —
  Unfit to govern, live, or die.

### ELEGIAC STANZAS ON THE DEATH OF SIR PETER PARKER, BART.

There is a tear for all that die,
  A mourner o'er the humblest grave;
But nations swell the funeral cry,
  And Triumph weeps above the brave.

For them is Sorrow's purest sigh
  O'er Ocean's heaving bosom sent:
In vain their bones unburied lie,
  All earth becomes their monument!

A tomb is theirs on every page,
  An epitaph on every tongue:
The present hours, the future age,
  For them bewail, to them belong.

For them the voice of festal mirth
  Grows hush'd, *their name* the only sound;
While deep Remembrance pours to Worth
  The goblet's tributary round.

A theme to crowds that knew them not,
 Lamented by admiring foes,
Who would not share their glorious lot?
 Who would not die the death they chose?

And, gallant Parker! thus enshrined
 Thy life, thy fall, thy fame shall be;
And early valour, glowing, find
 A model in thy memory.

But there are breasts that bleed with thee
 In woe, that glory cannot quell;
And shuddering hear of victory,
 Where one so dear, so dauntless, fell.

Where shall they turn to mourn thee less?
 When cease to hear thy cherish'd name?
Time cannot teach forgetfulness,
 While Grief's full heart is fed by Fame.

Alas! for them, though not for thee,
 They cannot choose but weep the more;
Deep for the dead the grief must be,
 Who ne'er gave cause to mourn before.
                                    October, 1814.

---

### STANZAS FOR MUSIC.

["THERE'S NOT A JOY THE WORLD CAN GIVE," &c.]

"O Lachrymarum fons, tenero sacros
Ducentium ortus ex animo: quater
Felix! in imo qui scatentem
Pectore te, pia Nympha, sensit."
                            GRAY'S *Poemata.*

THERE'S not a joy the world can give like that it takes away,
When the glow of early thought declines in feeling's dull decay;
'Tis not on youth's smooth cheek the blush alone, which fades so fast,
But the tender bloom of heart is gone, ere youth itself be past.

Then the few whose spirits float above the wreck of happiness
Are driven o'er the shoals of guilt or ocean of excess:
The magnet of their course is gone, or only points in vain
The shore to which their shiver'd sail shall never stretch
    again.

Then the mortal coldness of the soul like death itself comes
    down;
It cannot feel for others' woes, it dare not dream its own;
That heavy chill has frozen o'er the fountain of our tears,
And though the eye may sparkle still, 'tis where the ice ap-
    pears.

Though wit may flash from fluent lips, and mirth distract the
    breast,
Through midnight hours that yield no more their former hope
    of rest;
'Tis but as ivy-leaves around the ruin'd turret wreath,
All green and wildly fresh without, but worn and grey
    beneath.

Oh could I feel as I have felt, — or be what I have been,
Or weep as I could once have wept, o'er many a vanish'd
    scene;
As springs in deserts found seem sweet, all brackish though
    they be,
So, midst the wither'd waste of life, those tears would flow
    to me.

                                March, 1815.

## STANZAS FOR MUSIC.

["THERE BE NONE OF BEAUTY'S DAUGHTERS."]

    There be none of Beauty's daughters
        With a magic like thee;
    And like music on the waters
        Is thy sweet voice to me:

When, as if its sound were causing
The charmed ocean's pausing,
The waves lie still and gleaming,
And the lull'd winds seem dreaming.

And the midnight moon is weaving
　Her bright chain o'er the deep;
Whose breast is gently heaving,
　As an infant's asleep:
So the spirit bows before thee,
To listen and adore thee;
With a full but soft emotion,
Like the swell of Summer's ocean.

---

### ON NAPOLEON'S ESCAPE FROM ELBA.

ONCE fairly set out on his party of pleasure,
Taking towns at his liking, and crowns at his leisure,
From Elba to Lyons and Paris he goes,
Making *balls for* the ladies, and *bows to* his foes.

March 27. 1815.

---

### ODE FROM THE FRENCH.

["WE DO NOT CURSE THEE, WATERLOO!"]

I.

WE do not curse thee, Waterloo!
Though Freedom's blood thy plain bedew;
There 'twas shed, but is not sunk —
Rising from each gory trunk,
Like the water-spout from ocean,
With a strong and growing motion —
It soars, and mingles in the air,
With that of lost Labedoyère —
With that of him whose honour'd grave
Contains the "bravest of the brave."
A crimson cloud it spreads and glows,
But shall return to whence it rose;

When 'tis full 'twill burst asunder —.
Never yet was heard such thunder,
As then shall shake the world with wonder —
Never yet was seen such lightning
As o'er heaven shall then be bright'ning!
Like the Wormwood Star foretold
By the sainted Seer of old,
Show'ring down a fiery flood,
Turning rivers into blood.*

II.

The Chief has fallen, but not by you,
Vanquishers of Waterloo!
When the soldier citizen
Sway'd not o'er his fellow-men —
Save in deeds that led them on
Where Glory smiled on Freedom's son —
Who, of all the despots banded,
 With that youthful chief competed?
 Who could boast o'er France defeated,
Till lone Tyranny commanded?
Till, goaded by ambition's sting,
The Hero sunk into the King?
Then he fell: — so perish all,
Who would men by man enthral!

III.

And thou, too, of the snow-white plume!
Whose realm refused thee ev'n a tomb;**

---

* See Rev. chap. viii. v. 7, &c. "The first angel sounded, and there followed hail and fire mingled with blood," &c. v. 8. "And the second angel sounded, and as it were a great mountain burning with fire was cast into the sea; and the third part of the sea became blood," &c. v. 10. "And the third angel sounded, and there fell a great star from heaven, burning as it were a lamp; and it fell upon the third part of the rivers, and upon the fountains of waters." v. 11. "And the name of the star is called Wormwood: and the third part of the waters became wormwood; and many men died of the waters, because they were made bitter."

** Marat's remains are said to have been torn from the grave and burnt.

Better hadst thou still been leading
France o'er hosts of hirelings bleeding,
Than sold thyself to death and shame
For a meanly royal name;
Such as he of Naples wears,
Who thy blood-bought title bears.
Little didst thou deem, when dashing
　On thy war-horse through the ranks
　Like a stream which burst its banks,
While helmets cleft, and sabres clashing,
Shone and shiver'd fast around thee —
Of the fate at last which found thee:
Was that haughty plume laid low
By a slave's dishonest blow?
Once — as the Moon sways o'er the tide,
It roll'd in air, the warrior's guide;
Through the smoke-created night
Of the black and sulphurous fight,
The soldier raised his seeking eye
To catch that crest's ascendency, —
And, as it onward rolling rose,
So moved his heart upon our foes.
There, where death's brief pang was quickest,
And the battle's wreck lay thickest,
Strew'd beneath the advancing banner
　Of the eagle's burning crest —
(There with thunder-clouds to fan her,
　*Who* could then her wing arrest —
　Victory beaming from her breast?)
While the broken line enlarging
　Fell, or fled along the plain;
There be sure was Murat charging!
　There he ne'er shall charge again!

IV.

O'er glories gone the invaders march,
Weeps Triumph o'er each levell'd arch —

But let Freedom rejoice,
With her heart in her voice;
But, her hand on her sword,
Doubly shall she be adored;
France hath twice too well been taught
The "moral lesson" dearly bought —
Her safety sits not on a throne,
With Capet or Napoleon!
But in equal rights and laws,
Hearts and hands in one great cause —
Freedom, such as God hath given
Unto all beneath his heaven,
With their breath, and from their birth,
Though Guilt would sweep it from the earth;
With a fierce and lavish hand
Scattering nations' wealth like sand;
Pouring nations' blood like water,
In imperial seas of slaughter!

v.

But the heart and the mind,
And the voice of mankind,
Shall arise in communion —
And who shall resist that proud union?
The time is past when swords subdued —
Man may die — the soul's renew'd:
Even in this low world of care
Freedom ne'er shall want an heir;
Millions breathe but to inherit
Her for ever bounding spirit —
When once more her hosts assemble,
Tyrants shall believe and tremble —
Smile they at this idle threat?
Crimson tears will follow yet.

### FROM THE FRENCH.

["MUST THOU GO, MY GLORIOUS CHIEF?"]*

#### I.

Must thou go, my glorious Chief,
    Sever'd from thy faithful few?
Who can tell thy warrior's grief,
    Maddening o'er that long adieu?
Woman's love, and friendship's zeal,
    Dear as both have been to me —
What are they to all I feel,
    With a soldier's faith for thee?

#### II.

Idol of the soldier's soul!
    First in fight, but mightiest now:
Many could a world control;
    Thee alone no doom can bow.
By thy side for years I dared
    Death; and envied those who fell,
When their dying shout was heard,
    Blessing him they served so well.

#### III.

Would that I were cold with those,
    Since this hour I live to see;
When the doubts of coward foes
    Scarce dare trust a man with thee,
Dreading each should set thee free!
    Oh! although in dungeons pent,
All their chains were light to me,
    Gazing on thy soul unbent.

---

* "All wept, but particularly Savary, and a Polish officer who had been exalted from the ranks by Buonaparte. He clung to his master's knees; wrote a letter to Lord Keith, entreating permission to accompany him, even in the most menial capacity, which could not be admitted."

IV.

Would the sycophants of him
  Now so deaf to duty's prayer,
Were his borrow'd glories dim,
  In his native darkness share?
Were that world this hour his own,
  All thou calmly dost resign,
Could he purchase with that throne
  Hearts like those which still are thine?

V.

My chief, my king, my friend, adieu!
  Never did I droop before;
Never to my sovereign sue,
  As his foes I now implore:
All I ask is to divide
  Every peril he must brave;
Sharing by the hero's side
  His fall, his exile, and his grave.

---

ON THE STAR OF "THE LEGION OF HONOUR."

[FROM THE FRENCH.]

Star of the brave! — whose beam hath shed
Such glory o'er the quick and dead —
Thou radiant and adored deceit!
Which millions rush'd in arms to greet, —
Wild meteor of immortal birth!
Why rise in Heaven to set on Earth?

Souls of slain heroes form'd thy rays;
Eternity flash'd through thy blaze;
The music of thy martial sphere
Was fame on high and honour here;
And thy light broke on human eyes,
Like a volcano of the skies.

Like lava roll'd thy stream of blood,
And swept down empires with its flood;
Earth rock'd beneath thee to her base,
As thou didst lighten through all space;
And the shorn Sun grew dim in air,
And set while thou wert dwelling there.

Before thee rose, and with thee grew,
A rainbow of the loveliest hue
Of three bright colours*, each divine,
And fit for that celestial sign;
For Freedom's hand had blended them,
Like tints in an immortal gem.

One tint was of the sunbeam's dyes;
One, the blue depth of Seraph's eyes;
One, the pure Spirit's veil of white
Had robed in radiance of its light:
The three so mingled did beseem
The texture of a heavenly dream.

Star of the brave! thy ray is pale,
And darkness must again prevail!
But, oh thou Rainbow of the free!
Our tears and blood must flow for thee.
When thy bright promise fades away,
Our life is but a load of clay.

And Freedom hallows with her tread
The silent cities of the dead;
For beautiful in death are they
Who proudly fall in her array;
And soon, oh Goddess! may we be
For evermore with them or thee!

* The tricolour.

## NAPOLEON'S FAREWELL.

[FROM THE FRENCH.]

### I.

Farewell to the Land, where the gloom of my Glory
Arose and o'ershadow'd the earth with her name —
She abandons me now — but the page of her story,
The brightest or blackest, is fill'd with my fame.
I have warr'd with a world which vanquish'd me only
When the meteor of conquest allured me too far;
I have coped with the nations which dread me thus lonely,
The last single Captive to millions in war.

### II.

Farewell to thee, France! when thy diadem crown'd me,
I made thee the gem and the wonder of earth, —
But thy weakness decrees I should leave as I found thee,
Decay'd in thy glory, and sunk in thy worth.
Oh! for the veteran hearts that were wasted
In strife with the storm, when their battles were won —
Then the Eagle, whose gaze in that moment was blasted,
Had still soar'd with eyes fix'd on victory's sun!

### III.

Farewell to thee, France! — but when Liberty rallies
Once more in thy regions, remember me then, —
The violet still grows in the depth of thy valleys;
Though wither'd, thy tear will unfold it again —
Yet, yet, I may baffle the hosts that surround us,
And yet may thy heart leap awake to my voice —
There are links which must break in the chain that has
    bound us,
*Then* turn thee and call on the Chief of thy choice!

### ENDORSEMENT TO THE DEED OF SEPARATION,
### IN THE APRIL OF 1816.

A YEAR ago you swore, fond she!
"To love, to honour," and so forth:
Such was the vow you pledged to me,
And here's exactly what 'tis worth.

---

### DARKNESS.

I HAD a dream, which was not all a dream.
The bright sun was extinguish'd, and the stars
Did wander darkling in the eternal space,
Rayless, and pathless, and the icy earth
Swung blind and blackening in the moonless air;
Morn came and went — and came, and brought no day.
And men forgot their passions in the dread
Of this their desolation; and all hearts
Were chill'd into a selfish prayer for light:
And they did live by watchfires — and the thrones,
The palaces of crowned kings — the huts,
The habitations of all things which dwell,
Were burnt for beacons; cities were consumed,
And men were gather'd round their blazing homes
To look once more into each other's face;
Happy were those who dwelt within the eye
Of the volcanos, and their mountain-torch:
A fearful hope was all the world contain'd;
Forests were set on fire — but hour by hour
They fell and faded — and the crackling trunks
Extinguish'd with a crash — and all was black.
The brows of men by the despairing light
Wore an unearthly aspect, as by fits
The flashes fell upon them; some lay down
And hid their eyes and wept; and some did rest
Their chins upon their clenched hands, and smiled;

And others hurried to and fro, and fed
Their funeral piles with fuel, and look'd up
With mad disquietude on the dull sky,
The pall of a past world; and then again
With curses cast them down upon the dust,
And gnash'd their teeth and howl'd: the wild birds
    shriek'd,
And, terrified, did flutter on the ground,
And flap their useless wings; the wildest brutes
Came tame and tremulous; and vipers crawl'd
And twined themselves among the multitude,
Hissing, but stingless — they were slain for food:
And War, which for a moment was no more,
Did glut himself again; — a meal was bought
With blood, and each sate sullenly apart
Gorging himself in gloom: no love was left;
All earth was but one thought — and that was death,
Immediate and inglorious; and the pang
Of famine fed upon all entrails — men
Died, and their bones were tombless as their flesh;
The meagre by the meagre were devour'd,
Even dogs assail'd their masters, all save one,
And he was faithful to a corse, and kept
The birds and beasts and famish'd men at bay,
Till hunger clung them, or the dropping dead
Lured their lank jaws; himself sought out no food,
But with a piteous and perpetual moan,
And a quick desolate cry, licking the hand
Which answer'd not with a caress — he died.
The crowd was famish'd by degrees; but two
Of an enormous city did survive,
And they were enemies: they met beside
The dying embers of an altar-place
Where had been heap'd a mass of holy things
For an unholy usage; they raked up,
And shivering scraped with their cold skeleton hands
The feeble ashes, and their feeble breath

Blew for a little life, and made a flame
Which was a mockery; then they lifted up
Their eyes as it grew lighter, and beheld
Each other's aspects — saw, and shriek'd, and died —
Even of their mutual hideousness they died,
Unknowing who he was upon whose brow
Famine had written Fiend. The world was void,
The populous and the powerful was a lump,
Seasonless, herbless, treeless, manless, lifeless —
A lump of death — a chaos of hard clay.
The rivers, lakes, and ocean all stood still,
And nothing stirr'd within their silent depths;
Ships sailorless lay rotting on the sea,
And their masts fell down piecemeal; as they dropp'd
They slept on the abyss without a surge —
The waves were dead; the tides were in their grave,
The Moon, their mistress, had expired before;
The winds were wither'd in the stagnant air,
And the clouds perish'd; Darkness had no need
Of aid from them — She was the Universe.
Diodati, July, 1816.

## CHURCHILL'S GRAVE;

#### A FACT LITERALLY RENDERED.

I stood beside the grave of him who blazed
　The comet of a season, and I saw
The humblest of all sepulchres, and gazed
　With not the less of sorrow and of awe
On that neglected turf and quiet stone,
With name no clearer than the names unknown,
Which lay unread around it; and I ask'd
　The Gardener of that ground, why it might be
That for this plant strangers his memory task'd
　Through the thick deaths of half a century;
And thus he answer'd — "Well, I do not know
Why frequent travellers turn to pilgrims so;

He died before my day of Sextonship,
   And I had not the digging of this grave."
And is this all? I thought, — and do we rip
   The veil of Immortality? and crave
I know not what of honour and of light
Through unborn ages, to endure this blight?
So soon, and so successless? As I said,
The Architect of all on which we tread,
For Earth is but a tombstone, did essay
To extricate remembrance from the clay,
Whose minglings might confuse a Newton's thought,
   Were it not that all life must end in one,
Of which we are but dreamers; — as he caught
   As 'twere the twilight of a former Sun,
Thus spoke he, — "I believe the man of whom
You wot, who lies in this selected tomb,
Was a most famous writer in his day,
And therefore travellers step from out their way
To pay him honour, — and myself whate'er
   Your honour pleases," — then most pleased I shook
   From out my pocket's avaricious nook
Some certain coins of silver, which as 'twere
Perforce I gave this man, though I could spare
So much but inconveniently: — Ye smile,
I see ye, ye profane ones! all the while,
Because my homely phrase the truth would tell.
You are the fools, not I — for I did dwell
With a deep thought, and with a soften'd eye,
On that Old Sexton's natural homily,
In which there was Obscurity and Fame, —
The Glory and the Nothing of a Name.

*Diodati, 1816.*

## PROMETHEUS.

### I.

Titan! to whose immortal eyes
   The sufferings of mortality,
   Seen in their sad reality,
Were not as things that gods despise;
What was thy pity's recompense?
A silent suffering, and intense;
The rock, the vulture, and the chain,
All that the proud can feel of pain,
The agony they do not show,
The suffocating sense of woe,
   Which speaks but in its loneliness,
And then is jealous lest the sky
Should have a listener, nor will sigh
   Until its voice is echoless.

### II.

Titan! to thee the strife was given
   Between the suffering and the will,
   Which torture where they cannot kill;
And the inexorable Heaven,
And the deaf tyranny of Fate,
The ruling principle of Hate,
Which for its pleasure doth create
The things it may annihilate,
Refused thee even the boon to die:
The wretched gift eternity
Was thine — and thou hast borne it well.
All that the Thunderer wrung from thee
Was but the menace which flung back
On him the torments of thy rack;
The fate thou didst so well foresee,
But would not to appease him tell;

And in thy Silence was his Sentence,
And in his Soul a vain repentance,
And evil dread so ill dissembled
That in his hand the lightnings trembled.

III.

Thy Godlike crime was to be kind,
　To render with thy precepts less
　The sum of human wretchedness,
And strengthen Man with his own mind;
But baffled as thou wert from high,
Still in thy patient energy,
In the endurance, and repulse
　Of thine impenetrable Spirit,
Which Earth and Heaven could not convulse,
　A mighty lesson we inherit:
Thou art a symbol and a sign
　To Mortals of their fate and force;
Like thee, Man is in part divine,
　A troubled stream from a pure source;
And Man in portions can foresee
His own funereal destiny;
His wretchedness, and his resistance,
And his sad unallied existence:
To which his Spirit may oppose
Itself — and equal to all woes,
　And a firm will, and a deep sense,
Which even in torture can descry
　Its own concenter'd recompense,
Triumphant where it dares defy,
And making Death a Victory.

Diodati, July, 1816.

## A FRAGMENT.

["COULD I REMOUNT," &c.]

Could I remount the river of my years
To the first fountain of our smiles and tears,
I would not trace again the stream of hours
Between their outworn banks of wither'd flowers,
But bid it flow as now — until it glides
Into the number of the nameless tides.
\* \* \* \* \*

What is this Death? — a quiet of the heart?
The whole of that of which we are a part?
For life is but a vision — what I see
Of all which lives alone is life to me,
And being so — the absent are the dead,
Who haunt us from tranquillity, and spread
A dreary shroud around us, and invest
With sad remembrances our hours of rest.

The absent are the dead — for they are cold,
And ne'er can be what once we did behold;
And they are changed, and cheerless, — or if yet
The unforgotten do not all forget,
Since thus divided — equal must it be
If the deep barrier be of earth, or sea;
It may be both — but one day end it must
In the dark union of insensate dust.

The under-earth inhabitants — are they
But mingled millions decomposed to clay?
The ashes of a thousand ages spread
Wherever man has trodden or shall tread?
Or do they in their silent cities dwell
Each in his incommunicative cell?
Or have they their own language? and a sense
Of breathless being? — darken'd and intense
As midnight in her solitude? — Oh Earth!
Where are the past? — and wherefore had they birth?

The dead are thy inheritors — and we
But bubbles on thy surface; and the key
Of thy profundity is in the grave,
The ebon portal of thy peopled cave,
Where I would walk in spirit, and behold
Our elements resolved to things untold,
And fathom hidden wonders, and explore
The essence of great bosoms now no more.
  *  *  *  *  *

Diodati, July, 1816.

### SONNET TO LAKE LEMAN.

Rousseau — Voltaire — our Gibbon — and De Staël —
  Leman![a] these names are worthy of thy shore,
  Thy shore of names like these! wert thou no more,
Their memory thy remembrance would recall:
To them thy banks were lovely as to all,
  But they have made them lovelier, for the lore
  Of mighty minds doth hallow in the core
Of human hearts the ruin of a wall
  Where dwelt the wise and wondrous; but by *thee*,
How much more, Lake of Beauty! do we feel,
  In sweetly gliding o'er thy crystal sea,
The wild glow of that not ungentle zeal,
  Which of the heirs of immortality
Is proud, and makes the breath of glory real!

Diodati, July, 1816.

[a] Geneva, Ferney, Copet, Lausanne. —

# ROMANCE MUY DOLOROSO

### DEL

## SITIO Y TOMA DE ALHAMA.

The effect of the original ballad — which existed both in Spanish and Arabic — was such, that it was forbidden to be sung by the Moors, on pain of death, within Granada.

## ROMANCE MUY DOLOROSO
### DEL
#### SITIO Y TOMA DE ALHAMA.

*El qual dezia en Aravigo assi.*

I.

Passeavase el Rey Moro
Por la ciudad de Granada,
Desde las puertas de Elvira
Hasta las de Bivarambla.
   Ay de mi, Alhama!

II.

Cartas le fueron venidas
Que Alhama era ganada.
Las cartas echò en el fuego,
Y al mensagero matava.
   Ay de mi, Alhama!

III.

Descavalga de una mula,
Y en un cavallo cavalga.
Por el Zacatin arriba
Subido se avia al Alhambra.
   Ay de mi, Alhama!

IV.

Como en el Alhambra estuvo,
Al mismo punto mandave
Que se toquen las trompetas
Con añafiles de plata.
   Ay de mi, Alhama!

V.

Y que atambores de guerra
Apriessa toquen alarma;
Por que lo oygan sus Moros,
Los de la Vega y Granada.
   Ay de mi, Alhama!

## A VERY MOURNFUL BALLAD
### ON THE
### SIEGE AND CONQUEST OF ALHAMA.

*Which, in the Arabic language, is to the following purport.*

#### I.
The Moorish King rides up and down
Through Granada's royal town;
From Elvira's gates to those
Of Bivarambla on he goes.
           Woe is me, Alhama!

#### II.
Letters to the monarch tell
How Alhama's city fell:
In the fire the scroll he threw,
And the messenger he slew.
           Woe is me, Alhama!

#### III.
He quits his mule, and mounts his horse,
And through the street directs his course;
Through the street of Zacatin
To the Alhambra spurring in.
           Woe is me, Alhama!

#### IV.
When the Alhambra walls he gain'd,
On the moment he ordain'd
That the trumpet straight should sound
With the silver clarion round.
           Woe is me, Alhama!

#### V.
And when the hollow drums of war
Beat the loud alarm afar,
That the Moors of town and plain
Might answer to the martial strain,
           Woe is me, Alhama!

### VI.

Los Moros que el son oyeron,
Que al sangriento Marte llama,
Uno a uno, y dos a dos,
Un gran esquadron formavan.
   Ay de mi, Alhama!

### VII.

Alli hablò un Moro viejo;
Desta manera hablava: —
Para que nos llamas, Rey?
Para que es este llamada?
   Ay de mi, Alhama!

### VIII.

Aveys de saber, amigos,
Una nueva desdichada:
Que Christianos, con braveza,
Ya nos han tomado Alhama.
   Ay de mi, Alhama!

### IX.

Alli hablò un viejo Alfaqui,
De barba crecida y cana: —
Bien se te emplea, buen Rey,
Buen Rey; bien se te empleava.
   Ay de mi, Alhama!

### X.

Mataste los Bencerrages,
Que era la flor de Granada;
Cogiste los tornadizos
De Cordova la nombrada.
   Ay de mi, Alhama!

### XI.

Por esso mereces, Rey,
Una pene bien doblada;
Que te pierdas tu y el reyno,
Y que se pierda Granada.
   Ay de mi, Alhama!

### VI.

Then the Moors, by this aware
That bloody Mars recall'd them there,
One by one, and two by two,
To a mighty squadron grew.
Woe is me, Alhama!

### VII.

Out then spake an aged Moor
In these words the king before,
"Wherefore call on us, oh King?
What may mean this gathering?"
Woe is me, Alhama!

### VIII.

"Friends! ye have, alas! to know
Of a most disastrous blow,
That the Christians, stern and bold,
Have obtain'd Alhama's hold."
Woe is me, Alhama!

### IX.

Out then spake old Alfaqui,
With his beard so white to see,
"Good King! thou art justly served,
Good King! this thou hast deserved.
Woe is me, Alhama!

### X.

"By thee were slain, in evil hour,
The Abencerrage, Granada's flower;
And strangers were received by thee
Of Cordova the Chivalry.
Woe is me, Alhama!

### XI.

"And for this, oh King! is sent
On thee a double chastisement:
Thee and thine, thy crown and realm,
One last wreck shall overwhelm.
Woe is me, Alhama!

XII.

Si no se respetan leyes,
Es ley que todo se pierda;
Y que se pierda Granada,
Y que te pierdas en ella.
   Ay de mi, Alhama!

XIII.

Fuego por los ojos vierte,
El Rey que esto oyera,
Y como el otro de leyes
De leyes tambien hablava.
   Ay de mi, Alhama!

XIV.

Sabe un Rey que no ay leyes
De darle a Reyes disgusto —
Esso dize el Rey Moro
Relinchando de colera.
   Ay de mi, Alhama!

XV.

Moro Alfaqui, Moro Alfaqui,
El de la vellida barba,
El Rey te manda prender,
Por la perdida de Alhama.
   Ay de mi, Alhama!

XVI.

Y cortarte la cabeza,
Y ponerla en el Alhambra,
Por que a ti castigo sea,
Y otros tiemblen en miralla.
   Ay de mi, Alhama!

XVII.

Cavalleros, hombres buenos,
Dezid de mi parte al Rey,
Al Rey Moro de Granada,
Como no le devo nada.
   Ay de mi, Alhama!

## XII.

"He who holds no laws in awe,
He must perish by the law;
And Granada must be won,
And thyself with her undone."
    Woe is me, Alhama!

## XIII.

Fire flash'd from out the old Moor's eyes,
The Monarch's wrath began to rise,
Because he answer'd, and because
He spake exceeding well of laws.
    Woe is me, Alhama!

## XIV.

"There is no law to say such things
As may disgust the ear of kings:"—
Thus, snorting with his choler, said
The Moorish King, and doom'd him dead.
    Woe is me, Alhama!

## XV.

Moor Alfaqui! Moor Alfaqui!
Though thy beard so hoary be,
The King hath sent to have thee seized,
For Alhama's loss displeased.
    Woe is me, Alhama!

## XVI.

And to fix thy head upon
High Alhambra's loftiest stone;
That this for thee should be the law,
And others tremble when they saw.
    Woe is me, Alhama!

## XVII.

"Cavalier, and man of worth!
Let these words of mine go forth;
Let the Moorish Monarch know,
That to him I nothing owe.
    Woe is me, Alhama!

XVIII.
De averse Alhama perdido
A mi me pesa en el alma.
Que si el Rey perdió su tierra,
Otro mucho mas perdiera.
   Ay de mi, Alhama!

XIX.
Perdieran hijos padres,
Y casados las casadas:
Las cosas que mas amara
Perdió l' un y el otro fama.
   Ay de mi, Alhama!

XX.
Perdi una hija donzella
Que era la flor d' esta tierra,
Cien doblas dava por ella,
No me las estimo en nada.
   Ay de mi, Alhama!

XXI.
Diziendo assi al hacen Alfaqui,
Le cortaron la cabeça,
Y la elevan al Alhambra,
Assi come el Rey lo manda.
   Ay de mi, Alhama!

XXII.
Hombres, niños y mugeres,
Lloran tan grande perdida.
Lloravan todas las damas
Quantas en Granada avia.
   Ay de mi, Alhama!

XXIII.
Por las calles y ventanas
Mucho luto parecia;
Llora el Rey como fembra,
Qu' es mucho lo que perdia.
   Ay de mi, Alhama!

XVIII.

"But on my soul Alhama weighs,
And on my inmost spirit preys;
And if the King his land hath lost,
Yet others may have lost the most.
    Woe is me, Alhama!

XIX.

"Sires have lost their children, wives
Their lords, and valiant men their lives;
One what best his love might claim
Hath lost, another wealth, or fame.
    Woe is me, Alhama!

XX.

"I lost a damsel in that hour,
Of all the land the loveliest flower;
Doubloons a hundred I would pay,
And think her ransom cheap that day."
    Woe is me, Alhama!

XXI.

And as these things the old Moor said,
They sever'd from the trunk his head;
And to the Alhambra's wall with speed
'Twas carried, as the King decreed.
    Woe is me, Alhama!

XXII.

And men and infants therein weep
Their loss, so heavy and so deep;
Granada's ladies, all she rears
Within her walls, burst into tears.
    Woe is me, Alhama!

XXIII.

And from the windows o'er the walls
The sable web of mourning falls;
The King weeps as a woman o'er
His loss, for it is much and sore.
    Woe is me, Alhama!

### SONETTO DI VITTORELLI.

#### PER MONACA.

Sonetto composto in nome di un genitore, a cui era morta poco innanzi una figlia appena maritata; è diretto al genitore della sacra sposa.

Di duo vaghe donzelle, oneste, accorte
   Lieti e miseri padri il ciel ne feo,
   Il ciel, che degne di più nobil sorte
   L' una e l' altra veggendo, ambo chiedeo.
La mia fu tolta da veloce morte
   A le fumanti tede d' imeneo:
   La tua, Francesco, in sugellate porte
   Eterna prigioniera or si rendeo.
Ma tu almeno potrai de la gelosa
   Irremeabil soglia, ove s' asconde,
   La sua tenera udir voce pietosa.
Io verso un fiume d' amarissim' onde,
   Corro a quel marmo, in cui la figlia or posa
   Batto, e ribatto, ma nessun risponde.

### TRANSLATION FROM VITTORELLI.

#### ON A NUN.

*Sonnet composed in the name of a father, whose daughter had recently died shortly after her marriage; and addressed to the father of her who had lately taken the veil.*

Of two fair virgins, modest, though admired,
   Heaven made us happy; and now, wretched sires;
   Heaven for a nobler doom their worth desires,
   And gazing upon *either*, *both* required.
Mine, while the torch of Hymen newly fired
   Becomes extinguish'd, soon — too soon — expires;
   But thine, within the closing grate retired,
   Eternal captive, to her God aspires.
But *thou* at least from out the jealous door,
   Which shuts between your never-meeting eyes,
   May'st hear her sweet and pious voice once more:
I to the marble, where *my daughter* lies,
   Rush, — the swoln flood of bitterness I pour,
   And knock, and knock, and knock — but none replies.

### STANZAS FOR MUSIC.
["BRIGHT BE THE PLACE OF THY SOUL!"]

#### I.
Bright be the place of thy soul!
  No lovelier spirit than thine
E'er burst from its mortal control,
  In the orbs of the blessed to shine.
On earth thou wert all but divine,
  As thy soul shall immortally be;
And our sorrow may cease to repine
  When we know that thy God is with thee.

#### II.
Light be the turf of thy tomb!
  May its verdure like emeralds be!
There should not be the shadow of gloom,
  In aught that reminds us of thee.
Young flowers and an evergreen tree
  May spring from the spot of thy rest:
But nor cypress nor yew let us see;
  For why should we mourn for the blest?

---

### STANZAS FOR MUSIC.
["THEY SAY THAT HOPE IS HAPPINESS."]

#### I.
They say that Hope is happiness;
  But genuine Love must prize the past,
And Memory wakes the thoughts that bless:
  They rose the first — they set the last;

#### II.
And all that Memory loves the most
  Was once our only Hope to be,
And all that Hope adored and lost
  Hath melted into Memory.

### III.

Alas! it is delusion all:
The future cheats us from afar,
Nor can we be what we recall,
Nor dare we think on what we are.

---

## TO THOMAS MOORE.

### I.

My boat is on the shore,
 And my bark is on the sea;
But, before I go, Tom Moore,
 Here's a double health to thee!

### II.

Here's a sigh to those who love me,
 And a smile to those who hate;
And, whatever sky's above me,
 Here's a heart for every fate.

### III.

Though the ocean roar around me,
 Yet it still shall bear me on;
Though a desert should surround me,
 It hath springs that may be won.

### IV.

Were't the last drop in the well
 As I gasp'd upon the brink,
Ere my fainting spirit fell,
 'Tis to thee that I would drink.

### V.

With that water, as this wine,
 The libation I would pour
Should be — peace with thine and mine,
 And a health to thee, Tom Moore.

### SONG FOR THE LUDDITES.

#### I.

As the Liberty lads o'er the sea
Bought their freedom, and cheaply, with blood,
  So we, boys, we
  Will *die* fighting, or *live* free,
And down with all kings but King Ludd!

#### II.

When the web that we weave is complete,
And the shuttle exchanged for the sword,
  We will fling the winding sheet
  O'er the despot at our feet,
And die it deep in the gore he has pour'd.

#### III.

Though black as his heart its hue,
Since his veins are corrupted to mud,
    Yet this is the dew
    Which the tree shall renew
Of Liberty, planted by Ludd!

---

### SO, WE'LL GO NO MORE A ROVING.

#### I.

  So, we'll go no more a roving
    So late into the night,
  Though the heart be still as loving,
    And the moon be still as bright.

#### II.

  For the sword outwears its sheath,
    And the soul wears out the breast,
  And the heart must pause to breathe,
    And love itself have rest.

#### III.

  Though the night was made for loving,
    And the day returns too soon,
  Yet we'll go no more a roving
    By the light of the moon.

## ON THE BUST OF HELEN BY CANOVA.

In this beloved marble view,
  Above the works and thoughts of man,
What Nature *could,* but *would not,* do,
  And Beauty and Canova *can!*
Beyond imagination's power,
  Beyond the Bard's defeated art,
With immortality her dower,
  Behold the *Helen* of the *heart!*

## VERSICLES.

I READ the "Christabel;"
  Very well:
I read the "Missionary;"
  Pretty — very:
I tried at "Ilderim;"
  Ahem!
I read a sheet of "Marg'ret of *Anjou;*"
  *Can you?*
I turn'd a page of Scott's "Waterloo;"
  Pooh! pooh!
I look'd at Wordsworth's milk-white "Rylstone Doe;"
  Hillo!
  &c. &c. &c.

## TO MR. MURRAY.

To hook the reader, you, John Murray,
  Have publish'd "Anjou's Margaret,"
Which won't be sold off in a hurry
  (At least, it has not been as yet);
And then, still further to bewilder 'em,
  Without remorse you set up "Ilderim;"
So mind you don't get into debt,
  Because as how, if you should fail,
These books would be but baddish bail.

And mind you do *not* let escape
  These rhymes to Morning Post or Perry,
  Which would be *very* treacherous — *very*,
And get me into such a scrape!
  For, firstly, I should have to sally,
  All in my little boat, against a *Galley;*
  And, should I chance to slay the Assyrian wight,
  Have next to combat with the female knight.
                              March 25. 1817.

---

EPISTLE FROM MR. MURRAY TO DR. POLIDORI.

Dear Doctor, I have read your play,
Which is a good one in its way, —
Purges the eyes and moves the bowels,
And drenches handkerchiefs like towels
With tears, that, in a flux of grief,
Afford hysterical relief
To shatter'd nerves and quicken'd pulses,
Which your catastrophe convulses.

  I like your moral and machinery;
Your plot, too, has such scope for scenery;
Your dialogue is apt and smart;
The play's concoction full of art;
Your hero raves, your heroine cries,
All stab, and every body dies.
In short, your tragedy would be
The very thing to hear and see:
And for a piece of publication,
If I decline on this occasion,
It is not that I am not sensible
To merits in themselves ostensible,
But — and I grieve to speak it — plays
Are drugs — mere drugs, sir — now-a-days.
I had a heavy loss by "Manuel," —
Too lucky if it prove not annual, —

And Sotheby, with his "Orestes,"
(Which, by the by, the author's best is,)
Has lain so very long on hand
That I despair of all demand.
I've advertised, but see my books,
Or only watch my shopman's looks; —
Still Ivan, Ina, and such lumber,
My back-shop glut, my shelves encumber.

There's Byron too, who once did better,
Has sent me, folded in a letter,
A sort of — it's no more a drama
Than Darnley, Ivan, or Kehama;
So alter'd since last year his pen is,
I think he's lost his wits at Venice.
In short, sir, what with one and t'other,
I dare not venture on another.
I write in haste; excuse each blunder;
The coaches through the street so thunder!
My room's so full — we've Gifford here
Reading MS., with Hookham Frere,
Pronouncing on the nouns and particles
Of some of our forthcoming Articles.

The Quarterly — Ah, sir, if you
Had but the genius to review! —
A smart critique upon St. Helena,
Or if you only would but tell in a
Short compass what — but, to resume:
As I was saying, sir, the room —
The room's so full of wits and bards,
Crabbes, Campbells, Crokers, Freres, and Wards,
And others, neither bards nor wits: —
My humble tenement admits
All persons in the dress of gent.,
From Mr. Hammond to Dog Dent.

A party dines with me to-day,
All clever men, who make their way;

Crabbe, Malcolm, Hamilton, and Chantrey,
Are all partakers of my pantry.
They're at this moment in discussion
On poor De Staël's late dissolution.
Her book, they say, was in advance —
Pray Heaven, she tell the truth of France!
Thus run our time and tongues away. —
But, to return, sir, to your play:
Sorry, sir, but I can not deal,
Unless 'twere acted by O'Neill.
My hands so full, my head so busy,
I'm almost dead, and always dizzy;
And so, with endless truth and hurry,
Dear Doctor, I am yours,
     JOHN MURRAY.

### EPISTLE TO MR. MURRAY.

My dear Mr. Murray,
You're in a damn'd hurry
 To set up this ultimate Canto;\*
But (if they don't rob us)
You'll see Mr. Hobhouse
 Will bring it safe in his portmanteau.

For the Journal you hint of,
As ready to print off,
 No doubt you do right to commend it;
But as yet I have writ off
The devil a bit of
 Our "Beppo:" — when copied, I'll send it.

Then you've \* \* \* 's Tour, —
No great things, to be sure, —
 You could hardly begin with a less work;
For the pompous rascallion,
Who don't speak Italian
 Nor French, must have scribbled by guesswork.

\* The fourth Canto of "Childe Harold."

You can make any loss up
With "Spence" and his gossip,
　A work which must surely succeed;
Then Queen Mary's Epistle-craft,
With the new "Fytte" of "Whistlecraft,"
　Must make people purchase and read.

Then you've General Gordon,
Who girded his sword on,
　To serve with a Muscovite master,
And help him to polish
A nation so owlish,
　They thought shaving their beards a disaster.

For the man, "poor and shrewd,"
With whom you'd conclude
　A compact without more delay,
Perhaps some such pen is
Still extant in Venice;
　But please, sir, to mention *your pay*.

Venice, January 8. 1818.

---

### TO MR. MURRAY.

Strahan, Tonson, Lintot of the times,
Patron and publisher of rhymes,
For thee the bard up Pindus climbs,
　　　My Murray.

To thee, with hope and terror dumb,
The unfledged MS. authors come;
Thou printest all — and sellest some —
　　　My Murray.

Upon thy table's baize so green
The last new Quarterly is seen, —
But where is thy new Magazine,
　　　My Murray?

Along thy sprucest bookshelves shine
The works thou deemest most divine —
The "Art of Cookery," and mine,
    My Murray.

Tours, Travels, Essays, too, I wist,
And Sermons to thy mill bring grist;
And then thou hast the "Navy List,"
    My Murray.

And Heaven forbid I should conclude
Without "the Board of Longitude,"
Although this narrow paper would,
    My Murray!

Venice, March 25. 1818.

## TO THOMAS MOORE.

What are you doing now,
  Oh Thomas Moore?
What are you doing now,
  Oh Thomas Moore?
Sighing or suing now,
Rhyming or wooing now,
Billing or cooing now,
  Which, Thomas Moore?

But the Carnival's coming,
  Oh Thomas Moore!
The Carnival's coming,
  Oh Thomas Moore!
Masking and humming,
Fifing and drumming,
Guitarring and strumming,
  Oh Thomas Moore!

### EPITAPH FOR WILLIAM PITT.

With death doom'd to grapple,
  Beneath this cold slab, he
Who lied in the Chapel
  Now lies in the Abbey.

---

### SONNET TO GEORGE THE FOURTH,

#### ON THE REPEAL OF LORD EDWARD FITZGERALD'S FORFEITURE.

To be the father of the fatherless,
  To stretch the hand from the throne's height, and raise
  *His* offspring, who expired in other days
To make thy sire's sway by a kingdom less, —
*This* is to be a monarch, and repress
  Envy into unutterable praise.
Dismiss thy guard, and trust thee to such traits,
For who would lift a hand, except to bless?
  Were it not easy, sir, and is't not sweet
To make thyself beloved? and to be
Omnipotent by mercy's means? for thus
  Thy sovereignty would grow but more complete,
A despot thou, and yet thy people free,
  And by the heart, not hand, enslaving us.

Bologna, August 12, 1819.

---

### EPIGRAM.

#### FROM THE FRENCH OF RULHIERES.

If, for silver or for gold,
  You could melt ten thousand pimples
  Into half a dozen dimples,
Then your face we might behold,
  Looking, doubtless, much more snugly;
  Yet even *then* 'twould be d—d ugly.

### ON MY WEDDING-DAY.

Here's a happy new year! but with reason
    I beg you'll permit me to say —
Wish me *many* returns of the *season*,
    But as *few* as you please of the *day*.

---

### EPIGRAM.

In digging up your bones, Tom Paine,
    Will. Cobbett has done well:
You visit him on earth again,
    He'll visit you in hell.

---

### STANZAS.

When a man hath no freedom to fight for at home,
    Let him combat for that of his neighbours;
Let him think of the glories of Greece and of Rome,
    And get knock'd on the head for his labours.

To do good to mankind is the chivalrous plan,
    And is always as nobly requited;
Then battle for freedom wherever you can,
    And, if not shot or hang'd, you'll get knighted.

---

### EPIGRAM.

The world is a bundle of hay,
    Mankind are the asses who pull;
Each tugs it a different way,
    And the greatest of all is John Bull.

---

### THE IRISH AVATAR.

#### I.

Ere the daughter of Brunswick is cold in her grave,
    And her ashes still float to their home o'er the tide,
Lo! George the triumphant speeds over the wave,
    To the long-cherish'd isle which he loved like his — bride.

II.

True, the great of her bright and brief era are gone,
  The rainbow-like epoch where Freedom could pause
For the few little years, out of centuries won,
  Which betray'd not, or crush'd not, or wept not her cause.

III.

True, the chains of the Catholic clank o'er his rags,
  The castle still stands, and the senate's no more,
And the famine which dwelt on her freedomless crags
  Is extending its steps to her desolate shore.

IV.

To her desolate shore — where the emigrant stands
  For a moment to gaze ere he flies from his hearth;
Tears fall on his chain, though it drops from his hands,
  For the dungeon he quits is the place of his birth.

V.

But he comes! the Messiah of royalty comes!
  Like a goodly Leviathan roll'd from the waves!
Then receive him as best such an advent becomes,
  With a legion of cooks, and an army of slaves!

VI.

He comes in the promise and bloom of threescore,
  To perform in the pageant the sovereign's part —
But long live the shamrock which shadows him o'er!
  Could the green in his *hat* be transferr'd to his *heart!*

VII.

Could that long-wither'd spot but be verdant again,
  And a new spring of noble affections arise —
Then might freedom forgive thee this dance in thy chain,
  And this shout of thy slavery which saddens the skies.

VIII.

Is it madness or meanness which clings to thee now?
  Were he God — as he is but the commonest clay,
With scarce fewer wrinkles than sins on his brow —
  Such servile devotion might shame him away.

#### IX.

Ay, roar in his train! let thine orators lash
    Their fanciful spirits to pamper his pride —
Not thus did thy Grattan indignantly flash
    His soul o'er the freedom implored and denied.

#### X.

Ever glorious Grattan! the best of the good!
    So simple in heart, so sublime in the rest!
With all which Demosthenes wanted endued,
    And his rival or victor in all he possess'd.

#### XI.

Ere Tully arose in the zenith of Rome,
    Though unequall'd, preceded, the task was begun —
But Grattan sprung up like a god from the tomb
    Of ages, the first, last, the saviour, the *one!*

#### XII.

With the skill of an Orpheus to soften the brute:
    With the fire of Prometheus to kindle mankind;
Even Tyranny listening sate melted or mute,
    And Corruption shrunk scorch'd from the glance of his mind.

#### XIII.

But back to our theme! Back to despots and slaves!
    Feasts furnish'd by Famine! rejoicings by Pain!
True freedom but *welcomes*, while slavery still *raves*,
    When a week's saturnalia hath loosen'd her chain.

#### XIV.

Let the poor squalid splendour thy wreck can afford
    (As the bankrupt's profusion his ruin would hide)
Gild over the palace, Lo! Erin, thy lord!
    Kiss his foot with thy blessing, his blessings denied!

#### XV.

Or *if* freedom past hope be extorted at last,
    If the idol of brass find his feet are of clay,
Must what terror or policy wring forth be class'd
    With what monarchs ne'er give, but as wolves yield their prey?

### XVI.

Each brute hath its nature, a king's is to *reign*, —
  To *reign!* in that word see, ye ages, comprised
The cause of the curses all annals contain,
  From Cæsar the dreaded to George the despised!

### XVII.

Wear, Fingal, thy trapping! O'Connell, proclaim
  His accomplishments! *His!!!* and thy country convince
Half an age's contempt was an error of fame,
  And that "Hal is the rascaliest, sweetest *young* prince!"

### XVIII.

Will thy yard of blue riband, poor Fingal, recall
  The fetters from millions of Catholic limbs?
Or, has it not bound thee the fastest of all
  The slaves, who now hail their betrayer with hymns?

### XIX.

Ay! "Build him a dwelling!" let each give his mite!
  Till, like Babel, the new royal dome hath arisen!
Let thy beggars and helots their pittance unite —
  And a palace bestow for a poor-house and prison!

### XX.

Spread — spread, for Vitellius, the royal repast,
  Till the gluttonous despot be stuff'd to the gorge!
And the roar of his drunkards proclaim him at last
  The Fourth of the fools and oppressors call'd "George!"

### XXI.

Let the tables be loaded with feasts till they groan!
  'Till they *groan* like thy people, through ages of woe!
Let the wine flow around the old Bacchanal's throne,
  Like their blood which has flow'd, and which yet has to flow.

### XXII.

But let not *his* name be thine idol alone —
  On his right hand behold a Sejanus appears!
Thine own Castlereagh! let him still be thine own!
  A wretch, never named but with curses and jeers!

XXIII.

Till now, when the isle which should blush for his birth,
  Deep, deep as the gore which he shed on her soil,
Seems proud of the reptile which crawl'd from her earth,
  And for murder repays him with shouts and a smile!

XXIV.

Without one single ray of her genius, without
  The fancy, the manhood, the fire of her race —
The miscreant who well might plunge Erin in doubt
  If *she* ever gave birth to a being so base.

XXV.

If she did — let her long-boasted proverb be hush'd,
  Which proclaims that from Erin no reptile can spring —
See the cold-blooded serpent, with venom full flush'd,
  Still warming its folds in the breast of a king!

XXVI.

Shout, drink, feast, and flatter! Oh! Erin, how low
  Wert thou sunk by misfortune and tyranny, till
Thy welcome of tyrants hath plunged thee below
  The depth of thy deep in a deeper gulf still.

XXVII.

My voice, though but humble, was raised for thy right,
  My vote, as a freeman's, still voted thee free,
This hand, though but feeble, would arm in thy fight,
  And this heart, though outworn, had a throb still for *thee!*

XXVIII.

Yes, I loved thee and thine, though thou art not my land,
  I have known noble hearts and great souls in thy sons,
And I wept with the world o'er the patriot band
  Who are gone, but I weep them no longer as once.

XXIX.

For happy are they now reposing afar, —
  Thy Grattan, thy Curran, thy Sheridan, all
Who, for years, were the chiefs in the eloquent war,
  And redeem'd, if they have not retarded, thy fall.

### XXX.

Yes, happy are they in their cold English graves!
 Their shades cannot start to thy shouts of to-day —
Nor the steps of enslavers and chain-kissing slaves
 Be stamp'd in the turf o'er their fetterless clay.

### XXXI.

Till now I had envied thy sons and their shore,
 Though their virtues were hunted, their liberties fled;
There was something so warm and sublime in the core
 Of an Irishman's heart, that I envy — thy *dead*.

### XXXII.

Or, if aught in my bosom can quench for an hour
 My contempt for a nation so servile, though sore,
Which though trod like the worm will not turn upon power,
 'Tis the glory of Grattan, and genius of Moore!

---

## ON THE BIRTH OF JOHN WILLIAM RIZZO HOPPNER.

His father's sense, his mother's grace,
 In him, I hope, will always fit so;
With — still to keep him in good case —
 The health and appetite of Rizzo.

---

## STANZAS.

["COULD LOVE FOR EVER."]

### I.

Could Love for ever
Run like a river,
And Time's endeavour
 Be tried in vain —
No other pleasure
With this could measure;
And like a treasure
 We'd hug the chain.

But since our sighing
Ends not in dying,
And, form'd for flying,
   Love plumes his wing;
Then for this reason
Let's love a season;
But let that season be only Spring.

### II.

When lovers parted
Feel broken-hearted,
And, all hopes thwarted,
   Expect to die;
A few years older,
Ah! how much colder
They might behold her
   For whom they sigh!
When link'd together,
In every weather,
They pluck Love's feather
   From out his wing —
He'll stay for ever,
But sadly shiver
Without his plumage, when past the Spring.

### III.

Like Chiefs of Faction,
His life is action —
A formal paction
   That curbs his reign,
Obscures his glory,
Despot no more, he
Such territory
   Quits with disdain.
Still, still advancing,
With banners glancing,
His power enhancing,

He must move on —
Repose but cloys him,
Retreat destroys him,
Love brooks not a degraded throne.

### IV.

Wait not, fond lover!
Till years are over,
And then recover,
  As from a dream.
While each bewailing
The other's failing,
With wrath and railing,
  All hideous seem —
While first decreasing,
Yet not quite ceasing,
Wait not till teasing
  All passion blight:
If once diminish'd
Love's reign is finish'd —
Then part in friendship, — and bid good-night.

### V.

So shall Affection
To recollection
The dear connection
  Bring back with joy:
You had not waited
Till, tired or hated,
Your passions sated
  Began to cloy.
Your last embraces
Leave no cold traces —
The same fond faces
  As through the past;
And eyes, the mirrors
Of your sweet errors
Reflect but rapture — not least though last.

VI.

True, separations
Ask more than patience;
What desperations
 From such have risen!
But yet remaining,
What is't but chaining
Hearts which, once waning,
 Beat 'gainst their prison?
Time can but cloy love,
And use destroy love:
The winged boy, Love,
 Is but for boys —
You'll find it torture
Though sharper, shorter,
To wean, and not wear out your joys.

---

### THE CHARITY BALL.

What matter the pangs of a husband and father,
 If his sorrows in exile be great or be small,
So the Pharisee's glories around her she gather,
 And the saint patronizes her "charity ball!"
What matters — a heart which, though faulty, was feeling,
 Be driven to excesses which once could appal —
That the sinner should suffer is only fair dealing,
 As the saint keeps her charity back for "the ball!"*

* These lines were written on reading in the newspapers, that Lady Byron had been patroness of a ball in aid of some charity at Hinckley.

### EPIGRAM ON MY WEDDING-DAY.

#### TO PENELOPE.

This day, of all our days, has done
  The worst for me and you: —
'Tis just *six* years since we were *one*,
  And *five* since we were *two*.

January 2. 1821.

---

### ON MY THIRTY-THIRD BIRTH-DAY.

#### JANUARY 22. 1821.

Through life's dull road, so dim and dirty,
I have dragg'd to three and thirty.
What have these years left to me?
Nothing — except thirty-three.

---

### EPIGRAM,

#### ON THE BRASIERS' COMPANY HAVING RESOLVED TO PRESENT AN ADDRESS TO QUEEN CAROLINE.

The brasiers, it seems, are preparing to pass
An address, and present it themselves all in brass; —
A superfluous pageant — for, by the Lord Harry!
They'll find where they're going much more than they carry.

---

### TO MR. MURRAY.

For Orford and for Waldegrave
You give much more than me you gave;
Which is not fairly to behave,
          My Murray.

Because if a live dog, 'tis said,
Be worth a lion fairly sped,
A *live lord* must be worth *two* dead,
          My Murray.

And if, as the opinion goes,
Verse hath a better sale than prose —
Certes, I should have more than those,
      My Murray.

But now this sheet is nearly cramm'd,
So, if *you will*, *I* shan't be shamm'd,
And if you *won't*, *you* may be damn'd,
      My Murray.

## STANZAS TO THE PO.

#### I.

River, that rollest by the ancient walls,
  Where dwells the lady of my love, when she
Walks by thy brink, and there perchance recalls
  A faint and fleeting memory of me;

#### II.

What if thy deep and ample stream should be
  A mirror of my heart, where she may read
The thousand thoughts I now betray to thee,
  Wild as thy wave, and headlong as thy speed!

#### III.

What do I say — a mirror of my heart?
  Are not thy waters sweeping, dark, and strong?
Such as my feelings were and are, thou art;
  And such as thou art were my passions long.

#### IV

Time may have somewhat tamed them, — not for ever;
  Thou overflow'st thy banks, and not for aye
Thy bosom overboils, congenial river!
  Thy floods subside, and mine have sunk away.

#### V.

But left long wrecks behind, and now again,
  Borne in our old unchanged career, we move;
Thou tendest wildly onwards to the main,
  And I — to loving *one* I should not love.

#### VI.

The current I behold will sweep beneath
  Her native walls and murmur at her feet;
Her eyes will look on thee, when she shall breathe
  The twilight air, unharm'd by summer's heat.

#### VII.

She will look on thee, — I have look'd on thee,
  Full of that thought; and, from that moment, ne'er
Thy waters could I dream of, name, or see,
  Without the inseparable sigh for her!

#### VIII.

Her bright eyes will be imaged in thy stream, —
  Yes! they will meet the wave I gaze on now:
Mine cannot witness, even in a dream,
  That happy wave repass me in its flow!

#### IX.

The wave that bears my tears returns no more:
  Will she return by whom that wave shall sweep? —
Both tread thy banks, both wander on thy shore,
  I by thy source, she by the dark-blue deep.

#### X.

But that which keepeth us apart is not
  Distance, nor depth of wave, nor space of earth,
But the distraction of a various lot,
  As various as the climates of our birth.

#### XI.

A stranger loves the lady of the land,
  Born far beyond the mountains, but his blood
Is all meridian, as if never fann'd
  By the black wind that chills the polar flood.

#### XII.

My blood is all meridian; were it not,
  I had not left my clime, nor should I be,
In spite of tortures, ne'er to be forgot,
  A slave again of love, — at least of thee.

#### XIII.

'Tis vain to struggle — let me perish young —
  Live as I lived, and love as I have loved;
To dust if I return, from dust I sprung,
  And then, at least, my heart can ne'er be moved.

## STANZAS WRITTEN ON THE ROAD BETWEEN FLORENCE AND PISA.

### I.

Oh, talk not to me of a name great in story;
The days of our youth are the days of our glory;
And the myrtle and ivy of sweet two-and-twenty
Are worth all your laurels, though ever so plenty.

### II.

What are garlands and crowns to the brow that is wrinkled?
'Tis but as a dead-flower with May-dew besprinkled.
Then away with all such from the head that is hoary!
What care I for the wreaths that can *only* give glory?

### III.

Oh FAME! — if I e'er took delight in thy praises,
'Twas less for the sake of thy high sounding phrases,
Than to see the bright eyes of the dear one discover
She thought that I was not unworthy to love her.

### IV.

*There* chiefly I sought thee, *there* only I found thee;
Her glance was the best of the rays that surround thee;
When it sparkled o'er aught that was bright in my story,
I knew it was love, and I felt it was glory.

---

## STANZAS:

### TO A HINDOO AIR.

[These verses were written by Lord Byron a little before he left Italy for Greece. They were meant to suit the Hindostanee air — "Alla Malla Punca," which the Countess Guiccioli was fond of singing.]

Oh! — my lonely — lonely — lonely — Pillow!
Where is my lover? where is my lover?
Is it his bark which my dreary dreams discover?
Far — far away! and alone along the billow?

Oh! my lonely — lonely – lonely — Pillow!
Why must my head ache where his gentle brow lay?
How the long night flags lovelessly and slowly,
And my head droops over thee like the willow. —

Oh! thou, my sad and solitary Pillow!
Send me kind dreams to keep my heart from breaking,
In return for the tears I shed upon thee waking
Let me not die till he comes back o'er the billow. —

Then if thou wilt — no more my *lonely* Pillow,
In one embrace let these arms again enfold him,
And then expire of the joy — but to behold him!
Oh! my lone bosom! — oh! my lonely Pillow!

## ON THIS DAY I COMPLETE MY THIRTY-SIXTH YEAR.

*Missolonghi, Jan. 22. 1824.*

### 1.

"Tis time this heart should be unmoved,
   Since others it hath ceased to move:
Yet, though I cannot be beloved,
   Still let me love!

### 2.

My days are in the yellow leaf;
   The flowers and fruits of love are gone;
The worm, the canker, and the grief
   Are mine alone!

### 3.

The fire that on my bosom preys
   Is lone as some volcanic isle;
No torch is kindled at its blaze —
   A funeral pile!

### 4.

The hope, the fear, the jealous care,
   The exalted portion of the pain
And power of love, I cannot share,
   But wear the chain.

5.

But 'tis not *thus* — and 'tis not *here* —
  Such thoughts should shake my soul, nor *now*,
Where glory decks the hero's bier,
    Or binds his brow.

6.

The sword, the banner, and the field,
  Glory and Greece, around me see!
The Spartan, borne upon his shield,
    Was not more free.

7.

Awake! (not Greece — she *is* awake!)
  Awake, my spirit! Think through *whom*
Thy life-blood tracks its parent lake,
    And then strike home!

8.

Tread those reviving passions down,
  Unworthy manhood! — unto thee
Indifferent should the smile or frown
    Of beauty be.

9.

If thou regret'st thy youth, *why live?*
  The land of honourable death
Is here: — up to the field, and give
    Away thy breath!

10.

Seek out — less often sought than found —
  A soldier's grave, for thee the best;
Then look around, and choose thy ground,
    And take thy rest.

# APPENDIX.

### FAREWELL TO MALTA.

Adieu, ye joys of La Valette!
Adieu, sirocco, sun, and sweat!
Adieu, thou palace rarely enter'd!
Adieu, ye mansions where — I've ventured!
Adieu, ye cursed streets of stairs!
(How surely he who mounts you swears!)
Adieu, ye merchants often failing!
Adieu, thou mob for ever railing!
Adieu, ye packets — without letters!
Adieu, ye fools — who ape your betters!
Adieu, thou damned'st quarantine,
That gave me fever, and the spleen!
Adieu that stage which makes us yawn, Sirs,
Adieu his Excellency's dancers!
Adieu to Peter — whom no fault's in,
But could not teach a colonel waltzing;
Adieu, ye females fraught with graces!
Adieu red coats, and redder faces!
Adieu the supercilious air
Of all that strut "en militaire!"
I go — but God knows when, or why,
To smoky towns and cloudy sky,
To things (the honest truth to say)
As bad — but in a different way. —
Farewell to these, but not adieu,
Triumphant sons of truest blue!
While either Adriatic shore,
And fallen chiefs, and fleets no more,

And nightly smiles, and daily dinners,
Proclaim you war and women's winners.
Pardon my Muse, who apt to prate is,
And take my rhyme — because 't is "gratis."

And now I've got to Mrs. Fraser,
Perhaps you think I mean to praise her —
And were I vain enough to think
My praise was worth this drop of ink,
A line — or two — were no hard matter,
As here, indeed, I need not flatter:
But she must be content to shine
In better praises than in mine,
With lively air, and open heart,
And fashion's case, without its art;
Her hours can gaily glide along,
Nor ask the aid of idle song. —

And now, O Malta! since thou'st got us,
Thou little military hothouse!
I'll not offend with words uncivil,
And wish thee rudely at the Devil,
But only stare from out my casement,
And ask, for what is such a place meant?
Then, in my solitary nook,
Return to scribbling, or a book,
Or take my physic while I'm able
(Two spoonfuls hourly by the label),
Prefer my nightcap to my beaver,
And bless the gods — I've got a fever!

May 26th, 1811.

## TO DIVES.

### A FRAGMENT.

Unhappy Dives! in an evil hour
'Gainst Nature's voice seduced to deeds accurst!
Once Fortune's minion, now thou feel'st her power;
Wrath's vial on thy lofty head hath burst.
In Wit, in Genius, as in Wealth the first,
How wond'rous bright thy blooming morn arose!
But thou wert smitten with th' unhallow'd thirst
Of Crime un-named, and thy sad noon must close
In scorn, and solitude unsought, the worst of woes.

1811.

---

### FROM THE FRENCH.

Æolē, beauty and poet, has two little crimes;
She makes her own face, and does not make her rhymes.

---

### PARENTHETICAL ADDRESS*

#### BY DR. PLAGIARY.

*Half stolen*, with acknowledgments, to be spoken in an inarticulate voice by Master P. at the opening of the next new theatre. Stolen parts marked with the inverted commas of quotation — thus "—".

"When energising objects men pursue,"
Then Lord knows what is writ by Lord knows who.
"A modest monologue you here survey,"
Hiss'd from the theatre the "other day,"
As if Sir Fretful wrote "the slumberous" verse,
And gave his son "the rubbish" to rehearse.
"Yet at the thing you'd never be amazed,"
Knew you the rumpus which the author raised;

---

* [Among the addresses sent in to the Drury Lane Committee, (see *ante*, p. 81) was one by Dr. Busby, entitled "A Monologue," of which the above is a parody.]

"Nor even here your smiles would be represt,"
Knew you these lines — the badness of the best.
"Flame! fire! and flame!!" (words borrow'd from Lucretius,)
"Dread metaphors which open wounds" like issues!
"And sleeping pangs awake — and — but away"
(Confound me if I know what next to say).
"Lo! Hope reviving re-expands her wings,"
And Master G— recites what Doctor Busby sings! —
"If mighty things with small we may compare,"
(Translated from the grammar for the fair!)
Dramatic "spirit drives a conquering car,"
And burn'd poor Moscow like a tub of "tar."
"This spirit Wellington has shown in Spain,"
To furnish melodrames for Drury Lane.
"Another Marlborough points to Blenheim's story,"
And George and I will dramatise it for ye.

"In arts and sciences our isle hath shone"
(This deep discovery is mine alone).
"Oh British poesy, whose powers inspire"
My verse — or I'm a fool — and Fame's a liar,
"Thee we invoke, your sister arts implore"
With "smiles," and "lyres," and "pencils," and much more.
These, if we win the Graces, too, we gain
*Disgraces*, too! "inseparable train!"
"Three who have stolen their witching airs from Cupid"
(You all know what I mean, unless you're stupid):
"Harmonious throng" that I have kept in petto,
Now to produce in a "divine *sestetto*"!!
"While Poesy," with these delightful doxies,
"Sustains her part" in all the "upper" boxes!
"Thus lifted gloriously, you'll soar along,"
Borne in the vast balloon of Busby's song;
"Shine in your farce, masque, scenery, and play"
(For this last line George had a holiday).
"Old Drury never, never soar'd so high,"
So says the manager, and so says I.

"But hold, you say, this self-complacent boast;"
Is this the poem which the public lost?
"True — true — that lowers at once our mounting pride;"
But lo! — the papers print what you deride.
"'Tis ours to look on you — you hold the prize,"
'Tis *twenty guineas*, as they advertize!
"A double blessing your rewards impart" —
I wish I had them, then, with all my heart.
"Our *twofold* feeling *owns* its twofold cause,"
Why son and I both beg for your applause.
"When in your fostering beams you bid us live,"
My next subscription list shall say how much you give!

October, 1812.

---

### VERSES FOUND IN A SUMMER HOUSE AT HALES-OWEN.*

When Dryden's fool, "unknowing what he sought,"
His hours in whistling spent, "for want of thought,"**
This guiltless oaf his vacancy of sense
Supplied, and amply too by innocence;
Did modern swains, possess'd of Cymon's powers,
In Cymon's manner waste their leisure hours,
Th' offended guests would not, with blushing, see
These fair green walks disgraced by infamy.
Severe the fate of modern fools, alas!
When vice and folly mark them as they pass.
Like noxious reptiles o'er the whiten'd wall,
The filth they leave still points out where they crawl.

\* In Warwickshire.
\*\* See Cymon and Iphigenia.

### MARTIAL, LIB. I. EPIG. L.

*Hic est, quem legis, ille, quem requiris,*
*Toto notus in orbe Martialis, &c.*

He unto whom thou art so partial,
Oh, reader! is the well-known Martial,
The Epigrammatist: while living,
Give him the fame thou wouldst be giving:
So shall he hear, and feel, and know it —
Post-obits rarely reach a poet.

---

### NEW DUET.

To the tune of "Why, how now, saucy jade?"

Why, how now, saucy Tom?
If you thus must ramble,
I will publish some
Remarks on Mister Campbell.

---

### ANSWER.

Why, how now, Parson Bowles?
Sure the priest is maudlin!
*(To the public)* How can you, d—n your souls,
Listen to his twaddling?

---

### EPIGRAMS.

Oh, Castlereagh! thou art a patriot now;
Cato died for his country, so didst thou:
He perish'd rather than see Rome enslaved,
Thou cutt'st thy throat that Britain may be saved!

---

So Castlereagh has cut his throat! — The worst
Of this is, — that his own was not the first.

---

So *He* has cut his throat at last! — He! Who?
The man who cut his country's long ago.

### EPITAPH.

Posterity will ne'er survey
  A nobler grave than this:
Here lie the bones of Castlereagh:
  Stop, traveller——

---

### THE CONQUEST.

[This fragment was found amongst Lord Byron's papers, after his departure from Genoa for Greece.]

March 8—9. 1823.

I.

The Son of Love and Lord of War I sing;
  Him who bade England bow to Normandy,
And left the name of conqueror more than king
  To his unconquerable dynasty.
Not fann'd alone by Victory's fleeting wing,
  He rear'd his bold and brilliant throne on high:
The Bastard kept, like lions, his prey fast,
And Britain's bravest victor was the last.

# MANFRED,

A

DRAMATIC POEM.

---

"There are more things in heaven and earth, Horatio,
Than are dreamt of in your philosophy."

---

## DRAMATIS PERSONÆ.

MANFRED.  
CHAMOIS HUNTER.  
ABBOT OF ST. MAURICE.  
MANUEL.  
HERMAN.  

WITCH OF THE ALPS.  
ARIMANES.  
NEMESIS.  
THE DESTINIES.  
SPIRITS, &c.

---

*The Scene of the Drama is amongst the Higher Alps — partly in the Castle of Manfred, and partly in the Mountains.*

# MANFRED.

## ACT I.

### SCENE I.

*Manfred alone.— Scene, a Gothic Gallery.— Time, Midnight.*

*Man.* The lamp must be replenish'd, but even then
It will not burn so long as I must watch:
My slumbers — if I slumber — are not sleep,
But a continuance of enduring thought,
Which then I can resist not: in my heart
There is a vigil, and these eyes but close
To look within; and yet I live, and bear
The aspect and the form of breathing men.
But grief should be the instructor of the wise;
Sorrow is knowledge: they who know the most
Must mourn the deepest o'er the fatal truth,
The Tree of Knowledge is not that of Life.
Philosophy and science, and the springs
Of wonder, and the wisdom of the world,
I have essay'd, and in my mind there is
A power to make these subject to itself —
But they avail not: I have done men good,
And I have met with good even among men —
But this avail'd not: I have had my foes,
And none have baffled, many fallen before me —
But this avail'd not: — Good, or evil, life,
Powers, passions, all I see in other beings,
Have been to me as rain unto the sands,
Since that all-nameless hour. I have no dread,
And feel the curse to have no natural fear,
Nor fluttering throb, that beats with hopes or wishes,
Or lurking love of something on the earth. —
Now to my task. —

Mysterious Agency!
Ye spirits of the unbounded Universe!
Whom I have sought in darkness and in light —
Ye, who do compass earth about, and dwell
In subtler essence — ye, to whom the tops
Of mountains inaccessible are haunts,
And earth's and ocean's caves familiar things —
I call upon ye by the written charm
Which gives me power upon you — Rise! appear! [*A pause.*
They come not yet. — Now by the voice of him
Who is the first among you — by this sign,
Which makes you tremble — by the claims of him
Who is undying, — Rise! appear! — Appear! [*A pause.*
If it be so. — Spirits of earth and air,
Ye shall not thus elude me: by a power,
Deeper than all yet urged, a tyrant-spell,
Which had its birthplace in a star condemn'd,
The burning wreck of a demolish'd world,
A wandering hell in the eternal space;
By the strong curse which is upon my soul,
The thought which is within me and around me,
I do compel ye to my will. — Appear!

[*A star is seen at the darker end of the gallery: it is stationary; and a voice is heard singing.*

FIRST SPIRIT.

Mortal! to thy bidding bow'd,
From my mansion in the cloud,
Which the breath of twilight builds,
And the summer's sunset gilds
With the azure and vermilion,
Which is mix'd for my pavilion;
Though thy quest may be forbidden,
On a star-beam I have ridden;
To thine adjuration bow'd,
Mortal — be thy wish avow'd!

*Voice of the* SECOND SPIRIT.

Mont Blanc is the monarch of mountains;
  They crown'd him long ago
On a throne of rocks, in a robe of clouds,
  With a diadem of snow.
Around his waist are forests braced,
  The Avalanche in his hand;
But ere it fall, that thundering ball
  Must pause for my command.
The Glacier's cold and restless mass
  Moves onward day by day;
But I am he who bids it pass,
  Or with its ice delay.
I am the spirit of the place,
  Could make the mountain bow
And quiver to his cavern'd base—
  And what with me wouldst *Thou?*

*Voice of the* THIRD SPIRIT.

In the blue depth of the waters,
  Where the wave hath no strife,
Where the wind is a stranger,
  And the sea-snake hath life,
Where the Mermaid is decking
  Her green hair with shells;
Like the storm on the surface
  Came the sound of thy spells;
O'er my calm Hall of Coral
  The deep echo roll'd —
To the Spirit of Ocean
  Thy wishes unfold!

FOURTH SPIRIT.

Where the slumbering earthquake
  Lies pillow'd on fire,
And the lakes of bitumen
  Rise boilingly higher;

Where the roots of the Andes
  Strike deep in the earth,
As their summits to heaven
  Shoot soaringly forth;
I have quitted my birthplace,
  Thy bidding to bide —
Thy spell hath subdued me,
  Thy will be my guide!

### Fifth Spirit.

I am the Rider of the wind,
  The Stirrer of the storm;
The hurricane I left behind
  Is yet with lightning warm;
To speed to thee, o'er shore and sea
  I swept upon the blast:
The fleet I met sail'd well, and yet
  'Twill sink ere night be past.

### Sixth Spirit.

My dwelling is the shadow of the night,
Why doth thy magic torture me with light?

### Seventh Spirit.

The star which rules thy destiny
Was ruled, ere earth began, by me:
It was a world as fresh and fair
As e'er revolved round sun in air;
Its course was free and regular,
Space bosom'd not a lovelier star.
The hour arrived — and it became
A wandering mass of shapeless flame,
A pathless comet, and a curse,
The menace of the universe;
Still rolling on with innate force,
Without a sphere, without a course,
A bright deformity on high,
The monster of the upper sky!

And thou! beneath its influence born —
Thou worm! whom I obey and scorn —
Forced by a power (which is not thine,
And lent thee but to make thee mine)
For this brief moment to descend,
Where these weak spirits round thee bend
And parley with a thing like thee —
What wouldst thou, Child of Clay! with me?

*The* SEVEN SPIRITS.

Earth, ocean, air, night, mountains, winds, thy star,
Are at thy beck and bidding, Child of Clay!
Before thee at thy quest their spirits are —
What wouldst thou with us, son of mortals — say?

*Man.* Forgetfulness —
*First Spirit.* Of what — of whom — and why?
*Man.* Of that which is within me; read it there —
Ye know it, and I cannot utter it.
*Spirit.* We can but give thee that which we possess:
Ask of us subjects, sovereignty, the power
O'er earth, the whole, or portion, or a sign
Which shall control the elements, whereof
We are the dominators, each and all,
These shall be thine.
*Man.* Oblivion, self-oblivion —
Can ye not wring from out the hidden realms
Ye offer so profusely what I ask?
*Spirit.* It is not in our essence, in our skill;
But — thou mayst die.
*Man.* Will death bestow it on me?
*Spirit.* We are immortal, and do not forget;
We are eternal; and to us the past
Is, as the future, present. Art thou answer'd?
*Man.* Ye mock me — but the power which brought ye here
Hath made you mine. Slaves, scoff not at my will!
The mind, the spirit, the Promethean spark,
The lightning of my being, is as bright,

Pervading, and far darting as your own,
And shall not yield to yours, though coop'd in clay!
Answer, or I will teach you what I am.
  *Spirit.* We answer as we answer'd; our reply
Is even in thine own words.
  *Man.*                          Why say ye so?
  *Spirit.* If, as thou say'st, thine essence be as ours,
We have replied in telling thee, the thing
Mortals call death hath nought to do with us.
  *Man.* I then have call'd ye from your realms in vain;
Ye cannot, or ye will not, aid me.
  *Spirit.*                          Say;
What we possess we offer; it is thine:
Bethink ere thou dismiss us, ask again —
Kingdom, and sway, and strength, and length of days —
  *Man.* Accursed! what have I to do with days?
They are too long already. — Hence — begone!
  *Spirit.* Yet pause: being here, our will would do thee
               service;
Bethink thee, is there then no other gift
Which we can make not worthless in thine eyes?
  *Man.* No, none: yet stay — one moment, ere we part —
I would behold ye face to face. I hear
Your voices, sweet and melancholy sounds,
As music on the waters; and I see
The steady aspect of a clear large star;
But nothing more. Approach me as ye are,
Or one, or all, in your accustom'd forms.
  *Spirit.* We have no forms, beyond the elements
Of which we are the mind and principle:
But choose a form — in that we will appear.
  *Man.* I have no choice; there is no form on earth
Hideous or beautiful to me. Let him,
Who is most powerful of ye, take such aspect
As unto him may seem most fitting — Come!
  *Seventh Spirit. (Appearing in the shape of a beautiful female
               figure.)* Behold!

*Man.* Oh God! if it be thus, and *thou*
Art not a madness and a mockery,
I yet might be most happy. I will clasp thee,
And we again will be —         [*The figure vanishes.*
        My heart is crush'd!
                [MANFRED *falls senseless.*

(*A Voice is heard in the Incantation which follows.*)
  When the moon is on the wave,
    And the glow-worm in the grass,
  And the meteor on the grave,
    And the wisp on the morass;
  When the falling stars are shooting,
  And the answer'd owls are hooting,
  And the silent leaves are still
  In the shadow of the hill,
  Shall my soul be upon thine,
  With a power and with a sign.

  Though thy slumber may be deep,
  Yet thy spirit shall not sleep;
  There are shades which will not vanish,
  There are thoughts thou canst not banish;
  By a power to thee unknown,
  Thou canst never be alone;
  Thou art wrapt as with a shroud,
  Thou art gather'd in a cloud;
  And for ever shalt thou dwell
  In the spirit of this spell.

  Though thou seest me not pass by,
  Thou shalt feel me with thine eye
  As a thing that, though unseen,
  Must be near thee, and hath been;
  And when in that secret dread
  Thou hast turn'd around thy head,
  Thou shalt marvel I am not
  As thy shadow on the spot,

And the power which thou dost feel
Shall be what thou must conceal.

And a magic voice and verse
Hath baptized thee with a curse;
And a spirit of the air
Hath begirt thee with a snare;
In the wind there is a voice
Shall forbid thee to rejoice;
And to thee shall Night deny
All the quiet of her sky;
And the day shall have a sun,
Which shall make thee wish it done.

From thy false tears I did distil
An essence which hath strength to kill;
From thy own heart I then did wring
The black blood in its blackest spring;
From thy own smile I snatch'd the snake,
For there it coil'd as in a brake;
From thy own lip I drew the charm
Which gave all these their chiefest harm;
In proving every poison known,
I found the strongest was thine own.

By thy cold breast and serpent smile,
By thy unfathom'd gulfs of guile,
By that most seeming virtuous eye,
By thy shut soul's hypocrisy;
By the perfection of thine art
Which pass'd for human thine own heart;
By thy delight in others' pain,
And by thy brotherhood of Cain,
I call upon thee! and compel
Thyself to be thy proper Hell!

And on thy head I pour the vial
Which doth devote thee to this trial;
Nor to slumber, nor to die,
Shall be in thy destiny;

Though thy death shall still seem near
To thy wish, but as a fear;
Lo! the spell now works around thee,
And the clankless chain hath bound thee;
O'er thy heart and brain together
Hath the word been pass'd — now wither!

SCENE II.

*The Mountain of the Jungfrau. — Time, Morning. —* MANFRED
*alone upon the Cliffs.*

*Man.* The spirits I have raised abandon me —
The spells which I have studied baffle me —
The remedy I reck'd of tortured me;
I lean no more on super-human aid,
It hath no power upon the past, and for
The future, till the past be gulf'd in darkness,
It is not of my search. — My mother Earth!
And thou fresh breaking Day, and you, ye Mountains,
Why are ye beautiful? I cannot love ye.
And thou, the bright eye of the universe,
That openest over all, and unto all
Art a delight — thou shin'st not on my heart.
And you, ye crags, upon whose extreme edge
I stand, and on the torrent's brink beneath
Behold the tall pines dwindled as to shrubs
In dizziness of distance; when a leap,
A stir, a motion, even a breath, would bring
My breast upon its rocky bosom's bed
To rest for ever — wherefore do I pause?
I feel the impulse — yet I do not plunge;
I see the peril — yet do not recede;
And my brain reels — and yet my foot is firm:
There is a power upon me which withholds,
And makes it my fatality to live;
If it be life to wear within myself
This barrenness of spirit, and to be
My own soul's sepulchre, for I have ceased

To justify my deeds unto myself —
The last infirmity of evil.  Ay,
Thou winged and cloud-cleaving minister,    [*An eagle passes.*
Whose happy flight is highest into heaven,
Well may'st thou swoop so near me — I should be
Thy prey, and gorge thine eaglets; thou art gone
Where the eye cannot follow thee; but thine
Yet pierces downward, onward, or above,
With a pervading vision. — Beautiful!
How beautiful is all this visible world!
How glorious in its action and itself!
But we, who name ourselves its sovereigns, we,
Half dust, half deity, alike unfit
To sink or soar, with our mix'd essence make
A conflict of its elements, and breathe
The breath of degradation and of pride,
Contending with low wants and lofty will,
Till our mortality predominates,
And men are — what they name not to themselves,
And trust not to each other.  Hark! the note,
            [*The Shepherd's pipe in the distance is heard.*
The natural music of the mountain reed —
For here the patriarchal days are not
A pastoral fable — pipes in the liberal air,
Mix'd with the sweet bells of the sauntering herd;
My soul would drink those echoes. — Oh, that I were
The viewless spirit of a lovely sound,
A living voice, a breathing harmony,
A bodiless enjoyment — born and dying
With the blest tone which made me!

             *Enter from below a* CHAMOIS HUNTER.
    *Chamois Hunter.*                Even so
This way the chamois leapt: her nimble feet
Have baffled me; my gains to-day will scarce
Repay my break-neck travail. — What is here?
Who seems not of my trade, and yet hath reach'd

A height which none even of our mountaineers,
Save our best hunters, may attain: his garb
Is goodly, his mien manly, and his air
Proud as a free-born peasant's, at this distance —
I will approach him nearer.

  *Man.* (*not perceiving the other.*) To be thus —
Grey-hair'd with anguish, like these blasted pines,
Wrecks of a single winter, barkless, branchless,
A blighted trunk upon a cursed root,
Which but supplies a feeling to decay —
And to be thus, eternally but thus,
Having been otherwise! Now furrow'd o'er
With wrinkles, plough'd by moments, not by years
And hours — all tortured into ages — hours
Which I outlive! — Ye toppling crags of ice!
Ye avalanches, whom a breath draws down
In mountainous o'erwhelming, come and crush me!
I hear ye momently above, beneath,
Crash with a frequent conflict; but ye pass,
And only fall on things that still would live;
On the young flourishing forest, or the hut
And hamlet of the harmless villager.

  *C. Hun.* The mists begin to rise from up the valley;
I'll warn him to descend, or he may chance
To lose at once his way and life together.

  *Man.* The mists boil up around the glaciers; clouds
Rise curling fast beneath me, white and sulphury,
Like foam from the roused ocean of deep Hell,
Whose every wave breaks on a living shore,
Heap'd with the damn'd like pebbles. — I am giddy.

  *C. Hun.* I must approach him cautiously; if near,
A sudden step will startle him, and he
Seems tottering already.

  *Man.*     Mountains have fallen,
Leaving a gap in the clouds, and with the shock
Rocking their Alpine brethren; filling up
The ripe green valleys with destruction's splinters;

Damming the rivers with a sudden dash,
Which crush'd the waters into mist, and made
Their fountains find another channel — thus,
Thus, in its old age, did Mount Rosenberg —
Why stood I not beneath it?
   *C. Hun.*               Friend! have a care,
Your next step may be fatal! — for the love
Of him who made you, stand not on that brink!
   *Man.* (*not hearing him.*) Such would have been for me a
              fitting tomb;
My bones had then been quiet in their depth;
They had not then been strewn upon the rocks
For the wind's pastime — as thus — thus they shall be —
In this one plunge. — Farewell, ye opening heavens!
Look not upon me thus reproachfully —
Ye were not meant for me — Earth! take these atoms!
     [*As* MANFRED *is in act to spring from the cliff, the*
       CHAMOIS HUNTER *seizes and retains him with a*
       *sudden grasp.*
   *C. Hun.* Hold, madman! — though aweary of thy life,
Stain not our pure vales with thy guilty blood —
Away with me — I will not quit my hold.
   *Man.* I am most sick at heart — nay, grasp me not —
I am all feebleness — the mountains whirl
Spinning around me — I grow blind — What art thou?
   *C. Hun.* I'll answer that anon. — Away with me —
The clouds grow thicker — there — now lean on me —
Place your foot here — here, take this staff, and cling
A moment to that shrub — now give me your hand,
And hold fast by my girdle — softly — well —
The Chalet will be gain'd within an hour —
Come on, we'll quickly find a surer footing,
And something like a pathway, which the torrent
Hath wash'd since winter. — Come, 'tis bravely done —
You should have been a hunter. — Follow me.
     [*As they descend the rocks with difficulty, the scene*
       *closes.*

## ACT II.

### SCENE I.

*A Cottage amongst the Bernese Alps.*

MANFRED *and the* CHAMOIS HUNTER.

*C. Hun.* No, no — yet pause — thou must not yet go
            forth:
Thy mind and body are alike unfit
To trust each other, for some hours, at least;
When thou art better, I will be thy guide —
But whither?
   *Man.*      It imports not: I do know
My route full well, and need no further guidance.
   *C. Hun.* Thy garb and gait bespeak thee of high lineage —
One of the many chiefs, whose castled crags
Look o'er the lower valleys — which of these
May call thee lord? I only know their portals;
My way of life leads me but rarely down
To bask by the huge hearths of those old halls,
Carousing with the vassals; but the paths,
Which step from out our mountains to their doors,
I know from childhood — which of these is thine?
   *Man.* No matter.
   *C. Hun.*         Well, sir, pardon me the question,
And be of better cheer. Come, taste my wine;
'Tis of an ancient vintage; many a day
'T has thawed my veins among our glaciers, now
Let it do thus for thine — Come, pledge me fairly.
   *Man.* Away, away! there's blood upon the brim!
Will it then never — never sink in the earth?
   *C. Hun.* What dost thou mean? thy senses wander from
            thee.
   *Man.* I say 'tis blood -- my blood! the pure warm stream
Which ran in the veins of my fathers, and in ours
When we were in our youth, and had one heart,

And loved each other as we should not love,
And this was shed: but still it rises up,
Colouring the clouds, that shut me out from heaven,
Where thou art not — and I shall never be.

   *C. Hun.* Man of strange words, and some half-maddening sin,
Which makes thee people vacancy, whate'er
Thy dread and sufferance be, there's comfort yet —
The aid of holy men, and heavenly patience —

   *Man.* Patience and patience! Hence — that word was made
For brutes of burthen, not for birds of prey;
Preach it to mortals of a dust like thine, —
I am not of thine order.

   *C. Hun.*           Thanks to heaven!
I would not be of thine for the free fame
Of William Tell; but whatsoe'er thine ill,
It must be borne, and these wild starts are useless.

   *Man.* Do I not bear it? — Look on me — I live.

   *C. Hun.* This is convulsion, and no healthful life.

   *Man.* I tell thee, man! I have lived many years,
Many long years, but they are nothing now
To those which I must number: ages — ages —
Space and eternity — and consciousness,
With the fierce thirst of death — and still unslaked!

   *C. Hun.* Why, on thy brow the seal of middle age
Hath scarce been set; I am thine elder far.

   *Man.* Think'st thou existence doth depend on time?
It doth; but actions are our epochs: mine
Have made my days and nights imperishable,
Endless, and all alike, as sands on the shore,
Innumerable atoms! and one desert,
Barren and cold, on which the wild waves break,
But nothing rests, save carcasses and wrecks,
Rocks, and the salt-surf weeds of bitterness.

   *C. Hun.* Alas! he's mad — but yet I must not leave him.

   *Man.* I would I were — for then the things I see
Would be but a distemper'd dream.

*C. Hun.* What is it
That thou dost see, or think thou look'st upon?
　　*Man.* Myself, and thee — a peasant of the Alps —
Thy humble virtues, hospitable home,
And spirit patient, pious, proud, and free;
Thy self-respect, grafted on innocent thoughts;
Thy days of health, and nights of sleep; thy toils,
By danger dignified, yet guiltless; hopes
Of cheerful old age and a quiet grave,
With cross and garland over its green turf,
And thy grandchildren's love for epitaph;
This do I see — and then I look within —
It matters not — my soul was scorch'd already!
　　*C. Hun.* And would'st thou then exchange thy lot for
　　　　mine?
　　*Man.* No, friend! I would not wrong thee, nor exchange
My lot with living being: I can bear —
However wretchedly, 'tis still to bear —
In life what others could not brook to dream,
But perish in their slumber.
　　*C. Hun.* And with this —
This cautious feeling for another's pain,
Canst thou be black with evil? — say not so.
Can one of gentle thoughts have wreak'd revenge
Upon his enemies?
　　*Man.* Oh! no, no, no!
My injuries came down on those who loved me —
On those whom I best loved: I never quell'd
An enemy, save in my just defence —
But my embrace was fatal.
　　*C. Hun.* Heaven give thee rest!
And penitence restore thee to thyself;
My prayers shall be for thee.
　　*Man.* I need them not,
But can endure thy pity. I depart —
'Tis time — farewell! — Here's gold, and thanks for thee —
No words — it is thy due. — Follow me not —

I know my path — the mountain peril's past:
And once again, I charge thee, follow not! [*Exit* MANFRED.

### SCENE II.
*A lower Valley in the Alps. — A Cataract.*
*Enter* MANFRED.

It is not noon — the sunbow's rays* still arch
The torrent with the many hues of heaven,
And roll the sheeted silver's waving column
O'er the crag's headlong perpendicular,
And fling its lines of foaming light along,
And to and fro, like the pale courser's tail,
The Giant steed, to be bestrode by Death,
As told in the Apocalypse. No eyes
But mine now drink this sight of loveliness;
I should be sole in this sweet solitude,
And with the Spirit of the place divide
The homage of these waters. — I will call her.

[MANFRED *takes some of the water into the palm of his
hand, and flings it into the air, muttering the adjuration. After a pause, the* WITCH OF THE ALPS *rises
beneath the arch of the sunbow of the torrent.*

Beautiful Spirit! with thy hair of light,
And dazzling eyes of glory, in whose form
The charms of earth's least mortal daughters grow
To an unearthly stature, in an essence
Of purer elements; while the hues of youth, —
Carnation'd like a sleeping infant's cheek,
Rock'd by the beating of her mother's heart,
Or the rose tints, which summer's twilight leaves
Upon the lofty glacier's virgin snow,
The blush of earth embracing with her heaven, —
Tinge thy celestial aspect, and make tame
The beauties of the sunbow which bends o'er thee.
Beautiful Spirit! in thy calm clear brow,

* This Iris is formed by the rays of the sun over the lower part of the Alpine torrents: it is exactly like a rainbow come down to pay a visit, and so close that you may walk into it; this effect lasts till noon. —

Wherein is glass'd serenity of soul,
Which of itself shows immortality,
I read that thou wilt pardon to a Son
Of Earth, whom the abstruser powers permit
At times to commune with them — if that he
Avail him of his spells — to call thee thus,
And gaze on thee a moment.
    *Witch.*                Son of Earth!
I know thee, and the powers which give thee power;
I know thee for a man of many thoughts,
And deeds of good and ill, extreme in both,
Fatal and fated in thy sufferings.
I have expected this — what would'st thou with me?
    *Man.* To look upon thy beauty — nothing further.
The face of the earth hath madden'd me, and I
Take refuge in her mysteries, and pierce
To the abodes of those who govern her —
But they can nothing aid me. I have sought
From them what they could not bestow, and now
I search no further.
    *Witch.* What could be the quest
Which is not in the power of the most powerful,
The rulers of the invisible?
    *Man.*                A boon;
But why should I repeat it? 'twere in vain.
    *Witch.* I know not that; let thy lips utter it.
    *Man.* Well, though it torture me, 'tis but the same;
My pang shall find a voice. From my youth upwards
My spirit walk'd not with the souls of men,
Nor look'd upon the earth with human eyes;
The thirst of their ambition was not mine,
The aim of their existence was not mine;
My joys, my griefs, my passions, and my powers,
Made me a stranger; though I wore the form,
I had no sympathy with breathing flesh,
Nor midst the creatures of clay that girded me
Was there but one who — but of her anon.

ACT II.

I said with men, and with the thoughts of men,
I held but slight communion; but instead,
My joy was in the Wilderness, to breathe
The difficult air of the iced mountain's top,
Where the birds dare not build, nor insect's wing
Flit o'er the herbless granite; or to plunge
Into the torrent, and to roll along
On the swift whirl of the new breaking wave
Of river-stream, or ocean, in their flow.
In these my early strength exulted; or
To follow through the night the moving moon,
The stars and their development; or catch
The dazzling lightnings till my eyes grew dim;
Or to look, list'ning, on the scatter'd leaves,
While Autumn winds were at their evening song.
These were my pastimes, and to be alone;
For if the beings, of whom I was one, —
Hating to be so, — cross'd me in my path,
I felt myself degraded back to them,
And was all clay again. And then I dived,
In my lone wanderings, to the caves of death,
Searching its cause in its effect; and drew
From wither'd bones, and skulls, and heap'd up dust,
Conclusions most forbidden. Then I pass'd
The nights of years in sciences untaught,
Save in the old time; and with time and toil,
And terrible ordeal, and such penance
As in itself hath power upon the air,
And spirits that do compass air and earth,
Space, and the peopled infinite, I made
Mine eyes familiar with Eternity,
Such as, before me, did the Magi, and
He who from out their fountain dwellings raised
Eros and Anteros, at Gadara,*
As I do thee; — and with my knowledge grew

* The philosopher Jamblicus. The story of the raising of Eros and Anteros may be found in his life by Eunapius. It is well told. —

The thirst of knowledge, and the power and joy
Of this most bright intelligence, until —
   *Witch.* Proceed.
   *Man.*          Oh! I but thus prolong'd my words,
Boasting these idle attributes, because
As I approach the core of my heart's grief —
But to my task. I have not named to thee
Father or mother, mistress, friend, or being,
With whom I wore the chain of human ties;
If I had such, they seem'd not such to me —
Yet there was one —
   *Witch.*       Spare not thyself — proceed.
   *Man.* She was like me in lineaments — her eyes,
Her hair, her features, all, to the very tone
Even of her voice, they said were like to mine;
But soften'd all, and temper'd into beauty;
She had the same lone thoughts and wanderings,
The quest of hidden knowledge, and a mind
To comprehend the universe: nor these
Alone, but with them gentler powers than mine,
Pity, and smiles, and tears — which I had not;
And tenderness — but that I had for her;
Humility — and that I never had.
Her faults were mine — her virtues were her own —
I loved her, and destroy'd her!
   *Witch.*          With thy hand?
   *Man.* Not with my hand, but heart — which broke her
        heart —
It gazed on mine, and wither'd. I have shed
Blood, but not hers — and yet her blood was shed —
I saw — and could not stanch it.
   *Witch.*          And for this —
A being of the race thou dost despise,
The order which thine own would rise above,
Mingling with us and ours, thou dost forego
The gifts of our great knowledge, and shrink'st back
To recreant mortality — Away!

*Man.* Daughter of Air! I tell thee, since that hour —
But words are breath — look on me in my sleep,
Or watch my watchings — Come and sit by me!
My solitude is solitude no more,
But peopled with the Furies; — I have gnash'd
My teeth in darkness till returning morn,
Then cursed myself till sunset; — I have pray'd
For madness as a blessing — 'tis denied me.
I have affronted death — but in the war
Of elements the waters shrunk from me,
And fatal things pass'd harmless — the cold hand
Of an all-pitiless demon held me back,
Back by a single hair, which would not break.
In fantasy, imagination, all
The affluence of my soul — which one day was
A Crœsus in creation — I plunged deep,
But, like an ebbing wave, it dash'd me back
Into the gulf of my unfathom'd thought.
I plunged amidst mankind — Forgetfulness
I sought in all, save where 'tis to be found,
And that I have to learn — my sciences,
My long pursued and super-human art,
Is mortal here — I dwell in my despair —
And live — and live for ever.
   *Witch.* It may be
That I can aid thee.
   *Man.* To do this thy power
Must wake the dead, or lay me low with them.
Do so — in any shape — in any hour —
With any torture — so it be the last.
   *Witch.* That is not in my province; but if thou
Wilt swear obedience to my will, and do
My bidding, it may help thee to thy wishes.
   *Man.* I will not swear — Obey! and whom? the spirits
Whose presence I command, and be the slave
Of those who served me — Never!
   *Witch.* Is this all?

Hast thou no gentler answer? — Yet bethink thee,
And pause ere thou rejectest.
    *Man.*                      I have said it.
    *Witch.* Enough! — I may retire then — say!
    *Man.*                                  Retire!
                                [*The* WITCH *disappears.*
    *Man. (alone).* We are the fools of time and terror: Days
Steal on us and steal from us; yet we live,
Loathing our life, and dreading still to die.
In all the days of this detested yoke —
This vital weight upon the struggling heart,
Which sinks with sorrow, or beats quick with pain,
Or joy that ends in agony or faintness —
In all the days of past and future, for
In life there is no present, we can number
How few — how less than few — wherein the soul
Forbears to pant for death, and yet draws back
As from a stream in winter, though the chill
Be but a moment's. I have one resource
Still in my science — I can call the dead,
And ask them what it is we dread to be:
The sternest answer can but be the Grave,
And that is nothing — if they answer not —
The buried Prophet answered to the Hag
Of Endor; and the Spartan Monarch drew
From the Byzantine maid's unsleeping spirit
An answer and his destiny — he slew
That which he loved, unknowing what he slew,
And died unpardon'd — though he call'd in aid
The Phyxian Jove, and in Phigalia roused
The Arcadian Evocators to compel
The indignant shadow to depose her wrath,
Or fix her term of vengeance — she replied
In words of dubious import, but fulfill'd.*

    * The story of Pausanias, king of Sparta (who commanded the Greeks at the battle of Platea, and afterwards perished for an attempt to betray the Lacedæmonians), and Cleonice, is told in Plutarch's life of Cimon; and in the Laconics of Pausanias the sophist, in his description of Greece. —

If I had never lived, that which I love
Had still been living; had I never loved,
That which I love would still be beautiful —
Happy and giving happiness. What is she?
What is she now? — a sufferer for my sins —
A thing I dare not think upon — or nothing.
Within few hours I shall not call in vain —
Yet in this hour I dread the thing I dare:
Until this hour I never shrunk to gaze
On spirit, good or evil — now I tremble,
And feel a strange cold thaw upon my heart.
But I can act even what I most abhor,
And champion human fears. — The night approaches. [*Exit.*

### SCENE III.
*The Summit of the Jungfrau Mountain.*
*Enter* FIRST DESTINY.

The moon is rising broad, and round, and bright;
And here on snows, where never human foot
Of common mortal trod, we nightly tread,
And leave no traces; o'er the savage sea,
The glassy ocean of the mountain ice,
We skim its rugged breakers, which put on
The aspect of a tumbling tempest's foam,
Frozen in a moment — a dead whirlpool's image:
And this most steep fantastic pinnacle,
The fretwork of some earthquake — where the clouds
Pause to repose themselves in passing by —
Is sacred to our revels, or our vigils;
Here do I wait my sisters, on our way
To the Hall of Arimanes, for to-night
Is our great festival — 'tis strange they come not.

*A Voice without, singing.*

The Captive Usurper,
 Hurl'd down from the throne,
Lay buried in torpor,
 Forgotten and lone;

I broke through his slumbers,
I shiver'd his chain,
I leagued him with numbers —
He's Tyrant again!
With the blood of a million he'll answer my care,
With a nation's destruction — his flight and despair.

*Second Voice, without.*

The ship sail'd on, the ship sail'd fast,
But I left not a sail, and I left not a mast;
There is not a plank of the hull or the deck,
And there is not a wretch to lament o'er his wreck;
Save one, whom I held, as he swam, by the hair,
And he was a subject well worthy my care;
A traitor on land, and a pirate at sea —
But I saved him to wreak further havoc for me!

FIRST DESTINY, *answering.*

The city lies sleeping;
 The morn, to deplore it,
May dawn on it weeping:
 Sullenly, slowly,
The black plague flew o'er it —
 Thousands lie lowly;
Tens of thousands shall perish —
 The living shall fly from
The sick they should cherish;
 But nothing can vanquish
The touch that they die from.
 Sorrow and anguish,
And evil and dread,
 Envelope a nation —
The blest are the dead,
 Who see not the sight
 Of their own desolation —
 This work of a night —
This wreck of a realm — this deed of my doing —
For ages I've done, and shall still be renewing!

ACT II.

*Enter the* SECOND *and* THIRD DESTINIES.
*The Three.*
Our hands contain the hearts of men,
  Our footsteps are their graves;
We only give to take again
  The spirits of our slaves!
*First Des.* Welcome! — Where's Nemesis?
*Second Des.*                        At some great work;
But what I know not, for my hands were full.
*Third Des.* Behold she cometh.
*Enter* NEMESIS.
*First Des.*                  Say, where hast thou been?
My sisters and thyself are slow to-night.
  *Nem.* I was detain'd repairing shatter'd thrones,
Marrying fools, restoring dynasties,
Avenging men upon their enemies,
And making them repent their own revenge;
Goading the wise to madness; from the dull
Shaping out oracles to rule the world
Afresh, for they were waxing out of date,
And mortals dared to ponder for themselves,
To weigh kings in the balance, and to speak
Of freedom, the forbidden fruit. — Away!
We have outstay'd the hour — mount we our clouds! [*Exeunt.*

SCENE IV.

*The Hall of Arimanes — Arimanes on his Throne, a Globe of
Fire, surrounded by the Spirits.*
*Hymn of the* SPIRITS.
Hail to our Master! — Prince of Earth and Air!
  Who walks the clouds and waters — in his hand
The sceptre of the elements, which tear
  Themselves to chaos at his high command!
He breatheth — and a tempest shakes the sea;
  He speaketh — and the clouds reply in thunder;
He gazeth — from his glance the sunbeams flee;
  He moveth — earthquakes rend the world asunder.

Beneath his footsteps the volcanoes rise;
    His shadow is the Pestilence; his path
The comets herald through the crackling skies;
    And planets turn to ashes at his wrath.
To him War offers daily sacrifice;
    To him Death pays his tribute; Life is his,
With all its infinite of agonies —
    And his the spirit of whatever is!

*Enter the* DESTINIES *and* NEMESIS.

*First Des.* Glory to Arimanes! on the earth
His power increaseth — both my sisters did
His bidding, nor did I neglect my duty!

*Second Des.* Glory to Arimanes! we who bow
The necks of men, bow down before his throne!

*Third Des.* Glory to Arimanes! we await
His nod!

*Nem.* Sovereign of Sovereigns! we are thine,
And all that liveth, more or less, is ours,
And most things wholly so; still to increase
Our power, increasing thine, demands our care,
And we are vigilant — Thy late commands
Have been fulfill'd to the utmost.

*Enter* MANFRED.

*A Spirit.* What is here?
A mortal! — Thou most rash and fatal wretch,
Bow down and worship!

*Second Spirit.* I do know the man —
A Magian of great power, and fearful skill!

*Third Spirit.* Bow down and worship, slave! — What,
    know'st thou not
Thine and our Sovereign? — Tremble, and obey!

*All the Spirits.* Prostrate thyself, and thy condemned clay,
Child of the Earth! or dread the worst.

*Man.* I know it;
And yet ye see I kneel not.

*Fourth Spirit.* 'Twill be taught thee.

*Man.* 'Tis taught already; — many a night on the earth,
On the bare ground, have I bow'd down my face,
And strew'd my head with ashes; I have known
The fulness of humiliation, for
I sunk before my vain despair, and knelt
To my own desolation.
    *Fifth Spirit.*    Dost thou dare
Refuse to Arimanes on his throne
What the whole earth accords, beholding not
The terror of his Glory? — Crouch! I say.
    *Man.* Bid *him* bow down to that which is above him,
The overruling Infinite — the Maker
Who made him not for worship — let him kneel,
And we will kneel together.
    *The Spirits.*    Crush the worm!
Tear him in pieces! —
    *First Des.*    Hence! Avaunt! — he's mine.
Prince of the Powers invisible! This man
Is of no common order, as his port
And presence here denote; his sufferings
Have been of an immortal nature, like
Our own; his knowledge, and his powers and will,
As far as is compatible with clay,
Which clogs the ethereal essence, have been such
As clay hath seldom borne; his aspirations
Have been beyond the dwellers of the earth,
And they have only taught him what we know —
That knowledge is not happiness, and science
But an exchange of ignorance for that
Which is another kind of ignorance.
This is not all — the passions, attributes
Of earth and heaven, from which no power, nor being,
Nor breath from the worm upwards is exempt,
Have pierced his heart; and in their consequence
Made him a thing, which I, who pity not,
Yet pardon those who pity. He is mine,
And thine, it may be — be it so, or not,

No other Spirit in this region hath
A soul like his — or power upon his soul.
 *Nem.* What doth he here then?
 *First Des.*     Let him answer that.
 *Man.* Ye know what I have known; and without power
I could not be amongst ye: but there are
Powers deeper still beyond — I come in quest
Of such, to answer unto what I seek.
 *Nem.* What would'st thou?
 *Man.*     Thou canst not reply to me.
Call up the dead — my question is for them.
 *Nem.* Great Arimanes, doth thy will avouch
The wishes of this mortal?
 *Ari.*     Yea.
 *Nem.*     Whom would'st thou
Uncharnel?
 *Man.* One without a tomb — call up
Astarte.

     NEMESIS.
  Shadow! or Spirit!
   Whatever thou art,
  Which still doth inherit
   The whole or a part
  Of the form of thy birth,
   Of the mould of thy clay,
  Which return'd to the earth,
   Re-appear to the day!
  Bear what thou borest,
   The heart and the form,
  And the aspect thou worest
   Redeem from the worm.
  Appear! — Appear! — Appear!
  Who sent thee there requires thee here!
 [*The Phantom of* ASTARTE *rises and stands in the midst.*
 *Man.* Can this be death? there's bloom upon her cheek;
But now I see it is no living hue
But a strange hectic — like the unnatural red

Which Autumn plants upon the perish'd leaf.
It is the same! Oh, God! that I should dread
To look upon the same — Astarte! — No,
I cannot speak to her — but bid her speak —
Forgive me or condemn me.

NEMESIS.
By the power which hath broken
The grave which enthrall'd thee,
Speak to him who hath spoken,
Or those who have call'd thee!

*Man.* She is silent,
And in that silence I am more than answer'd.
*Nem.* My power extends no further. Prince of air!
It rests with thee alone — command her voice.
*Ari.* Spirit — obey this sceptre!
*Nem.* Silent still!
She is not of our order, but belongs
To the other powers. Mortal! thy quest is vain,
And we are baffled also.
*Man.* Hear me, hear me—
Astarte! my beloved! speak to me:
I have so much endured — so much endure —
Look on me! the grave hath not changed thee more
Than I am changed for thee. Thou lovedst me
Too much, as I loved thee: we were not made
To torture thus each other, though it were
The deadliest sin to love as we have loved.
Say that thou loath'st me not — that I do bear
This punishment for both — that thou wilt be
One of the blessed — and that I shall die;
For hitherto all hateful things conspire
To bind me in existence — in a life
Which makes me shrink from immortality —
A future like the past. I cannot rest.
I know not what I ask, nor what I seek:
I feel but what thou art — and what I am;

And I would hear yet once before I perish
The voice which was my music — Speak to me!
For I have call'd on thee in the still night,
Startled the slumbering birds from the hush'd boughs,
And woke the mountain wolves, and made the caves
Acquainted with thy vainly echoed name,
Which answer'd me — many things answer'd me —
Spirits and men — but thou wert silent all.
Yet speak to me! I have outwatch'd the stars,
And gazed o'er heaven in vain in search of thee.
Speak to me! I have wander'd o'er the earth,
And never found thy likeness — Speak to me!
Look on the fiends around — they feel for me:
I fear them not, and feel for thee alone —
Speak to me! though it be in wrath; — but say —
I reck not what — but let me hear thee once —
This once — once more!

  *Phantom of Astarte.* Manfred!
  *Man.*       Say on, say on —
I live but in the sound — it is thy voice!
  *Phan.* Manfred! To-morrow ends thine earthly ills.
Farewell!
  *Man.* Yet one word more — am I forgiven?
  *Phan.* Farewell!
  *Man.*     Say, shall we meet again?
  *Phan.* Farewell!
  *Man.* One word for mercy! Say, thou lovest me.
  *Phan.* Manfred!

        [*The Spirit of* ASTARTE *disappears.*
  *Nem.*    She's gone, and will not be recall'd;
Her words will be fulfill'd. Return to the earth.
  *A Spirit.* He is convulsed — This is to be a mortal
And seek the things beyond mortality.
  *Another Spirit.* Yet, see, he mastereth himself, and makes
His torture tributary to his will.
Had he been one of us, he would have made
An awful spirit.

*Nem.*     Hast thou further question
Of our great sovereign, or his worshippers?
 *Man.* None.
 *Nem.*     Then for a time farewell.
 *Man.* We meet then! Where? On the earth? —
Even as thou wilt: and for the grace accorded
I now depart a debtor. Fare ye well!   [*Exit* MANFRED.
     (*Scene closes.*)

## ACT III.

### SCENE I.

*A Hall in the Castle of Manfred.*

MANFRED *and* HERMAN.

 *Man.* What is the hour?
 *Her.*     It wants but one till sunset,
And promises a lovely twilight.
 *Man.*     Say,
Are all things so disposed of in the tower
As I directed?
 *Her.*  All, my lord, are ready:
Here is the key and casket.
 *Man.*     It is well:
Thou may'st retire.      [*Exit* HERMAN.
 *Man. (alone).* There is a calm upon me —
Inexplicable stillness! which till now
Did not belong to what I knew of life.
If that I did not know philosophy
To be of all our vanities the motliest,
The merest word that ever fool'd the ear
From out the schoolman's jargon, I should deem
The golden secret, the sought "Kalon," found,
And seated in my soul. It will not last,
But it is well to have known it, though but once:
It hath enlarged my thoughts with a new sense,
And I within my tablets would note down
That there is such a feeling. Who is there?

*Re-enter* HERMAN.

*Her.* My lord, the abbot of St. Maurice craves
To greet your presence.

*Enter the* ABBOT OF ST. MAURICE.

*Abbot.* Peace be with Count Manfred!
*Man.* Thanks, holy father! welcome to these walls;
Thy presence honours them, and blesseth those
Who dwell within them.
*Abbot.* Would it were so, Count! —
But I would fain confer with thee alone.
*Man.* Herman, retire. — What would my reverend guest?
*Abbot.* Thus, without prelude: — Age and zeal, my office,
And good intent, must plead my privilege;
Our near, though not acquainted neighbourhood,
May also be my herald. Rumours strange,
And of unholy nature, are abroad,
And busy with thy name; a noble name
For centuries: may he who bears it now
Transmit it unimpair'd!
*Man.* Proceed, — I listen.
*Abbot.* 'Tis said thou holdest converse with the things
Which are forbidden to the search of man;
That with the dwellers of the dark abodes,
The many evil and unheavenly spirits
Which walk the valley of the shade of death,
Thou communest. I know that with mankind,
Thy fellows in creation, thou dost rarely
Exchange thy thoughts, and that thy solitude
Is as an anchorite's, were it but holy.
*Man.* And what are they who do avouch these things?
*Abbot.* My pious brethren — the scared peasantry —
Even thy own vassals — who do look on thee
With most unquiet eyes. Thy life's in peril.
*Man.* Take it.
*Abbot.* I come to save, and not destroy —
I would not pry into thy secret soul;

But if these things be sooth, there still is time
For penitence and pity: reconcile thee
With the true church, and through the church to heaven.
*Man.* I hear thee. This is my reply: whate'er
I may have been, or am, doth rest between
Heaven and myself. — I shall not choose a mortal
To be my mediator. Have I sinn'd
Against your ordinances? prove and punish!
*Abbot.* My son! I did not speak of punishment,
But penitence and pardon; — with thyself
The choice of such remains — and for the last,
Our institutions and our strong belief
Have given me power to smooth the path from sin
To higher hope and better thoughts; the first
I leave to heaven, — "Vengeance is mine alone!"
So saith the Lord, and with all humbleness
His servant echoes back the awful word.
*Man.* Old man! there is no power in holy men,
Nor charm in prayer — nor purifying form
Of penitence — nor outward look — nor fast —
Nor agony — nor, greater than all these,
The innate tortures of that deep despair,
Which is remorse without the fear of hell,
But all in all sufficient to itself
Would make a hell of heaven — can exorcise
From out the unbounded spirit the quick sense
Of its own sins, wrongs, sufferance, and revenge
Upon itself; there is no future pang
Can deal that justice on the self-condemn'd
He deals on his own soul.
*Abbot.* All this is well;
For this will pass away, and be succeeded
By an auspicious hope, which shall look up
With calm assurance to that blessed place,
Which all who seek may win, whatever be
Their earthly errors, so they be atoned:
And the commencement of atonement is

The sense of its necessity. — Say on —
And all our church can teach thee shall be taught;
And all we can absolve thee shall be pardon'd.

*Man.* When Rome's sixth emperor was near his last,
The victim of a self-inflicted wound,
To shun the torments of a public death
From senates once his slaves, a certain soldier,
With show of loyal pity, would have stanch'd
The gushing throat with his officious robe;
The dying Roman thrust him back, and said —
Some empire still in his expiring glance,
"It is too late — is this fidelity?"

*Abbot.* And what of this?

*Man.* I answer with the Roman —
"It is too late!"

*Abbot.* It never can be so,
To reconcile thyself with thy own soul,
And thy own soul with heaven. Hast thou no hope?
'Tis strange — even those who do despair above,
Yet shape themselves some fantasy on earth,
To which frail twig they cling, like drowning men.

*Man.* Ay — father! I have had those earthly visions
And noble aspirations in my youth,
To make my own the mind of other men,
The enlightener of nations; and to rise
I knew not whither — it might be to fall;
But fall, even as the mountain-cataract,
Which having leapt from its more dazzling height,
Even in the foaming strength of its abyss,
(Which casts up misty columns that become
Clouds raining from the re-ascended skies,)
Lies low but mighty still. — But this is past,
My thoughts mistook themselves.

*Abbot.* And wherefore so?

*Man.* I could not tame my nature down; for he
Must serve who fain would sway — and soothe — and sue —
And watch all time — and pry into all place —

And be a living lie — who would become
A mighty thing amongst the mean, and such
The mass are; I disdain'd to mingle with
A herd, though to be leader — and of wolves.
The lion is alone, and so am I.

*Abbot.* And why not live and act with other men?

*Man.* Because my nature was averse from life;
And yet not cruel; for I would not make,
But find a desolation: — like the wind,
The red-hot breath of the most lone Simoom,
Which dwells but in the desert, and sweeps o'er
The barren sands which bear no shrubs to blast,
And revels o'er their wild and arid waves,
And seeketh not, so that it is not sought,
But being met is deadly; such hath been
The course of my existence; but there came
Things in my path which are no more.

*Abbot.* Alas!
I 'gin to fear that thou art past all aid
From me and from my calling; yet so young,
I still would —

*Man.* Look on me! there is an order
Of mortals on the earth, who do become
Old in their youth, and die ere middle age,
Without the violence of warlike death;
Some perishing of pleasure — some of study —
Some worn with toil — some of mere weariness —
Some of disease — and some insanity —
And some of wither'd, or of broken hearts;
For this last is a malady which slays
More than are number'd in the lists of Fate,
Taking all shapes, and bearing many names.
Look upon me! for even of all these things
Have I partaken; and of all these things,
One were enough; then wonder not that I
Am what I am, but that I ever was,
Or having been, that I am still on earth.

*Abbot.* Yet, hear me still —
*Man.*                    Old man! I do respect
Thine order, and revere thine years; I deem
Thy purpose pious, but it is in vain:
Think me not churlish; I would spare thyself,
Far more than me, in shunning at this time
All further colloquy — and so — farewell.    [*Exit* Manfred.
    *Abbot.* This should have been a noble creature: he
Hath all the energy which would have made
A goodly frame of glorious elements,
Had they been wisely mingled; as it is,
It is an awful chaos — light and darkness —
And mind and dust — and passions and pure thoughts
Mix'd, and contending without end or order,
All dormant or destructive: he will perish,
And yet he must not; I will try once more,
For such are worth redemption; and my duty
Is to dare all things for a righteous end.
I'll follow him — but cautiously, though surely.    [*Exit* Abbot.

### SCENE II.
*Another Chamber.*
Manfred *and* Herman.

*Her.* My lord, you bade me wait on you at sunset:
He sinks behind the mountain.
    *Man.*                    Doth he so?
I will look on him.
                [Manfred *advances to the Window of the Hall.*
            Glorious Orb! the idol
Of early nature, and the vigorous race
Of undiseased mankind, the giant sons*
Of the embrace of angels, with a sex

---

* "And it came to pass, that the *Sons of God* saw the daughters of men, that they were fair," &c. — "There were giants in the earth in those days; and also after that, when the *Sons of God* came in unto the daughters of men, and they bare children to them, the same became mighty men which were of old, men of renown." — *Genesis*, ch. vi. verses 2 and 4.

More beautiful than they, which did draw down
The erring spirits who can ne'er return. —
Most glorious orb! that wert a worship, ere
The mystery of thy making was reveal'd!
Thou earliest minister of the Almighty,
Which gladden'd, on their mountain tops, the hearts
Of the Chaldean shepherds, till they pour'd
Themselves in orisons! Thou material God!
And representative of the Unknown —
Who chose thee for his shadow! Thou chief star!
Centre of many stars! which mak'st our earth
Endurable, and temperest the hues
And hearts of all who walk within thy rays!
Sire of the seasons! Monarch of the climes,
And those who dwell in them! for near or far,
Our inborn spirits have a tint of thee
Even as our outward aspects; — thou dost rise,
And shine, and set in glory. Fare thee well!
I ne'er shall see thee more. As my first glance
Of love and wonder was for thee, then take
My latest look: thou wilt not beam on one
To whom the gifts of life and warmth have been
Of a more fatal nature. He is gone:
I follow. [*Exit* MANFRED.

### SCENE III.

*The Mountains — The Castle of Manfred at some distance — A Terrace before a Tower. — Time, Twilight.*

HERMAN, MANUEL, *and other Dependants of* MANFRED.

*Her.* "Tis strange enough; night after night, for years,
He hath pursued long vigils in this tower,
Without a witness. I have been within it, —
So have we all been oft-times; but from it,
Or its contents, it were impossible
To draw conclusions absolute, of aught
His studies tend to. To be sure, there is
One chamber where none enter: I would give

The fee of what I have to come these three years,
To pore upon its mysteries.
  *Manuel.*      'Twere dangerous;
Content thyself with what thou know'st already.
  *Her.* Ah! Manuel! thou art elderly and wise,
And couldst say much; thou hast dwelt within the castle —
How many years is't?
  *Manuel.*     Ere Count Manfred's birth,
I served his father, whom he nought resembles.
  *Her.* There be more sons in like predicament.
But wherein do they differ?
  *Manuel.*      I speak not
Of features or of form, but mind and habits;
Count Sigismund was proud, — but gay and free, —
A warrior and a reveller; he dwelt not
With books and solitude, nor made the night
A gloomy vigil, but a festal time,
Merrier than day; he did not walk the rocks
And forests like a wolf, nor turn aside
From men and their delights.
  *Her.*      Beshrew the hour,
But those were jocund times! I would that such
Would visit the old walls again; they look
As if they had forgotten them.
  *Manuel.*     These walls
Must change their chieftain first. Oh! I have seen
Some strange things in them, Herman.
  *Her.*      Come, be friendly;
Relate me some to while away our watch:
I've heard thee darkly speak of an event
Which happen'd hereabouts, by this same tower.
  *Manuel.* That was a night indeed! I do remember
'Twas twilight, as it may be now, and such
Another evening; — yon red cloud, which rests
On Eigher's pinnacle, so rested then, —
So like that it might be the same; the wind
Was faint and gusty, and the mountain snows

Began to glitter with the climbing moon;
Count Manfred was, as now, within his tower, —
How occupied, we knew not, but with him
The sole companion of his wanderings
And watchings — her, whom of all earthly things
That lived, the only thing he seem'd to love, —
As he, indeed, by blood was bound to do,
The lady Astarte, his —
      Hush! who comes here?
    *Enter the* ABBOT.
*Abbot.* Where is your master?
*Her.*       Yonder in the tower.
*Abbot.* I must speak with him.
*Manuel.*       'Tis impossible;
He is most private, and must not be thus
Intruded on.
 *Abbot.*   Upon myself I take
The forfeit of my fault, if fault there be —
But I must see him.
 *Her.*   Thou hast seen him once
This eve already.
 *Abbot.*   Herman! I command thee,
Knock, and apprize the Count of my approach.
 *Her.* We dare not.
 *Abbot.*   Then it seems I must be herald
Of my own purpose.
 *Manuel.*   Reverend father, stop —
I pray you pause.
 *Abbot.*   Why so?
 *Manuel.*     But step this way,
And I will tell you further.     [*Exeunt.*

### SCENE IV.
*Interior of the Tower.*
MANFRED *alone.*

The stars are forth, the moon above the tops
Of the snow-shining mountains. — Beautiful!

I linger yet with Nature, for the night
Hath been to me a more familiar face
Than that of man; and in her starry shade
Of dim and solitary loveliness,
I learn'd the language of another world.
I do remember me, that in my youth,
When I was wandering,— upon such a night
I stood within the Coliseum's wall,
Midst the chief relics of almighty Rome;
The trees which grew along the broken arches
Waved dark in the blue midnight, and the stars
Shone through the rents of ruin; from afar
The watchdog bay'd beyond the Tiber; and
More near from out the Cæsars' palace came
The owl's long cry, and, interruptedly,
Of distant sentinels the fitful song
Begun and died upon the gentle wind.
Some cypresses beyond the time-worn breach
Appear'd to skirt the horizon, yet they stood
Within a bowshot — Where the Cæsars dwelt,
And dwell the tuneless birds of night, amidst
A grove which springs through levell'd battlements,
And twines its roots with the imperial hearths,
Ivy usurps the laurel's place of growth;—
But the gladiators' bloody Circus stands,
A noble wreck in ruinous perfection!
While Cæsar's chambers, and the Augustan halls,
Grovel on earth in indistinct decay. —
And thou didst shine, thou rolling moon, upon
All this, and cast a wide and tender light,
Which soften'd down the hoar austerity
Of rugged desolation, and fill'd up,
As 'twere anew, the gaps of centuries;
Leaving that beautiful which still was so,
And making that which was not, till the place
Became religion, and the heart ran o'er
With silent worship of the great of old! —

The dead, but sceptred sovereigns, who still rule
Our spirits from their urns. —
'Twas such a night!
'Tis strange that I recall it at this time;
But I have found our thoughts take wildest flight
Even at the moment when they should array
Themselves in pensive order.

*Enter the Abbot.*

*Abbot.* My good lord!
I crave a second grace for this approach;
But yet let not my humble zeal offend
By its abruptness — all it hath of ill
Recoils on me; its good in the effect
May light upon your head — could I say *heart* —
Could I touch *that*, with words or prayers, I should
Recall a noble spirit which hath wander'd;
But is not yet all lost.
*Man.* Thou know'st me not;
My days are number'd, and my deeds recorded:
Retire, or 'twill be dangerous — Away!
*Abbot.* Thou dost not mean to menace me?
*Man.* Not I;
I simply tell thee peril is at hand,
And would preserve thee.
*Abbot.* What dost thou mean?
*Man.* Look there!
What dost thou see?
*Abbot.* Nothing.
*Man.* Look there, I say,
And steadfastly; — now tell me what thou seest?
*Abbot.* That which should shake me, — but I fear it not —
I see a dusk and awful figure rise,
Like an infernal god, from out the earth;
His face wrapt in a mantle, and his form
Robed as with angry clouds: he stands between
Thyself and me — but I do fear him not.

*Man.* Thou hast no cause — he shall not harm thee — but
His sight may shock thine old limbs into palsy.
I say to thee — Retire!

*Abbot.* And I reply —
Never — till I have battled with this fiend: —
What doth he here?

*Man.* Why — ay — what doth he here? —
I did not send for him, — he is unbidden.

*Abbot.* Alas! lost mortal! what with guests like these
Hast thou to do? I tremble for thy sake:
Why doth he gaze on thee, and thou on him?
Ah! he unveils his aspect: on his brow
The thunder-scars are graven; from his eye
Glares forth the immortality of hell —
Avaunt! —

*Man.* Pronounce — what is thy mission?
*Spirit.* Come!
*Abbot.* What art thou, unknown being? answer! — speak!
*Spirit.* The genius of this mortal. — Come! 'tis time.
*Man.* I am prepared for all things, but deny
The power which summons me. Who sent thee here?
*Spirit.* Thou'lt know anon — Come! come!
*Man.* I have commanded
Things of an essence greater far than thine,
And striven with thy masters. Get thee hence!
*Spirit.* Mortal! thine hour is come — Away! I say.
*Man.* I knew, and know my hour is come, but not
To render up my soul to such as thee:
Away! I'll die as I have lived — alone.
*Spirit.* Then I must summon up my brethren. — Rise!

[*Other Spirits rise up.*

*Abbot.* Avaunt! ye evil ones! — Avaunt! I say, —
Ye have no power where piety hath power,
And I do charge ye in the name —
*Spirit.* Old man!
We know ourselves, our mission, and thine order;
Waste not thy holy words on idle uses,

It were in vain: this man is forfeited.
Once more I summon him — Away! away!

   *Man.* I do defy ye, — though I feel my soul
Is ebbing from me, yet I do defy ye;
Nor will I hence, while I have earthly breath
To breathe my scorn upon ye — earthly strength
To wrestle, though with spirits; what ye take
Shall be ta'en limb by limb.

   *Spirit.*            Reluctant mortal!
Is this the Magian who would so pervade
The world invisible, and make himself
Almost our equal? — Can it be that thou
Art thus in love with life? the very life
Which made thee wretched!

   *Man.*           Thou false fiend, thou liest!
My life is in its last hour, — *that* I know,
Nor would redeem a moment of that hour;
I do not combat against death, but thee
And thy surrounding angels; my past power
Was purchased by no compact with thy crew,
But by superior science — penance — daring —
And length of watching — strength of mind — and skill
In knowledge of our fathers — when the earth
Saw men and spirits walking side by side,
And gave ye no supremacy: I stand
Upon my strength — I do defy — deny —
Spurn back, and scorn ye! —

   *Spirit.*          But thy many crimes
Have made thee —

   *Man.*       What are they to such as thee?
Must crimes be punish'd but by other crimes,
And greater criminals? — Back to thy hell!
Thou hast no power upon me, *that* I feel;
Thou never shalt possess me, *that* I know:
What I have done is done; I bear within
A torture which could nothing gain from thine:
The mind which is immortal makes itself

Requital for its good or evil thoughts —
Is its own origin of ill and end —
And its own place and time — its innate sense,
When stripp'd of this mortality, derives
No colour from the fleeting things without;
But is absorb'd in sufferance or in joy,
Born from the knowledge of its own desert.
Thou didst not tempt me, and thou couldst not tempt me;
I have not been thy dupe, nor am thy prey —
But was my own destroyer, and will be
My own hereafter. — Back, ye baffled fiends!
The hand of death is on me — but not yours!

[*The Demons disappear.*

*Abbot.* Alas! how pale thou art — thy lips are white —
And thy breast heaves — and in thy gasping throat
The accents rattle — Give thy prayers to Heaven —
Pray — albeit but in thought, — but die not thus.

*Man.* 'Tis over — my dull eyes can fix thee not;
But all things swim around me, and the earth
Heaves as it were beneath me. Fare thee well —
Give me thy hand.

*Abbot.* Cold — cold — even to the heart —
But yet one prayer — Alas! how fares it with thee?

*Man.* Old man! 'tis not so difficult to die.

[MANFRED *expires.*

*Abbot.* He's gone — his soul hath ta'en its earthless flight —
Whither? I dread to think — but he is gone.

# CAIN,

## A MYSTERY.

---

"Now the Serpent was more subtil than any beast of the field which the LORD God had made." — *Gen.* ch. III. ver. 1.

---

TO
## SIR WALTER SCOTT, BART.

THIS MYSTERY OF CAIN

IS INSCRIBED,

BY HIS OBLIGED FRIEND,

AND FAITHFUL SERVANT,

THE AUTHOR.

---

## PREFACE.

THE following scenes are entitled "A Mystery," in conformity with the ancient title annexed to dramas upon similar subjects, which were styled "Mysteries, or Moralities." The author has by no means taken the same liberties with his subject which were common formerly, as may be seen by any reader curious enough to refer to those very profane productions, whether in English, French, Italian, or Spanish. The author has endeavoured to preserve the language adapted to his characters; and where it is (and this is but rarely) taken from actual *Scripture*, he has made as little alteration, even of words, as the rhythm would permit. The reader will recollect that the book of Genesis does not state that Eve was tempted by a demon, but by "the Serpent;" and that only because he was "the most subtil of all the beasts of the field." Whatever interpretation the Rabbins and the Fathers may have put upon this, I take the words as I find them, and reply, with Bishop Watson upon similar occasions, when the Fathers were quoted to him, as Moderator in the schools of Cambridge, "Behold the Book!" — holding up the Scripture. It is to be recollected, that my present subject has nothing to do with the *New Testament*, to which no reference can be here made without anachronism. With the poems upon similar topics I have not been recently familiar. Since I was twenty, I have never read Milton; but I had read him so frequently before, that this may make little difference. Gesner's "Death of Abel" I have never read since I was eight years of age, at Aberdeen. The general impression of my recollection is delight; but of the contents I remember only that Cain's wife was called Mahala, and Abel's Thirza: in the following pages I have called them "Adah" and "Zillah," the earliest female names which occur in Genesis; they were those of Lamech's wives: those of Cain and Abel are not called by their names. Whether, then, a coincidence of subject may have caused the same in expression, I know nothing, and care as little.

The reader will please to bear in mind (what few choose to recollect), that there is no allusion to a future state in any of the books of Moses, nor indeed in the Old Testament. For a reason for this extraordinary omission he may consult Warburton's "Divine Legation;" whether satisfactory or not, no better has yet been assigned. I have therefore supposed it new to Cain, without, I hope, any perversion of Holy Writ.

With regard to the language of Lucifer, it was difficult for me to make him talk like a clergyman upon the same subjects; but I have done what I could to restrain him within the bounds of spiritual politeness. If he disclaims having tempted Eve in the shape of the Serpent, it is only because the book of Genesis has not the most distant allusion to any thing of the kind, but merely to the Serpent in his serpentine capacity.

*Note.* — The reader will perceive that the author has partly adopted in this poem the notion of Cuvier, that the world had been destroyed several times before the creation of man. This speculation, derived from the different strata and the bones of enormous and unknown animals found in them, is not contrary to the Mosaic account, but rather confirms it; as no human bones have yet been discovered in those strata, although those of many known animals are found near the remains of the unknown. The assertion of Lucifer, that the pre-Adamite world was also peopled by rational beings much more intelligent than man, and proportionably powerful to the mammoth, &c. &c. is, of course, a poetical fiction to help him to make out his case.

I ought to add, that there is a "tramelogedia" of Alfieri, called "Abele." — I have never read that, nor any other of the posthumous works of the writer, except his Life.

Ravenna, Sept. 20. 1821.

## DRAMATIS PERSONÆ.

*Men.* — ADAM.
CAIN.
ABEL.

*Spirits.* — ANGEL OF THE LORD.
LUCIFER.

*Women.* — EVE.
ADAH.
ZILLAH.

# CAIN.

## ACT I.

### SCENE 1.

*The Land without Paradise. — Time, Sunrise.*

ADAM, EVE, CAIN, ABEL, ADAH, ZILLAH, *offering a Sacrifice.*

    *Adam.* GOD, the Eternal! Infinite! All-wise! —
Who out of darkness on the deep didst make
Light on the waters with a word — all hail!
Jehovah, with returning light, all hail!
    *Eve.* God! who didst name the day, and separate
Morning from night, till then divided never —
Who didst divide the wave from wave, and call
Part of thy work the firmament — all hail!
    *Abel.* God! who didst call the elements into
Earth — ocean — air — and fire, and with the day
And night, and worlds which these illuminate,
Or shadow, madest beings to enjoy them,
And love both them and thee — all hail! all hail!
    *Adah.* God, the Eternal! Parent of all things!
Who didst create these best and beauteous beings,
To be beloved, more than all, save thee —
Let me love thee and them: — All hail! all hail!
    *Zillah.* Oh, God! who loving, making, blessing all,
Yet didst permit the Serpent to creep in,
And drive my father forth from Paradise,
Keep us from further evil: — Hail! all hail!
    *Adam.* Son Cain, my first-born, wherefore art thou silent?
    *Cain.* Why should I speak?
    *Adam.*                   To pray.
    *Cain.*                            Have ye not pray'd?
    *Adam.* We have, most fervently.

ACT I.

*Cain.* And loudly: I
Have heard you.
*Adam.* So will God, I trust.
*Abel.* Amen!
*Adam.* But thou, my eldest born, art silent still.
*Cain.* 'Tis better I should be so.
*Adam.* Wherefore so?
*Cain.* I have nought to ask.
*Adam.* Nor aught to thank for?
*Cain.* No.
*Adam.* Dost thou not live?
*Cain.* Must I not die?
*Eve.* Alas!
The fruit of our forbidden tree begins
To fall.
*Adam.* And we must gather it again.
Oh, God! why didst thou plant the tree of knowledge?
*Cain.* And wherefore pluck'd ye not the tree of life?
Ye might have then defied him.
*Adam.* Oh! my son,
Blaspheme not: these are serpent's words.
*Cain.* Why not?
The snake spoke *truth:* it *was* the tree of knowledge;
It *was* the tree of life: knowledge is good,
And life is good; and how can both be evil?
*Eve.* My boy! thou speakest as I spoke, in sin,
Before thy birth: let me not see renew'd
My misery in thine. I have repented.
Let me not see my offspring fall into
The snares beyond the walls of Paradise,
Which e'en in Paradise destroy'd his parents.
Content thee with what *is.* Had we been so,
Thou now hadst been contented. — Oh, my son!

*Adam.* Our orisons completed, let us hence,
Each to his task of toil — not heavy, though
Needful: the earth is young, and yields us kindly
Her fruits with little labour.

*Eve.* Cain, my son,
Behold thy father cheerful and resign'd,
And do as he doth.  [*Exeunt* ADAM *and* EVE.
*Zillah.* Wilt thou not, my brother?
*Abel.* Why wilt thou wear this gloom upon thy brow,
Which can avail thee nothing, save to rouse
The Eternal anger?
*Adah.* My beloved Cain,
Wilt thou frown even on me?
*Cain.* No, Adah! no;
I fain would be alone a little while.
Abel, I'm sick at heart; but it will pass.
Precede me, brother — I will follow shortly.
And you, too, sisters, tarry not behind;
Your gentleness must not be harshly met:
I'll follow you anon.
*Adah.* If not, I will
Return to seek you here.
*Abel.* The peace of God
Be on your spirit, brother!
 [*Exeunt* ABEL, ZILLAH, *and* ADAH.
*Cain (solus).* And this is
Life! — Toil! and wherefore should I toil? — because
My father could not keep his place in Eden.
What had *I* done in this? — I was unborn:
I sought not to be born; nor love the state
To which that birth has brought me. Why did he
Yield to the serpent and the woman? or,
Yielding, why suffer? What was there in this?
The tree was planted, and why not for him?
If not, why place him near it, where it grew,
The fairest in the centre? They have but
One answer to all questions, "'Twas *his* will,
And *he* is good." How know I that? Because
He is all-powerful, must all-good, too, follow?
I judge but by the fruits — and they are bitter —
Which I must feed on for a fault not mine.

Whom have we here? — A shape like to the angels
Yet of a sterner and a sadder aspect
Of spiritual essence: why do I quake?
Why should I fear him more than other spirits,
Whom I see daily wave their fiery swords
Before the gates round which I linger oft,
In twilight's hour, to catch a glimpse of those
Gardens which are my just inheritance,
Ere the night closes o'er the inhibited walls
And the immortal trees which overtop
The cherubim-defended battlements?
If I shrink not from these, the fire-arm'd angels,
Why should I quail from him who now approaches?
Yet he seems mightier far than them, nor less
Beauteous, and yet not all as beautiful
As he hath been, and might be: sorrow seems
Half of his immortality. And is it
So? and can aught grieve save humanity?
He cometh.

*Enter* Lucifer.

*Lucifer.* Mortal!
*Cain.*         Spirit, who art thou?
*Lucifer.* Master of spirits.
*Cain.*         And being so, canst thou
Leave them, and walk with dust?
*Lucifer.*         I know the thoughts
Of dust, and feel for it, and with you.
*Cain.*         How!
You know my thoughts?
*Lucifer.*         They are the thoughts of all
Worthy of thought; — 'tis your immortal part
Which speaks within you.
*Cain.*         What immortal part?
This has not been reveal'd: the tree of life
Was withheld from us by my father's folly,
While that of knowledge, by my mother's haste,
Was pluck'd too soon; and all the fruit is death!

*Lucifer.* They have deceived thee; thou shalt live.
*Cain.* I live,
But live to die: and, living, see nothing
To make death hateful, save an innate clinging,
A loathsome, and yet all invincible
Instinct of life, which I abhor, as I
Despise myself, yet cannot overcome —
And so I live. Would I had never lived!

*Lucifer.* Thou livest, and must live for ever: think not
The earth, which is thine outward cov'ring, is
Existence — it will cease, and thou wilt be
No less than thou art now.

*Cain.* No *less!* and why
No more?

*Lucifer.* It may be thou shalt be as we.

*Cain.* And ye?

*Lucifer.* Are everlasting.

*Cain.* Are ye happy?

*Lucifer.* We are mighty.

*Cain.* Are ye happy?

*Lucifer.* No: art thou?

*Cain.* How should I be so? Look on me!

*Lucifer.* Poor clay!
And thou pretendest to be wretched! Thou!

*Cain.* I am: — and thou, with all thy might, what art thou?

*Lucifer.* One who aspired to be what made thee, and
Would not have made thee what thou art.

*Cain.* Ah!
Thou look'st almost a god; and —

*Lucifer.* I am none:
And having fail'd to be one, would be nought
Save what I am. He conquer'd; let him reign!

*Cain.* Who?

*Lucifer.* Thy sire's Maker, and the earth's.

*Cain.* And heaven's,
And all that in them is. So I have heard
His seraphs sing; and so my father saith.

*Lucifer.* They say — what they must sing and say, on pain
Of being that which I am — and thou art —
Of spirits and of men.
    *Cain.*              And what is that?
    *Lucifer.* Souls who dare use their immortality —
Souls who dare look the Omnipotent tyrant in
His everlasting face, and tell him that
His evil is not good! If he has made,
As he saith — which I know not, nor believe —
But, if he made us — he cannot unmake:
We are immortal! — nay, he'd *have* us so,
That he may torture: — let him! He is great —
But, in his greatness, is no happier than
We in our conflict! Goodness would not make
Evil; and what else hath he made? But let him
Sit on his vast and solitary throne,
Creating worlds, to make eternity
Less burthensome to his immense existence
And unparticipated solitude;
Let him crowd orb on orb: he is alone
Indefinite, indissoluble tyrant;
Could he but crush himself, 'twere the best boon
He ever granted: but let him reign on,
And multiply himself in misery!
Spirits and Men, at least we sympathise —
And, suffering in concert, make our pangs
Innumerable, more endurable,
By the unbounded sympathy of all
With all! But *He!* so wretched in his height,
So restless in his wretchedness, must still
Create, and re-create —
    *Cain.* Thou speak'st to me of things which long have swum
In visions through my thought: I never could
Reconcile what I saw with what I heard.
My father and my mother talk to me
Of serpents, and of fruits and trees: I see
The gates of what they call their Paradise

Guarded by fiery-sworded cherubim,
Which shut them out, and me: I feel the weight
Of daily toil, and constant thought: I look
Around a world where I seem nothing, with
Thoughts which arise within me, as if they
Could master all things — but I thought alone
This misery was *mine*. — My father is
Tamed down; my mother has forgot the mind
Which made her thirst for knowledge at the risk
Of an eternal curse; my brother is
A watching shepherd boy, who offers up
The firstlings of the flock to him who bids
The earth yield nothing to us without sweat;
My sister Zillah sings an earlier hymn
Than the birds' matins; and my Adah, my
Own and beloved, she, too, understands not
The mind which overwhelms me: never till
Now met I aught to sympathise with me.
'Tis well — I rather would consort with spirits.

 *Lucifer.* And hadst thou not been fit by thine own soul
For such companionship, I would not now
Have stood before thee as I am: a serpent
Had been enough to charm ye, as before.

 *Cain.* Ah! didst *thou* tempt my mother?
 *Lucifer.*          I tempt none,
Save with the truth: was not the tree, the tree
Of knowledge? and was not the tree of life
Still fruitful? Did *I* bid her pluck them not?
Did *I* plant things prohibited within
The reach of beings innocent, and curious
By their own innocence? I would have made ye
Gods; and even He who thrust ye forth, so thrust ye
Because "ye should not eat the fruits of life,
"And become gods as we." Were those his words?

 *Cain.* They were, as I have heard from those who heard
   them,
In thunder.

## ACT I.

*Lucifer.* Then who was the demon? He
Who would not let ye live, or he who would
Have made ye live for ever in the joy
And power of knowledge?
  *Cain.*      Would they had snatch'd both
The fruits, or neither!
  *Lucifer.*     One is yours already;
The other may be still.
  *Cain.*     How so?
  *Lucifer.*     By being
Yourselves, in your resistance. Nothing can
Quench the mind, if the mind will be itself
And centre of surrounding things — 'tis made
To sway.
  *Cain.* But didst thou tempt my parents?
  *Lucifer.*        I?
Poor clay! what should I tempt them for, or how?
  *Cain.* They say the serpent was a spirit.
  *Lucifer.*       Who
Saith that? It is not written so on high:
The proud One will not so far falsify,
Though man's vast fears and little vanity
Would make him cast upon the spiritual nature
His own low failing. The snake *was* the snake —
No more; and yet not less than those he tempted,
In nature being earth also — *more* in *wisdom*,
Since he could overcome them, and foreknew
The knowledge fatal to their narrow joys.
Think'st thou I'd take the shape of things that die?
  *Cain.* But the thing had a demon?
  *Lucifer.*      He but woke one
In those he spake to with his forky tongue.
I tell thee that the serpent was no more
Than a mere serpent: ask the cherubim
Who guard the tempting tree. When thousand ages
Have roll'd o'er your dead ashes, and your seed's,
The seed of the then world may thus array

Their earliest fault in fable, and attribute
To me a shape I scorn, as I scorn all
That bows to him, who made things but to bend
Before his sullen, sole eternity;
But we, who see the truth, must speak it. Thy
Fond parents listen'd to a creeping thing,
And fell. For what should spirits tempt them? What
Was there to envy in the narrow bounds
Of Paradise, that spirits who pervade
Space — but I speak to thee of what thou know'st not,
With all thy tree of knowledge.
  *Cain.*      But thou canst not
Speak aught of knowledge which I would not know,
And do not thirst to know, and bear a mind
To know.
  *Lucifer.* And heart to look on?
  *Cain.*      Be it proved.
  *Lucifer.* Darest thou to look on Death?
  *Cain.*      He has not yet
Been seen.
  *Lucifer.* But must be undergone.
  *Cain.*      My father
Says he is something dreadful, and my mother
Weeps when he's named; and Abel lifts his eyes
To heaven, and Zillah casts hers to the earth,
And sighs a prayer; and Adah looks on me,
And speaks not.
  *Lucifer.* And thou?
  *Cain.*      Thoughts unspeakable
Crowd in my breast to burning, when I hear
Of this almighty Death, who is, it seems,
Inevitable. Could I wrestle with him?
I wrestled with the lion, when a boy,
In play, till he ran roaring from my gripe.
  *Lucifer.* It has no shape; but will absorb all things
That bear the form of earth-born being.
  *Cain.*      Ah!

I thought it was a being: who could do
Such evil things to beings save a being?
    *Lucifer.* Ask the Destroyer.
    *Cain.*                Who?
    *Lucifer.*               The Maker — call him
Which name thou wilt: he makes but to destroy.
    *Cain.* I knew not that, yet thought it, since I heard
Of death: although I know not what it is,
Yet it seems horrible. I have look'd out
In the vast desolate night in search of him;
And when I saw gigantic shadows in
The umbrage of the walls of Eden, chequer'd
By the far-flashing of the cherubs' swords,
I watch'd for what I thought his coming; for
With fear rose longing in my heart to know
What 'twas which shook us all — but nothing came.
And then I turn'd my weary eyes from off
Our native and forbidden Paradise,
Up to the lights above us, in the azure,
Which are so beautiful: shall they, too, die?
    *Lucifer.* Perhaps — but long outlive both thine and
        thee.
    *Cain.* I'm glad of that: I would not have them die —
They are so lovely. What is death? I fear,
I feel, it is a dreadful thing; but what,
I cannot compass: 'tis denounced against us,
Both them who sinn'd and sinn'd not, as an ill —
What ill?
    *Lucifer.* To be resolved into the earth.
    *Cain.* But shall I know it?
    *Lucifer.*             As I know not death,
I cannot answer.
    *Cain.*        Were I quiet earth
That were no evil: would I ne'er had been
Aught else but dust!
    *Lucifer.*        That is a groveling wish,
Less than thy father's, for he wish'd to know.

*Cain.* But not to live, or wherefore pluck'd he not
The life-tree?
　　*Lucifer.* He was hinder'd.
　　*Cain.* 　　　　　　　　　　Deadly error!
Not to snatch first that fruit: — but ere he pluck'd
The knowledge, he was ignorant of death.
Alas! I scarcely now know what it is,
And yet I fear it — fear I know not what!
　　*Lucifer.* And I, who know all things, fear nothing:
　　　　see
What is true knowledge.
　　*Cain.* 　　　　　　Wilt thou teach me all?
　　*Lucifer.* Ay, upon one condition.
　　*Cain.* 　　　　　　　　　Name it.
　　*Lucifer.* 　　　　　　　　　　　That
Thou dost fall down and worship me — thy Lord.
　　*Cain.* Thou art not the Lord my father worships.
　　*Lucifer.* 　　　　　　　　　　　　　No.
　　*Cain.* His equal?
　　*Lucifer.* No; — I have nought in common with him!
Nor would: I would be aught above — beneath —
Aught save a sharer or a servant of
His power. I dwell apart; but I am great: —
Many there are who worship me, and more
Who shall — be thou amongst the first.
　　*Cain.* 　　　　　　　　　　　I never
As yet have bow'd unto my father's God,
Although my brother Abel oft implores
That I would join with him in sacrifice: —
Why should I bow to thee?
　　*Lucifer.* 　　　　　Hast thou ne'er bow'd
To him?
　　*Cain.* Have I not said it? — need I say it?
Could not thy mighty knowledge teach thee that?
　　*Lucifer.* He who bows not to him has bow'd to me!
　　*Cain.* But I will bend to neither.
　　*Lucifer.* 　　　　　　　　Ne'er the less,

ACT I.

Thou art my worshipper: not worshipping
Him makes thee mine the same.
    *Cain.*                     And what is that?
    *Lucifer.* Thou'lt know here — and hereafter.
    *Cain.*                          Let me but
Be taught the mystery of my being.
    *Lucifer.*                   Follow
Where I will lead thee.
    *Cain.*              But I must retire
To till the earth — for I had promised —
    *Lucifer.*                  What?
    *Cain.* To cull some first-fruits.
    *Lucifer.*                  Why?
    *Cain.*                        To offer up
With Abel on an altar.
    *Lucifer.*        Saidst thou not
Thou ne'er hadst bent to him who made thee?
    *Cain.*                          Yes —
But Abel's earnest prayer has wrought upon me;
The offering is more his than mine — and Adah —
    *Lucifer.* Why dost thou hesitate?
    *Cain.*                   She is my sister,
Born on the same day, of the same womb; and
She wrung from me, with tears, this promise; and
Rather than see her weep, I would, methinks,
Bear all — and worship aught.
    *Lucifer.*              Then follow me!
    *Cain.* I will.

              *Enter* ADAH.

    *Adah.*       My brother, I have come for thee;
It is our hour of rest and joy — and we
Have less without thee. Thou hast labour'd not
This morn; but I have done thy task: the fruits
Are ripe, and glowing as the light which ripens:
Come away.
    *Cain.*     See'st thou not?
    *Adah.*                 I see an angel;

We have seen many: will he share our hour
Of rest? — he is welcome.
  *Cain.*       But he is not like
The angels we have seen.
  *Adah.*       Are there, then, others?
But he is welcome, as they were: they deign'd
To be our guests — will he?
  *Cain (to Lucifer).*    Wilt thou?
  *Lucifer.*        I ask
Thee to be mine.
  *Cain.*    I must away with him.
  *Adah.* And leave us?
  *Cain.*     Ay.
  *Adah.*      And *me?*
  *Cain.*        Beloved Adah!
  *Adah.* Let me go with thee.
  *Lucifer.*       No, she must not.
  *Adah.*          Who
Art thou that steppest between heart and heart?
  *Cain.* He is a god.
  *Adah.*     How know'st thou?
  *Cain.*        He speaks like
A god.
  *Adah.* So did the serpent, and it lied.
  *Lucifer.* Thou errest, Adah! — was not the tree that
Of knowledge?
  *Adah.*    Ay — to our eternal sorrow.
  *Lucifer.* And yet that grief is knowledge — so he lied
     not:
And if he did betray you, 'twas with truth;
And truth in its own essence cannot be
But good.
  *Adah.* But all we know of it has gather'd
Evil on ill: expulsion from our home,
And dread, and toil, and sweat, and heaviness;
Remorse of that which was — and hope of that
Which cometh not. Cain! walk not with this spirit.

Bear with what we have borne, and love me — I
Love thee.
    *Lucifer.* More than thy mother, and thy sire?
    *Adah.* I do. Is that a sin, too?
    *Lucifer.*                      No, not yet:
It one day will be in your children.
    *Adah.*                         What!
Must not my daughter love her brother Enoch?
    *Lucifer.* Not as thou lovest Cain.
    *Adah.*                  Oh, my God!
Shall they not love and bring forth things that love
Out of their love? have they not drawn their milk
Out of this bosom? was not he, their father,
Born of the same sole womb, in the same hour
With me? did we not love each other? and
In multiplying our being multiply
Things which will love each other as we love
Them? — And as I love thee, my Cain! go not
Forth with this spirit: he is not of ours.
    *Lucifer.* The sin I speak of is not of my making,
And cannot be a sin in you — whate'er
It seem in those who will replace ye in
Mortality.
    *Adah.* What is the sin which is not
Sin in itself? Can circumstance make sin
Or virtue? — if it doth, we are the slaves
Of —
    *Lucifer.* Higher things than ye are slaves: and higher
Than them or ye would be so, did they not
Prefer an independency of torture
To the smooth agonies of adulation,
In hymns and harpings, and self-seeking prayers,
To that which is omnipotent, because
It is omnipotent, and not from love,
But terror and self-hope.
    *Adah.*             Omnipotence
Must be all goodness.

*Lucifer.* Was it so in Eden?

*Adah.* Fiend! tempt me not with beauty; thou art fairer
Than was the serpent, and as false.

*Lucifer.* As true.
Ask Eve, your mother: bears she not the knowledge
Of good and evil?

*Adah.* Oh, my mother! thou
Hast pluck'd a fruit more fatal to thine offspring
Than to thyself; thou at the least hast pass'd
Thy youth in Paradise, in innocent
And happy intercourse with happy spirits:
But we, thy children, ignorant of Eden,
Are girt about by demons, who assume
The words of God, and tempt us with our own
Dissatisfied and curious thoughts — as thou
Wert work'd on by the snake, in thy most flush'd
And heedless, harmless wantonness of bliss.
I cannot answer this immortal thing
Which stands before me; I cannot abhor him;
I look upon him with a pleasing fear,
And yet I fly not from him: in his eye
There is a fastening attraction which
Fixes my fluttering eyes on his; my heart
Beats quick; he awes me, and yet draws me near,
Nearer and nearer: — Cain — Cain — save me from him!

*Cain.* What dreads my Adah? This is no ill spirit.

*Adah.* He is not God — nor God's: I have beheld
The cherubs and the seraphs; he looks not
Like them.

*Cain.* But there are spirits loftier still —
The archangels.

*Lucifer.* And still loftier than the archangels.

*Adah.* Ay — but not blessed.

*Lucifer.* If the blessedness
Consists in slavery — no.

*Adah.* I have heard it said,

The seraphs *love most* — cherubim *know most* —
And this should be a cherub — since he loves not.
 *Lucifer.* And if the higher knowledge quenches love,
What must *he be* you cannot love when known?
Since the all-knowing cherubim love least,
The seraphs' love can be but ignorance:
That they are not compatible, the doom
Of thy fond parents, for their daring, proves.
Choose betwixt love and knowledge — since there is
No other choice: your sire hath chosen already;
His worship is but fear.
 *Adah.*    Oh, Cain! choose love.
 *Cain.* For thee, my Adah, I choose not — it was
Born with me — but I love nought else.
 *Adah.*     Our parents?
 *Cain.* Did they love us when they snatch'd from the tree
That which hath driven us all from Paradise?
 *Adah.* We were not born then — and if we had been,
Should we not love them and our children, Cain?
 *Cain.* My little Enoch! and his lisping sister!
Could I but deem them happy, I would half
Forget — but it can never be forgotten
Through thrice a thousand generations! never
Shall men love the remembrance of the man
Who sow'd the seed of evil and mankind
In the same hour! They pluck'd the tree of science
And sin — and, not content with their own sorrow,
Begot *me* — *thee* — and all the few that are,
And all the unnumber'd and innumerable
Multitudes, millions, myriads, which may be,
To inherit agonies accumulated
By ages! — and *I* must be sire of such things!
Thy beauty and thy love — my love and joy,
The rapturous moment and the placid hour,
All we love in our children and each other,
But lead them and ourselves through many years
Of sin and pain — or few, but still of sorrow,

Intercheck'd with an instant of brief pleasure,
To Death — the unknown! Methinks the tree of knowledge
Hath not fulfill'd its promise: — if they sinn'd,
At least they ought to have known all things that are
Of knowledge — and the mystery of death.
What do they know? — that they are miserable.
What need of snakes and fruits to teach us that?

   *Adah.* I am not wretched, Cain, and if thou
Wert happy —
   *Cain.*      Be thou happy, then, alone —
I will have nought to do with happiness,
Which humbles me and mine.
   *Adah.*          Alone I could not,
Nor *would* be happy: but with those around us
I think I could be so, despite of death,
Which, as I know it not, I dread not, though
It seems an awful shadow — if I may
Judge from what I have heard.
   *Lucifer.*        And thou couldst not
Alone, thou say'st, be happy?
   *Adah.*         Alone! Oh, my God!
Who could be happy and alone, or good?
To me my solitude seems sin; unless
When I think how soon I shall see my brother,
His brother, and our children, and our parents.
   *Lucifer.* Yet thy God is alone; and is he happy,
Lonely, and good?
   *Adah.*       He is not so; he hath
The angels and the mortals to make happy,
And thus becomes so in diffusing joy.
What else can joy be, but the spreading joy?
   *Lucifer.* Ask of your sire, the exile fresh from Eden;
Or of his first-born son: ask your own heart;
It is not tranquil.
   *Adah.*    Alas! no! and you —
Are you of heaven?
   *Lucifer.*      If I am not, enquire

## ACT I.

The cause of this all-spreading happiness
(Which you proclaim) of the all-great and good
Maker of life and living things; it is
His secret, and he keeps it. *We* must bear,
And some of us resist, and both in vain,
His seraphs say: but it is worth the trial,
Since better may not be without: there is
A wisdom in the spirit, which directs
To right, as in the dim blue air the eye
Of you, young mortals, lights at once upon
The star which watches, welcoming the morn.

   *Adah.* It is a beautiful star; I love it for
Its beauty.
     *Lucifer.*   And why not adore?
     *Adah.*                     Our father
Adores the Invisible only.
     *Lucifer.*               But the symbols
Of the Invisible are the loveliest
Of what is visible; and you bright star
Is leader of the host of heaven.
     *Adah.*                   Our father
Saith that he has beheld the God himself
Who made him and our mother.
     *Lucifer.*               Hast *thou* seen him?
     *Adah.* Yes — in his works.
     *Lucifer.*               But in his being?
     *Adah.*                                 No —
Save in my father, who is God's own image;
Or in his angels, who are like to thee —
And brighter, yet less beautiful and powerful
In seeming: as the silent sunny noon,
All light, they look upon us; but thou seem'st
Like an ethereal night, where long white clouds
Streak the deep purple, and unnumber'd stars
Spangle the wonderful mysterious vault
With things that look as if they would be suns;
So beautiful, unnumber'd, and endearing,

Not dazzling, and yet drawing us to them,
They fill my eyes with tears, and so dost thou.
Thou seem'st unhappy: do not make us so,
And I will weep for thee.

  *Lucifer.*     Alas! those tears!
Could'st thou but know what oceans will be shed —
  *Adah.* By me?
  *Lucifer.*   By all.
  *Adah.*     What all?
  *Lucifer.*      The million millions —
The myriad myriads — the all-peopled earth —
The unpeopled earth — and the o'er-peopled Hell,
Of which thy bosom is the germ.
  *Adah.*     O Cain!
This spirit curseth us.
  *Cain.*    Let him say on;
Him will I follow.
  *Adah.*   Whither?
  *Lucifer.*     To a place
Whence he shall come back to thee in an hour;
But in that hour see things of many days.
  *Adah.* How can that be?
  *Lucifer.*     Did not your Maker make
Out of old worlds this new one in few days?
And cannot I, who aided in this work,
Show in an hour what he hath made in many,
Or hath destroy'd in few?
  *Cain.*     Lead on.
  *Adah.*      Will he,
In sooth, return within an hour?
  *Lucifer.*     He shall.
With us acts are exempt from time, and we
Can crowd eternity into an hour,
Or stretch an hour into eternity:
We breathe not by a mortal measurement —
But that's a mystery. Cain, come on with me.
  *Adah.* Will he return?

*Lucifer.* Ay, woman! he alone
Of mortals from that pla . (the first and last
Who shall return, save ONE), shall come back to thee,
To make that silent and expectant world
As populous as this: at present there
Are few inhabitants.
    *Adah.* Where dwellest thou?
    *Lucifer.* Throughout all space. Where should I dwell?
        Where are
Thy God or Gods — there am I: all things are
Divided with me; life and death — and time —
Eternity — and heaven and earth — and that
Which is not heaven nor earth, but peopled with
Those who once peopled or shall people both —
These are my realms! So that I do divide
His, and possess a kingdom which is not
His. If I were not that which I have said,
Could I stand here? His angels are within
Your vision.
    *Adah.* So they were when the fair serpent
Spoke with our mother first.
    *Lucifer.* Cain! thou hast heard,
If thou dost long for knowledge, I can satiate
That thirst; nor ask thee to partake of fruits
Which shall deprive thee of a single good
The conqueror has left thee. Follow me.
    *Cain.* Spirit, I have said it. [*Exeunt* LUCIFER *and* CAIN.
    *Adah (follows, exclaiming).* Cain! my brother! Cain!

## ACT II.

### SCENE I.

*The Abyss of Space.*

    *Cain.* I tread on air, and sink not; yet I fear
To sink.
    *Lucifer.* Have faith in me, and thou shalt be
Borne on the air, of which I am the prince.

*Cain.* Can I do so without impiety?
*Lucifer.* Believe — and sink not! doubt — and perish! thus
Would run the edict of the other God,
Who names me demon to his angels; they
Echo the sound to miserable things,
Which, knowing nought beyond their shallow senses,
Worship the word which strikes their ear, and deem
Evil or good what is proclaim'd to them
In their abasement. I will have none such:
Worship or worship not, thou shalt behold
The worlds beyond thy little world, nor be
Amerced for doubts beyond thy little life,
With torture of *my* dooming. There will come
An hour, when, toss'd upon some water-drops,
A man shall say to a man, "Believe in me,
And walk the waters;" and the man shall walk
The billows and be safe. *I* will not say,
Believe in *me*, as a conditional creed
To save thee; but fly with me o'er the gulf
Of space an equal flight, and I will show
What thou dar'st not deny, — the history
Of past, and present, and of future worlds.
*Cain.* Oh, god, or demon, or whate'er thou art,
Is yon our earth?
*Lucifer.* Dost thou not recognise
The dust which form'd your father?
*Cain.* Can it be?
Yon small blue circle, swinging in far ether,
With an inferior circlet near it still,
Which looks like that which lit our earthly night?
Is this our Paradise? Where are its walls,
And they who guard them?
*Lucifer.* Point me out the site
Of Paradise.
*Cain.* How should I? As we move
Like sunbeams onward, it grows small and smaller,
And as it waxes little, and then less,

## ACT II.

Gathers a halo round it, like the light
Which shone the roundest of the stars, when I
Beheld them from the skirts of Paradise:
Methinks they both, as we recede from them,
Appear to join the innumerable stars
Which are around us; and, as we move on,
Increase their myriads.
  *Lucifer.*   And if there should be
Worlds greater than thine own, inhabited
By greater things, and they themselves far more
In number than the dust of thy dull earth,
Though multiplied to animated atoms,
All living, and all doom'd to death, and wretched,
What wouldst thou think?
  *Cain.*   I should be proud of thought
Which knew such things.
  *Lucifer.*   But if that high thought were
Link'd to a servile mass of matter, and,
Knowing such things, aspiring to such things,
And science still beyond them, were chain'd down
To the most gross and petty paltry wants,
All foul and fulsome, and the very best
Of thine enjoyments a sweet degradation,
A most enervating and filthy cheat
To lure thee on to the renewal of
Fresh souls and bodies, all foredoom'd to be
As frail, and few so happy —
  *Cain.*    Spirit! I
Know nought of death, save as a dreadful thing
Of which I have heard my parents speak, as of
A hideous heritage I owe to them
No less than life; a heritage not happy,
If I may judge, till now. But, spirit! if
It be as thou hast said (and I within
Feel the prophetic torture of its truth),
Here let me die: for to give birth to those
Who can but suffer many years, and die,

Methinks is merely propagating death,
And multiplying murder.
  *Lucifer.*     Thou canst not
*All* die — there is what must survive.
  *Cain.*         The Other
Spake not of this unto my father, when
He shut him forth from Paradise, with death
Written upon his forehead. But at least
Let what is mortal of me perish, that
I may be in the rest as angels are.
  *Lucifer. I* am angelic: wouldst thou be as I am?
  *Cain.* I know not what thou art: I see thy power,
And see thou show'st me things beyond *my* power,
Beyond all power of my born faculties,
Although inferior still to my desires
And my conceptions.
  *Lucifer.*    What are they which dwell
So humbly in their pride, as to sojourn
With worms in clay?
  *Cain.*     And what art thou who dwellest
So haughtily in spirit, and canst range
Nature and immortality — and yet
Seem'st sorrowful?
  *Lucifer.*   I seem that which I am;
And therefore do I ask of thee, if thou
Wouldst be immortal?
  *Cain.*     Thou hast said, I must be
Immortal in despite of me. I knew not
This until lately — but since it must be,
Let me, or happy or unhappy, learn
To anticipate my immortality.
  *Lucifer.* Thou didst before I came upon thee.
  *Cain.*         How?
  *Lucifer.* By suffering.
  *Cain.*     And must torture be immortal?
  *Lucifer.* We and thy sons will try. But now, behold!
Is it not glorious?

*Cain.* Oh, thou beautiful
And unimaginable ether! and
Ye multiplying masses of increased
And still increasing lights! what are ye? what
Is this blue wilderness of interminable
Air, where ye roll along, as I have seen
The leaves along the limpid streams of Eden?
Is your course measured for ye? Or do ye
Sweep on in your unbounded revelry
Through an aërial universe of endless
Expansion — at which my soul aches to think —
Intoxicated with eternity?
Oh God! Oh Gods! or whatsoe'er ye are!
How beautiful ye are! how beautiful
Your works, or accidents, or whatsoe'er
They may be! Let me die, as atoms die,
(If that they die) or know ye in your might
And knowledge! My thoughts are not in this hour
Unworthy what I see, though my dust is;
Spirit! let me expire, or see them nearer.

*Lucifer.* Art thou not nearer? look back to thine earth!

*Cain.* Where is it? I see nothing save a mass
Of most innumerable lights.

*Lucifer.* Look there!

*Cain.* I cannot see it.

*Lucifer.* Yet it sparkles still.

*Cain.* That! — yonder!

*Lucifer.* Yea.

*Cain.* And wilt thou tell me so?
Why, I have seen the fire-flies and fire-worms
Sprinkle the dusky groves and the green banks
In the dim twilight, brighter than yon world
Which bears them.

*Lucifer.* Thou hast seen both worms and worlds,
Each bright and sparkling — what dost think of them?

*Cain.* That they are beautiful in their own sphere
And that the night, which makes both beautiful,

The little shining fire-fly in its flight,
And the immortal star in its great course,
Must both be guided.
  *Lucifer.*    But by whom or what?
  *Cain.* Show me.
  *Lucifer.*   Dar'st thou behold?
  *Cain.*       How know I what
I *dare* behold? As yet, thou hast shown nought
I dare not gaze on further.
  *Lucifer.*   On, then, with me.
Wouldst thou behold things mortal or immortal?
  *Cain.* Why, what are things?
  *Lucifer.*    Both partly: but what doth
Sit next thy heart?
  *Cain.*   The things I see.
  *Lucifer.*     But what
Sate nearest it?
  *Cain.*   The things I have not seen,
Nor ever shall — the mysteries of death..
  *Lucifer.* What, if I show to thee things which have died,
As I have shown thee much which cannot die?
  *Cain.* Do so.
  *Lucifer.*  Away, then! on our mighty wings.
  *Cain.* Oh! how we cleave the blue! The stars fade from us!
The earth! where is my earth? Let me look on it,
For I was made of it.
  *Lucifer.*   'Tis now beyond thee,
Less, in the universe, than thou in it;
Yet deem not that thou canst escape it; thou
Shalt soon return to earth, and all its dust;
'Tis part of thy eternity, and mine.
  *Cain.* Where dost thou lead me?
  *Lucifer.*     To what was before thee!
The phantasm of the world; of which thy world
Is but the wreck.
  *Cain.*  What! is it not then new?
  *Lucifer.* No more than life is; and that was ere thou

Or *I* were, or the things which seem to us
Greater than either: many things will have
No end; and some, which would pretend to have
Had no beginning, have had one as mean
As thou; and mightier things have been extinct
To make way for much meaner than we can
Surmise; for *moments* only and the *space*
Have been and must be all *unchangeable*.
But changes make not death, except to clay;
But thou art clay — and canst but comprehend
That which was clay, and such thou shalt behold.

 *Cain.* Clay, spirit! what thou wilt, I can survey.
 *Lucifer.* Away, then!
 *Cain.*      But the lights fade from me fast,
And some till now grew larger as we approach'd,
And wore the look of worlds.
 *Lucifer.*     And such they are.
 *Cain.* And Edens in them?
 *Lucifer.*     It may be.
 *Cain.*       And men?
 *Lucifer.* Yea, or things higher.
 *Cain.*      Ay? and serpents too?
 *Lucifer.* Wouldst thou have men without them? must no reptiles
Breathe, save the erect ones?
 *Cain.*      How the lights recede!
Where fly we?
 *Lucifer.*  To the world of phantoms, which
Are beings past, and shadows still to come.
 *Cain.* But it grows dark, and dark — the stars are gone!
 *Lucifer.* And yet thou seest.
 *Cain.*      'Tis a fearful light!
No sun, no moon, no lights innumerable.
The very blue of the empurpled night
Fades to a dreary twilight, yet I see
Huge dusky masses; but unlike the worlds
We were approaching, which, begirt with light,

Seem'd full of life even when their atmosphere
Of light gave way, and show'd them taking shapes
Unequal, of deep valleys and vast mountains;
And some emitting sparks, and some displaying
Enormous liquid plains, and some begirt
With luminous belts, and floating moons, which took,
Like them, the features of fair earth: — instead,
All here seems dark and dreadful.
  *Lucifer.*      But distinct.
Thou seekest to behold death, and dead things?
  *Cain.* I seek it not; but as I know there are
Such, and that my sire's sin makes him and me,
And all that we inherit, liable
To such, I would behold at once, what I
Must one day see perforce.
  *Lucifer.*    Behold!
  *Cain.*       'Tis darkness.
  *Lucifer.* And so it shall be ever; but we will
Unfold its gates!
  *Cain.*   Enormous vapours roll
Apart — what's this?
  *Lucifer.*  Enter!
  *Cain.*     Can I return?
  *Lucifer.* Return! be sure: how else should death be
   peopled?
Its present realm is thin to what it will be,
Through thee and thine.
  *Cain.*    The clouds still open wide
And wider, and make widening circles round us.
  *Lucifer.* Advance!
  *Cain.*   And thou!
  *Lucifer.*     Fear not — without me thou
Couldst not have gone beyond thy world. On! on!
      [*They disappear through the clouds.*

ACT II.

SCENE II.
*Hades.*
*Enter* LUCIFER *and* CAIN.

 *Cain.* How silent and how vast are these dim worlds!
For they seem more than one, and yet more peopled
Than the huge brilliant luminous orbs which swung
So thickly in the upper air, that I
Had deem'd them rather the bright populace
Of some all unimaginable Heaven,
Than things to be inhabited themselves,
But that on drawing near them I beheld
Their swelling into palpable immensity
Of matter, which seem'd made for life to dwell on,
Rather than life itself. But here, all is
So shadowy and so full of twilight, that
It speaks of a day past.
 *Lucifer.*    It is the realm
Of death. — Wouldst have it present?
 *Cain.*       Till I know
That which it really is, I cannot answer.
But if it be as I have heard my father
Deal out in his long homilies, 'tis a thing —
Oh God! I dare not think on't! Cursed be
He who invented life that leads to death!
Or the dull mass of life, that, being life,
Could not retain, but needs must forfeit it —
Even for the innocent!
 *Lucifer.*   Dost thou curse thy father?
 *Cain.* Cursed he not me in giving me my birth?
Cursed he not me before my birth, in daring
To pluck the fruit forbidden?
 *Lucifer.*     Thou say'st well:
The curse is mutual 'twixt thy sire and thee —
But for thy sons and brother?
 *Cain.*      Let them share it
With me, their sire and brother! What else is

Bequeath'd to me? I leave them my inheritance.
Oh, ye interminable gloomy realms
Of swimming shadows and enormous shapes,
Some fully shown, some indistinct, and all
Mighty and melancholy — what are ye?
Live ye, or have ye lived?
    *Lucifer.*               Somewhat of both.
    *Cain.* Then what is death?
    *Lucifer.*               What? Hath not he who made ye
Said 'tis another life?
    *Cain.*             Till now he hath
Said nothing, save that all shall die.
    *Lucifer.*               Perhaps
He one day will unfold that further secret.
    *Cain.* Happy the day!
    *Lucifer.*               Yes; happy! when unfolded,
Through agonies unspeakable, and clogg'd
With agonies eternal, to innumerable
Yet unborn myriads of unconscious atoms,
All to be animated for this only!
    *Cain.* What are these mighty phantoms which I see
Floating around me? — They wear not the form
Of the intelligences I have seen
Round our regretted and unenter'd Eden,
Nor wear the form of man as I have view'd it
In Adam's and in Abel's, and in mine,
Nor in my sister-bride's, nor in my children's:
And yet they have an aspect, which, though not
Of men nor angels, looks like something, which
If not the last, rose higher than the first,
Haughty, and high, and beautiful, and full
Of seeming strength, but of inexplicable
Shape; for I never saw such. They bear not
The wing of seraph, nor the face of man,
Nor form of mightiest brute, nor aught that is
Now breathing; mighty yet and beautiful
As the most beautiful and mighty which

Live, and yet so unlike them, that I scarce
Can call them living.
  *Lucifer.*     Yet they lived.
  *Cain.*         Where?
  *Lucifer.*          Where
Thou livest.
  *Cain.*   When?
  *Lucifer.*     On what thou callest earth
They did inhabit.
  *Cain.*     Adam is the first.
  *Lucifer.* Of thine, I grant thee — but too mean to be
The last of these.
  *Cain.*     And what are they?
  *Lucifer.*        That which
Thou shalt be.
  *Cain.*   But what *were* they?
  *Lucifer.*       Living, high,
Intelligent, good, great, and glorious things,
As much superior unto all thy sire,
Adam, could e'er have been in Eden, as
The sixty-thousandth generation shall be,
In its dull damp degeneracy, to
Thee and thy son; — and how weak they are, judge
By thy own flesh.
  *Cain.*   Ah me! and did *they* perish?
  *Lucifer.* Yes, from their earth, as thou wilt fade from thine.
  *Cain.* But was *mine* theirs?
  *Lucifer.*     It was.
  *Cain.*       But not as now.
It is too little and too lowly to
Sustain such creatures.
  *Lucifer.*     True, it was more glorious.
  *Cain.* And wherefore did it fall?
  *Lucifer.*     Ask him who fells.
  *Cain.* But how?
  *Lucifer.*   By a most crushing and inexorable
Destruction and disorder of the elements,

Which struck a world to chaos, as a chaos
Subsiding has struck out a world: such things,
Though rare in time, are frequent in eternity. —
Pass on, and gaze upon the past.
    *Cain.*                   'Tis awful!
    *Lucifer.* And true. Behold these phantoms! they were once
Material as thou art.
    *Cain.*       And must I be
Like them?
    *Lucifer.* Let He who made thee answer that.
I show thee what thy predecessors are,
And what they *were* thou feelest, in degree
Inferior as thy petty feelings and
Thy pettier portion of the immortal part
Of high intelligence and earthly strength.
What ye in common have with what they had
Is life, and what ye *shall* have — death: the rest
Of your poor attributes is such as suits
Reptiles engender'd out of the subsiding
Slime of a mighty universe, crush'd into
A scarcely-yet shaped planet, peopled with
Things whose enjoyment was to be in blindness —
A Paradise of Ignorance, from which
Knowledge was barr'd as poison. But behold
What these superior beings are or were;
Or, if it irk thee, turn thee back and till
The earth, thy task — I'll waft thee there in safety.
    *Cain.* No: I'll stay here.
    *Lucifer.*             How long?
    *Cain.*                     For ever! Since
I must one day return here from the earth,
I rather would remain; I am sick of all
That dust has shown me — let me dwell in shadows.
    *Lucifer.* It cannot be: thou now beholdest as
A vision that which is reality.
To make thyself fit for this dwelling, thou

Must pass through what the things thou see'st have pass'd —
The gates of death.

  *Cain.*    By what gate have we enter'd
Even now?

  *Lucifer.* By mine! But, plighted to return,
My spirit buoys thee up to breathe in regions
Where all is breathless save thyself. Gaze on,
But do not think to dwell here till thine hour
Is come.

  *Cain.* And these, too; can they ne'er repass
To earth again?

  *Lucifer.*  Their earth is gone for ever —
So changed by its convulsion, they would not
Be conscious to a single present spot
Of its new scarcely harden'd surface — 'twas —
Oh, what a beautiful world it *was!*

  *Cain.*       And is.
It is not with the earth, though I must till it,
I feel at war, but that I may not profit
By what it bears of beautiful, untoiling,
Nor gratify my thousand swelling thoughts
With knowledge, nor allay my thousand fears
Of death and life.

  *Lucifer.*  What thy world is, thou see'st,
But canst not comprehend the shadow of
That which it was.

  *Cain.*    And those enormous creatures,
Phantoms inferior in intelligence
(At least so seeming) to the things we have pass'd,
Resembling somewhat the wild habitants
Of the deep woods of earth, the hugest which
Roar nightly in the forest, but ten-fold
In magnitude and terror; taller than
The cherub-guarded walls of Eden, with
Eyes flashing like the fiery swords which fence them,
And tusks projecting like the trees stripp'd of
Their bark and branches — what were they?

*Lucifer.*                              That which
The Mammoth is in thy world; — but these lie
By myriads underneath its surface.
    *Cain.*                    But
None on it?
    *Lucifer.* No: for thy frail race to war
With them would render the curse on it useless —
'T would be destroy'd so early.
    *Cain.*                But why *war?*
    *Lucifer.* You have forgotten the denunciation
Which drove your race from Eden — war with all things,
And death to all things, and disease to most things,
And pangs, and bitterness; these were the fruits
Of the forbidden tree.
    *Cain.*           But animals —
Did they, too, eat of it, that they must die?
    *Lucifer.* Your Maker told ye, *they* were made for you,
As you for him. — You would not have their doom
Superior to your own? Had Adam not
Fallen, all had stood.
    *Cain.*          Alas! the hopeless wretches!
They too must share my sire's fate, like his sons;
Like them, too, without having shared the apple;
Like them, too, without the so dear-bought *knowledge!*
It was a lying tree — for we *know* nothing.
At least it *promised knowledge* at the *price*
Of death — but *knowledge* still: but what *knows* man?
    *Lucifer.* It may be death leads to the *highest* knowledge;
And being of all things the sole thing certain,
At least leads to the *surest* science: therefore
The tree was true, though deadly.
    *Cain.*                These dim realms!
I see them, but I know them not.
    *Lucifer.*               Because
Thy hour is yet afar, and matter cannot
Comprehend spirit wholly — but 't is something
To know there are such realms.

*Cain.* We knew already
That there was death.
*Lucifer.* But not what was beyond it.
*Cain.* Nor know I now.
*Lucifer.* Thou knowest that there is
A state, and many states beyond thine own —
And this thou knewest not this morn.
*Cain.* But all
Seems dim and shadowy.
*Lucifer.* Be content; it will
Seem clearer to thine immortality.
*Cain.* And yon immeasurable liquid space
Of glorious azure which floats on beyond us,
Which looks like water, and which I should deem
The river which flows out of Paradise
Past my own dwelling, but that it is bankless
And boundless, and of an ethereal hue —
What is it?
*Lucifer.* There is still some such on earth,
Although inferior, and thy children shall
Dwell near it — 'tis the phantasm of an ocean.
*Cain.* 'Tis like another world; a liquid sun —
And those inordinate creatures sporting o'er
Its shining surface?
*Lucifer.* Are its habitants,
The past leviathans.
*Cain.* And yon immense
Serpent, which rears his dripping mane and vasty
Head ten times higher than the haughtiest cedar
Forth from the abyss, looking as he could coil
Himself around the orbs we lately look'd on —
Is he not of the kind which bask'd beneath
The tree in Eden?
*Lucifer.* Eve, thy mother, best
Can tell what shape of serpent tempted her.
*Cain.* This seems too terrible. No doubt the other
Had more of beauty.

*Lucifer.* Hast thou ne'er beheld him?
*Cain.* Many of the same kind (at least so call'd),
But never that precisely which persuaded
The fatal fruit, nor even of the same aspect.
*Lucifer.* Your father saw him not?
*Cain.* No: 'twas my mother
Who tempted him — she tempted by the serpent.
*Lucifer.* Good man! whene'er thy wife, or thy sons' wives,
Tempt thee or them to aught that's new or strange,
Be sure thou see'st first who hath tempted *them*.
*Cain.* Thy precept comes too late: there is no more
For serpents to tempt woman to.
*Lucifer.* But there
Are some things still which woman may tempt man to,
And man tempt woman: — let thy sons look to it!
My counsel is a kind one; for 'tis even
Given chiefly at my own expense; 'tis true,
'Twill not be follow'd, so there's little lost.
*Cain.* I understand not this.
*Lucifer.* The happier thou! —
Thy world and thou are still too young! Thou thinkest
Thyself most wicked and unhappy: is it
Not so?
*Cain.* For crime, I know not; but for pain,
I have felt much.
*Lucifer.* First-born of the first man!
Thy present state of sin — and thou art evil,
Of sorrow — and thou sufferest, are both Eden
In all its innocence compared to what
*Thou* shortly may'st be; and that state again,
In its redoubled wretchedness, a Paradise
To what thy sons' sons' sons, accumulating
In generations like to dust (which they
In fact but add to), shall endure and do. —
Now let us back to earth!
*Cain.* And wherefore didst thou
Lead me here only to inform me this?

*Lucifer.* Was not thy quest for knowledge?
*Cain.*                                   Yes: as being
The road to happiness.
*Lucifer.*            If truth be so,
Thou hast it.
*Cain.*        Then my father's God did well
When he prohibited the fatal tree.
*Lucifer.* But had done better in not planting it.
But ignorance of evil doth not save
From evil; it must still roll on the same,
A part of all things.
*Cain.*           Not of all things. No:
I'll not believe it — for I thirst for good.
*Lucifer.* And who and what doth not? *Who* covets evil
For its own bitter sake? — *None* — nothing! 'tis
The leaven of all life, and lifelessness.
*Cain.* Within those glorious orbs which we behold,
Distant and dazzling, and innumerable,
Ere we came down into this phantom realm,
Ill cannot come: they are too beautiful.
*Lucifer.* Thou hast seen them from afar —
*Cain.*                                   And what of that?
Distance can but diminish glory — they,
When nearer, must be more ineffable.
*Lucifer.* Approach the things of earth most beautiful,
And judge their beauty near.
*Cain.*           I have done this —
The loveliest thing I know is loveliest nearest.
*Lucifer.* Then there must be delusion. — What is that,
Which being nearest to thine eyes is still
More beautiful than beauteous things remote?
*Cain.* My sister Adah. — All the stars of heaven,
The deep blue noon of night, lit by an orb
Which looks a spirit, or a spirit's world —
The hues of twilight — the sun's gorgeous coming —
His setting indescribable, which fills
My eyes with pleasant tears as I behold

Him sink, and feel my heart float softly with him
Along that western paradise of clouds —
The forest shade — the green bough — the bird's voice —
The vesper bird's, which seems to sing of love,
And mingles with the song of cherubim,
As the day closes over Eden's walls; —
All these are nothing, to my eyes and heart,
Like Adah's face: I turn from earth and heaven
To gaze on it.
  *Lucifer.*  'Tis fair as frail mortality,
In the first dawn and bloom of young creation
And earliest embraces of earth's parents,
Can make its offspring; still it is delusion.
  *Cain.* You think so, being not her brother.
  *Lucifer.*        Mortal!
My brotherhood's with those who have no children.
  *Cain.* Then thou canst have no fellowship with us.
  *Lucifer.* It may be that thine own shall be for me.
But if thou dost possess a beautiful
Being beyond all beauty in thine eyes,
Why art thou wretched?
  *Cain.*    Why do I exist?
Why art *thou* wretched? why are all things so?
Ev'n he who made us must be, as the maker
Of things unhappy! To produce destruction
Can surely never be the task of joy,
And yet my sire says he's omnipotent:
Then why is evil — he being good? I ask'd
This question of my father; and he said,
Because this evil only was the path
To good. Strange good, that must arise from out
Its deadly opposite. I lately saw
A lamb stung by a reptile: the poor suckling
Lay foaming on the earth, beneath the vain
And piteous bleating of its restless dam;
My father pluck'd some herbs, and laid them to
The wound; and by degrees the helpless wretch

ACT II.

Resumed its careless life, and rose to drain
The mother's milk, who o'er it tremulous
Stood licking its reviving limbs with joy.
Behold, my son! said Adam, how from evil
Springs good!
    *Lucifer.*    What didst thou answer?
    *Cain.*                    Nothing; for
He is my father: but I thought, that 't were
A better portion for the animal
Never to have been *stung at all*, than to
Purchase renewal of its little life
With agonies unutterable, though
Dispell'd by antidotes.
    *Lucifer.*            But as thou saidst
Of all beloved things thou lovest her
Who shared thy mother's milk, and giveth hers
Unto thy children —
    *Cain.*            Most assuredly:
What should I be without her?
    *Lucifer.*                What am I?
    *Cain.* Dost thou love nothing?
    *Lucifer.*                What does thy God love?
    *Cain.* All things, my father says; but I confess
I see it not in their allotment here.
    *Lucifer.* And, therefore, thou canst not see if *I* love
Or no, except some vast and general purpose,
To which particular things must melt like snows.
    *Cain.* Snows! what are they?
    *Lucifer.*            Be happier in not knowing
What thy remoter offspring must encounter;
But bask beneath the clime which knows no winter.
    *Cain.* But dost thou not love something like thyself?
    *Lucifer.* And dost thou love *thyself?*
    *Cain.*                Yes, but love more
What makes my feelings more endurable,
And is more than myself, because I love it.
    *Lucifer.* Thou lovest it, because 'tis beautiful,

17*

As was the apple in thy mother's eye;
And when it ceases to be so, thy love
Will cease, like any other appetite.
   *Cain.* Cease to be beautiful! how can that be?
   *Lucifer.* With time.
   *Cain.*               But time has past, and hitherto
Even Adam and my mother both are fair:
Not fair like Adah and the seraphim —
But very fair.
   *Lucifer.*    All that must pass away
In them and her.
   *Cain.*          I'm sorry for it; but
Cannot conceive my love for her the less.
And when her beauty disappears, methinks
He who creates all beauty will lose more
Than me in seeing perish such a work.
   *Lucifer.* I pity thee who lovest what must perish.
   *Cain.* And I thee who lov'st nothing.
   *Lucifer.*                   And thy brother —
Sits he not near thy heart?
   *Cain.*            Why should he not?
   *Lucifer.* Thy father loves him well — so does thy God.
   *Cain.* And so do I.
   *Lucifer.*       'Tis well and meekly done.
   *Cain.* Meekly!
   *Lucifer.*       He is the second born of flesh,
And is his mother's favourite.
   *Cain.*             Let him keep
Her favour, since the serpent was the first
To win it.
   *Lucifer.* And his father's?
   *Cain.*               What is that
To me? should I not love that which all love?
   *Lucifer.* And the Jehovah — the indulgent Lord,
And bounteous planter of barr'd Paradise —
He, too, looks smilingly on Abel.

    *Cain.*                                I
Ne'er saw him, and I know not if he smiles.
    *Lucifer.* But you have seen his angels.
    *Cain.*                          Rarely.
    *Lucifer.*                          But
Sufficiently to see they love your brother;
His sacrifices are acceptable.
    *Cain.* So be they! wherefore speak to me of this?
    *Lucifer.* Because thou hast thought of this ere now.
    *Cain.*                         And if
I *have* thought, why recall a thought that — *(he pauses, as
        agitated)* — Spirit!
*Here* we are in *thy* world; speak not of *mine.*
Thou hast shown me wonders; thou hast shown me those
Mighty pre-Adamites who walk'd the earth
Of which ours is the wreck; thou hast pointed out
Myriads of starry worlds, of which our own
Is the dim and remote companion, in
Infinity of life: thou hast shown me shadows
Of that existence with the dreaded name
Which my sire brought us — Death; thou hast shown me
        much —
But not all: show me where Jehovah dwells,
In his especial Paradise — or *thine:*
Where is it?
    *Lucifer.*   *Here,* and o'er all space.
    *Cain.*                         But ye
Have some allotted dwelling — as all things;
Clay has its earth, and other worlds their tenants;
All temporary breathing creatures their
Peculiar element; and things which have
Long ceased to breathe *our* breath, have theirs, thou say'st;
And the Jehovah and thyself have thine —
Ye do not dwell together?
    *Lucifer.*               No, we reign
Together; but our dwellings are asunder.
    *Cain.* Would there were only one of ye! perchance

An unity of purpose might make union
In elements which seem now jarr'd in storms.
How came ye, being spirits, wise and infinite,
To separate? Are ye not as brethren in
Your essence, and your nature, and your glory?

    *Lucifer.* Art thou not Abel's brother?
    *Cain.*                      We are brethren,
And so we shall remain; but were it not so,
Is spirit like to flesh? can it fall out?
Infinity with Immortality?
Jarring and turning space to misery —
For what?
    *Lucifer.* To reign.
    *Cain.*            Did ye not tell me that
Ye are both eternal?
    *Lucifer.*       Yea!
    *Cain.*               And what I have seen,
Yon blue immensity, is boundless?
    *Lucifer.*             Ay.
    *Cain.* And cannot ye both *reign* then? — is there not
Enough? — why should ye differ?
    *Lucifer.*            We *both* reign.
    *Cain.* But one of you makes evil.
    *Lucifer.*            Which?
    *Cain.*                      Thou! for
If thou canst do man good, why dost thou not?
    *Lucifer.* And why not he who made? *I* made ye not;
Ye are *his* creatures, and not mine.
    *Cain.*                 Then leave us
*His* creatures, as thou say'st we are, or show me
Thy dwelling, or *his* dwelling.
    *Lucifer.*                I could show thee
Both; but the time will come thou shalt see one
Of them for evermore.
    *Cain.*           And why not now?
    *Lucifer.* Thy human mind hath scarcely grasp to gather
The little I have shown thee into calm

And clear thought; and *thou* wouldst go on aspiring
To the great double Mysteries! the *two Principles!*
And gaze upon them on their secret thrones!
Dust! limit thy ambition; for to see
Either of these, would be for thee to perish!

    *Cain.* And let me perish, so I see them!
    *Lucifer.*                               There
The son of her who snatch'd the apple spake!
But thou wouldst only perish, and not see them;
That sight is for the other state.
    *Cain.*                         Of death?
    *Lucifer.* That is the prelude.
    *Cain.*                       Then I dread it less,
Now that I know it leads to something definite.
    *Lucifer.* And now I will convey thee to thy world,
Where thou shalt multiply the race of Adam,
Eat, drink, toil, tremble, laugh, weep, sleep, and die.
    *Cain.* And to what end have I beheld these things
Which thou hast shown me?
    *Lucifer.*                  Didst thou not require
Knowledge? And have I not, in what I show'd,
Taught thee to know thyself?
    *Cain.*                 Alas! I seem
Nothing.
    *Lucifer.* And this should be the human sum
Of knowledge, to know mortal nature's nothingness;
Bequeath that science to thy children, and
'Twill spare them many tortures.
    *Cain.*                 Haughty spirit!
Thou speak'st it proudly; but thyself, though proud,
Hast a superior.
    *Lucifer.*    No! By heaven, which He
Holds, and the abyss, and the immensity
Of worlds and life, which I hold with him — No!
I have a victor — true; but no superior.
Homage he has from all — but none from me:
I battle it against him, as I battled

In highest heaven. Through all eternity,
And the unfathomable gulfs of Hades,
And the interminable realms of space,
And the infinity of endless ages,
All, all, will I dispute! And world by world,
And star by star, and universe by universe,
Shall tremble in the balance, till the great
Conflict shall cease, if ever it shall cease,
Which it ne'er shall, till he or I be quench'd!
And what can quench our immortality,
Or mutual and irrevocable hate?
He as a conqueror will call the conquer'd
*Evil;* but what will be the *good* he gives?
Were I the victor, *his* works would be deem'd
The only evil ones. And you, ye new
And scarce-born mortals, what have been his gifts
To you already, in your little world?

    *Cain.* But few; and some of those but bitter.
    *Lucifer.*                                      Back
With me, then, to thine earth, and try the rest
Of his celestial boons to you and yours.
Evil and good are things in their own essence,
And not made good or evil by the giver;
But if he gives you good — so call him; if
Evil springs from *him,* do not name it *mine,*
Till ye know better its true fount; and judge
Not by words, though of spirits, but the fruits
Of your existence, such as it must be.
*One good* gift has the fatal apple given —
Your *reason:* — let it not be over-sway'd
By tyrannous threats to force you into faith
'Gainst all external sense and inward feeling:
Think and endure, — and form an inner world
In your own bosom — where the outward fails;
So shall you nearer be the spiritual
Nature, and war triumphant with your own.
                                               *[They disappear.*

## ACT III.

### SCENE I.

*The Earth, near Eden, as in Act I.*
*Enter* CAIN *and* ADAH.

*Adah.* Hush! tread softly, Cain.
*Cain.*                      I will; but wherefore?
*Adah.* Our little Enoch sleeps upon yon bed
Of leaves, beneath the cypress.
*Cain.*                    Cypress! 'tis
A gloomy tree, which looks as if it mourn'd
O'er what it shadows; wherefore didst thou choose it
For our child's canopy?
*Adah.*                   Because its branches
Shut out the sun like night, and therefore seem'd
Fitting to shadow slumber.
*Cain.*                   Ay, the last —
And longest; but no matter — lead me to him.
                             [*They go up to the child.*
How lovely he appears! his little cheeks,
In their pure incarnation, vying with
The rose leaves strewn beneath them.
*Adah.*                       And his lips, too,
How beautifully parted! No; you shall not
Kiss him, at least not now: he will awake soon —
His hour of mid-day rest is nearly over;
But it were pity to disturb him till
'Tis closed.
*Cain.*     You have said well; I will contain
My heart till then. He smiles, and sleeps! — Sleep on
And smile, thou little, young inheritor
Of a world scarce less young: sleep on, and smile!
Thine are the hours and days when both are cheering
And innocent! *thou* hast not pluck'd the fruit —
Thou know'st not thou art naked! Must the time
Come thou shalt be amerced for sins unknown,

Which were not thine nor mine? But now sleep on!
His checks are reddening into deeper smiles,
And shining lids are trembling o'er his long
Lashes, dark as the cypress which waves o'er them;
Half open, from beneath them the clear blue
Laughs out, although in slumber. He must dream —
Of what? Of Paradise! — Ay! dream of it,
My disinherited boy! 'Tis but a dream;
For never more thyself, thy sons, nor fathers,
Shall walk in that forbidden place of joy!

    *Adah.* Dear Cain! Nay, do not whisper o'er our son
Such melancholy yearnings o'er the past:
Why wilt thou always mourn for Paradise?
Can we not make another?

    *Cain.*              Where?

    *Adah.*                   Here, or
Where'er thou wilt: where'er thou art, I feel not
The want of this so much regretted Eden.
Have I not thee, our boy, our sire, and brother,
And Zillah — our sweet sister, and our Eve,
To whom we owe so much besides our birth?

    *Cain.* Yes — death, too, is amongst the debts we owe her.

    *Adah.* Cain! that proud spirit, who withdrew thee hence,
Hath sadden'd thine still deeper. I had hoped
The promised wonders which thou hast beheld,
Visions, thou say'st, of past and present worlds,
Would have composed thy mind into the calm
Of a contented knowledge; but I see
Thy guide hath done thee evil: still I thank him,
And can forgive him all, that he so soon
Hath given thee back to us.

    *Cain.*              So soon?

    *Adah.*                   'Tis scarcely
Two hours since ye departed: two *long* hours
To *me*, but only *hours* upon the sun.

    *Cain.* And yet I have approach'd that sun, and seen
Worlds which he once shone on, and never more

ACT III.

Shall light; and worlds he never lit: methought
Years had roll'd o'er my absence.
    *Adah.*                        Hardly hours.
    *Cain.* The mind then hath capacity of time,
And measures it by that which it beholds,
Pleasing or painful; little or almighty.
I had beheld the immemorial works
Of endless beings; skirr'd extinguish'd worlds;
And, gazing on eternity, methought
I had borrow'd more by a few drops of ages
From its immensity: but now I feel
My littleness again. Well said the spirit,
That I was nothing!
    *Adah.*                  Wherefore said he so?
Jehovah said not that.
    *Cain.*                  No; *he* contents him
With making us the *nothing* which we are;
And after flattering dust with glimpses of
Eden and Immortality, resolves
It back to dust again — for what?
    *Adah.*                  Thou know'st —
Even for our parents' error.
    *Cain.*                  What is that
To us? they sinn'd, then *let them* die!
    *Adah.* Thou hast not spoken well, nor is that thought
Thy own, but of the spirit who was with thee.
Would I could die for them, so *they* might live!
    *Cain.* Why, so say I — provided that one victim
Might satiate the insatiable of life,
And that our little rosy sleeper there
Might never taste of death nor human sorrow,
Nor hand it down to those who spring from him.
    *Adah.* How know we that some such atonement one day
May not redeem our race?
    *Cain.*                 By sacrificing
The harmless for the guilty? what atonement
Were there? why, *we* are innocent: what have we

Done, that we must be victims for a deed
Before our birth, or need have victims to
Atone for this mysterious, nameless sin —
If it be such a sin to seek for knowledge?

  *Adah.* Alas! thou sinnest now, my Cain: thy words
Sound impious in mine ears.
  *Cain.*       Then leave me!
  *Adah.*           Never,
Though thy God left thee.
  *Cain.*     Say, what have we here?
  *Adah.* Two altars, which our brother Abel made
During thine absence, whereupon to offer
A sacrifice to God on thy return.
  *Cain.* And how knew *he*, that *I* would be so ready
With the burnt offerings, which he daily brings
With a meek brow, whose base humility
Shows more of fear than worship, as a bribe
To the Creator?
  *Adah.*   Surely, 'tis well done.
  *Cain.* One altar may suffice; *I* have no offering.
  *Adah.* The fruits of the earth, the early, beautiful
Blossom and bud, and bloom of flowers, and fruits;
These are a goodly offering to the Lord,
Given with a gentle and a contrite spirit.
  *Cain.* I have toil'd, and till'd, and sweaten in the sun
According to the curse: — must I do more?
For what should I be gentle? for a war
With all the elements ere they will yield
The bread we eat? For what must I be grateful?
For being dust, and groveling in the dust,
Till I return to dust? If I am nothing —
For nothing shall I be an hypocrite,
And seem well-pleased with pain? For what should I
Be contrite? for my father's sin, already
Expiate with what we all have undergone,
And to be more than expiated by
The ages prophesied, upon our seed.

Little deems our young blooming sleeper, there,
The germs of an eternal misery
To myriads is within him! better 't were
I snatch'd him in his sleep, and dash'd him 'gainst
The rocks, than let him live to —
    *Adah.*                        Oh, my God!
Touch not the child — my child! *thy* child! Oh Cain!
    *Cain.* Fear not! for all the stars, and all the power
Which sways them, I would not accost yon infant
With ruder greeting than a father's kiss.
    *Adah.* Then, why so awful in thy speech?
    *Cain.*                                  I said,
'T were better that he ceased to live, than give
Life to so much of sorrow as he must
Endure, and, harder still, bequeath; but since
That saying jars you, let us only say —
'T were better that he never had been born.
    *Adah.* Oh, do not say so! Where were then the
        joys,
The mother's joys of watching, nourishing,
And loving him? Soft! he awakes. Sweet Enoch!
                                          [*She goes to the child.*
Oh Cain! look on him; see how full of life,
Of strength, of bloom, of beauty, and of joy,
How like to me — how like to thee, when gentle,
For *then* we are *all* alike; is't not so, Cain?
Mother, and sire, and son, our features are
Reflected in each other; as they are
In the clear waters, when *they* are *gentle*, and
When *thou* art *gentle*. Love us, then, my Cain!
And love thyself for our sakes, for we love thee.
Look! how he laughs and stretches out his arms,
And opens wide his blue eyes upon thine,
To hail his father; while his little form
Flutters as wing'd with joy. Talk not of pain!
The childless cherubs well might envy thee
The pleasures of a parent! Bless him, Cain!

As yet he hath no words to thank thee, but
His heart will, and thine own too.
  *Cain.*       Bless thee, boy!
If that a mortal blessing may avail thee,
To save thee from the serpent's curse!
  *Adah.*         It shall.
Surely a father's blessing may avert
A reptile's subtlety.
  *Cain.*    Of that I doubt;
But bless him ne'er the less.
  *Adah.*       Our brother comes.
  *Cain.* Thy brother Abel.

      *Enter* ABEL.

  *Abel.*     Welcome, Cain! My brother,
The peace of God be on thee!
  *Cain.*       Abel, hail!
  *Abel.* Our sister tells me that thou hast been wandering,
In high communion with a spirit, far
Beyond our wonted range. Was he of those
We have seen and spoken with, like to our father?
  *Cain.* No.
  *Abel.* Why then commune with him? he may be
A foe to the Most High.
  *Cain.*     And friend to man.
Has the Most High been so — if so you term him?
  *Abel. Term him!* your words are strange to-day, my
    brother.
My sister Adah, leave us for awhile —
We mean to sacrifice.
  *Adah.*    Farewell, my Cain;
But first embrace thy son. May his soft spirit,
And Abel's pious ministry, recall thee
To peace and holiness!
         [*Exit* ADAH, *with her child.*
  *Abel.*     Where hast thou been?
  *Cain.* I know not.

## ACT III.

*Abel.*         Nor what thou hast seen?
*Cain.*                               The dead,
The immortal, the unbounded, the omnipotent,
The overpowering mysteries of space —
The innumerable worlds that were and are —
A whirlwind of such overwhelming things,
Suns, moons, and earths, upon their loud-voiced spheres
Singing in thunder round me, as have made me
Unfit for mortal converse: leave me, Abel.

  *Abel.* Thine eyes are flashing with unnatural light —
Thy cheek is flush'd with an unnatural hue —
Thy words are fraught with an unnatural sound —
What may this mean?
  *Cain.*         It means — I pray thee, leave me.
  *Abel.* Not till we have pray'd and sacrificed together.
  *Cain.* Abel, I pray thee, sacrifice alone —
Jehovah loves thee well.
  *Abel.*         Both well, I hope.
  *Cain.* But thee the better: I care not for that;
Thou art fitter for his worship than I am;
Revere him, then — but let it be alone —
At least, without me.
  *Abel.*         Brother, I should ill
Deserve the name of our great father's son,
If, as my elder, I revered thee not,
And in the worship of our God call'd not
On thee to join me, and precede me in
Our priesthood — 'tis thy place.
  *Cain.*         But I have ne'er
Asserted it.
  *Abel.* The more my grief; I pray thee
To do so now: thy soul seems labouring in
Some strong delusion; it will calm thee.
  *Cain.*         No;
Nothing can calm me more. *Calm!* say I? Never
Knew I what calm was in the soul, although

I have seen the elements still'd. My Abel, leave me!
Or let me leave thee to thy pious purpose.
  *Abel.* Neither; we must perform our task together.
Spurn me not.
  *Cain.*     If it must be so — well, then,
What shall I do?
  *Abel.*         Choose one of those two altars.
  *Cain.* Choose for me: they to me are so much turf
And stone.
  *Abel.*    Choose thou!
  *Cain.*             I have chosen.
  *Abel.*                     'Tis the highest,
And suits thee, as the elder. Now prepare
Thine offerings.
  *Cain.*         Where are thine?
  *Abel.*                  Behold them here —
The firstlings of the flock, and fat thereof —
A shepherd's humble offering.
  *Cain.*               I have no flocks;
I am a tiller of the ground, and must
Yield what it yieldeth to my toil — its fruit:
                       [*He gathers fruits.*
Behold them in their various bloom and ripeness.
       [*They dress their altars, and kindle a flame
              upon them.*
  *Abel.* My brother, as the elder, offer first
Thy prayer and thanksgiving with sacrifice.
  *Cain.* No — I am new to this; lead thou the way,
And I will follow — as I may.
  *Abel (kneeling).*        Oh God!
Who made us, and who breathed the breath of life
Within our nostrils, who hath blessed us,
And spared, despite our father's sin, to make
His children all lost, as they might have been,
Had not thy justice been so temper'd with
The mercy which is thy delight, as to
Accord a pardon like a Paradise,

Compared with our great crimes: — Sole Lord of light!
Of good, and glory, and eternity;
Without whom all were evil, and with whom
Nothing can err, except to some good end
Of thine omnipotent benevolence —
Inscrutable, but still to be fulfill'd —
Accept from out thy humble first of shepherd's
First of the first-born flocks — an offering,
In itself nothing — as what offering can be
Aught unto thee? — but yet accept it for
The thanksgiving of him who spreads it in
The face of thy high heaven, bowing his own
Even to the dust, of which he is, in honour
Of thee, and of thy name, for evermore!

  *Cain (standing erect during this speech).*  Spirit! whate'er or
    whosoe'er thou art,
Omnipotent, it may be — and, if good,
Shown in the exemption of thy deeds from evil;
Jehovah upon earth! and God in heaven!
And it may be with other names, because
Thine attributes seem many, as thy works: —
If thou must be propitiated with prayers,
Take them! If thou must be induced with altars,
And soften'd with a sacrifice, receive them!
Two beings here erect them unto thee.
If thou lov'st blood, the shepherd's shrine, which smokes
On my right hand, hath shed it for thy service
In the first of his flock, whose limbs now reek
In sanguinary incense to thy skies;
Or if the sweet and blooming fruits of earth,
And milder seasons, which the unstain'd turf
I spread them on now offers in the face
Of the broad sun which ripen'd them, may seem
Good to thee, inasmuch as they have not
Suffer'd in limb or life, and rather form
A sample of thy works, than supplication
To look on ours! If a shrine without victim,

And altar without gore, may win thy favour,
Look on it! and for him who dresseth it,
He is — such as thou mad'st him; and seeks nothing
Which must be won by kneeling: if he's evil,
Strike him! thou art omnipotent, and may'st —
For what can he oppose? If he be good,
Strike him, or spare him, as thou wilt! since all
Rests upon thee; and good and evil seem
To have no power themselves, save in thy will;
And whether that be good or ill I know not,
Not being omnipotent, nor fit to judge
Omnipotence, but merely to endure
Its mandate; which thus far I have endured.

    [*The fire upon the altar of* ABEL *kindles into a column of the brightest flame, and ascends to heaven; while a whirlwind throws down the altar of* CAIN, *and scatters the fruits abroad upon the earth.*

  *Abel (kneeling).* Oh, brother, pray! Jehovah's wroth with thee.

  *Cain.* Why so?

  *Abel.*         Thy fruits are scatter'd on the earth.

  *Cain.* From earth they came, to earth let them return;
Their seed will bear fresh fruit there ere the summer:
Thy burnt flesh-off'ring prospers better; see
How heav'n licks up the flames, when thick with blood!

  *Abel.* Think not upon my offering's acceptance,
But make another of thine own before
It is too late.

  *Cain.*    I will build no more altars,
Nor suffer any. —

  *Abel (rising).*   Cain! what meanest thou?

  *Cain.* To cast down yon vile flatt'rer of the clouds,
The smoky harbinger of thy dull pray'rs —
Thine altar, with its blood of lambs and kids,
Which fed on milk, to be destroy'd in blood.

  *Abel (opposing him).* Thou shalt not: — add not impious works to impious

ACT III.

Words! let that altar stand — 'tis hallow'd now
By the immortal pleasure of Jehovah,
In his acceptance of the victims.
    *Cain.*                     *His!*
*His pleasure!* what was his high pleasure in
The fumes of scorching flesh and smoking blood,
To the pain of the bleating mothers, which
Still yearn for their dead offspring? or the pangs
Of the sad ignorant victims underneath
Thy pious knife? Give way! this bloody record
Shall not stand in the sun, to shame creation!
    *Abel.* Brother, give back! thou shalt not touch my altar
With violence: if that thou wilt adopt it,
To try another sacrifice, 'tis thine.
    *Cain.* Another sacrifice! Give way, or else
That sacrifice may be —
    *Abel.*              What mean'st thou?
    *Cain.*                        Give —
Give way! — thy God loves blood! — then look to it: —
Give way, ere he hath *more!*
    *Abel.*            In *his* great name,
I stand between thee and the shrine which hath
Had his acceptance.
    *Cain.*         If thou lov'st thyself,
Stand back till I have strew'd this turf along
Its native soil: — else —
    *Abel (opposing him).* I love God far more
Than life.
    *Cain (striking him with a brand, on the temples, which he
        snatches from the altar).* Then take thy life unto
        thy God,
Since he loves lives.
    *Abel (falls).* What hast thou done, my brother?
    *Cain.* Brother!
    *Abel.*           Oh, God! receive thy servant, and
Forgive his slayer, for he knew not what

18*

He did. — Cain, give me — give me thy hand; and tell
Poor Zillah —
    *Cain (after a moment's stupefaction).* My hand! 'tis all red,
        and with —
What?
                      [*A long pause. — Looking slowly round.*
        Where am I? alone! Where's Abel? where
Cain? Can it be that I am he? My brother,
Awake! — why liest thou so on the green earth?
'Tis not the hour of slumber: — why so pale?
What, hast thou! — thou wert full of life this morn!
Abel! I pray thee, mock me not! I smote
Too fiercely, but not fatally. Ah, why
Wouldst thou oppose me? This is mockery;
And only done to daunt me: — 'twas a blow —
And but a blow. Stir — stir — nay, only stir!
Why, so — that's well! — thou breath'st! breathe upon me!
Oh, God! Oh, God!
    *Abel (very faintly).* What's he who speaks of God?
    *Cain.* Thy murderer.
    *Abel.*            Then may God forgive him! Cain,
Comfort poor Zillah: — she has but one brother
Now.                                          [ABEL *dies.*
    *Cain.* And I none! — Who makes me brotherless?
His eyes are open! then he is not dead!
Death is like sleep; and sleep shuts down our lids.
His lips, too, are apart; why then he breathes;
And yet I feel it not. — His heart! — his heart! —
Let me see, doth it beat? methinks — No! — no!
This is a vision, else I am become
The native of another and worse world.
The earth swims round me: — what is this? — 'tis wet;
                [*Puts his hand to his brow, and then looks at it.*
And yet there are no dews! 'Tis blood — my blood —
My brother's and my own; and shed by me!
Then what have I further to do with life,
Since I have taken life from my own flesh?

## ACT III.

But he can not be dead! — Is silence death?
No; he will wake; then let me watch by him.
Life cannot be so slight, as to be quench'd
Thus quickly! — he hath spoken to me since —
What shall I say to him? — My brother! — No:
He will not answer to that name; for brethren
Smite not each other. Yet — yet — speak to me.
Oh! for a word more of that gentle voice,
That I may bear to hear my own again!

*Enter* ZILLAH.

*Zillah.* I heard a heavy sound; what can it be?
'Tis Cain; and watching by my husband. What
Dost thou there, brother? Doth he sleep? Oh, heav'n!
What means this paleness, and yon stream? — No, no!
It is not blood; for who would shed his blood?
Abel! what's this? — who hath done this? He moves not;
He breathes not: and his hands drop down from mine
With stony lifelessness! Ah! cruel Cain!
Why cam'st thou not in time to save him from
This violence? Whatever hath assail'd him,
Thou wert the stronger, and should'st have stepp'd in
Between him and aggression! Father! — Eve! —
Adah! — come hither! Death is in the world!
  [*Exit* ZILLAH, *calling on her Parents, &c.*
*Cain (solus).* And who hath brought him there? — I — who abhor
The name of Death so deeply, that the thought
Empoison'd all my life, before I knew
His aspect — I have led him here, and giv'n
My brother to his cold and still embrace,
As if he would not have asserted his
Inexorable claim without my aid.
I am awake at last — a dreary dream
Had madden'd me; — but *he* shall ne'er awake!

*Enter* ADAM, EVE, ADAH, *and* ZILLAH.

 *Adam.* A voice of woe from Zillah brings me here. —
What do I see? — 'Tis true! — My son! — my son!
Woman, behold the serpent's work, and thine!
                [*To* EVE.
 *Eve.* Oh! speak not of it now: the serpent's fangs
Are in my heart. My best beloved, Abel!
Jehovah! this is punishment beyond
A mother's sin, to take *him* from me!
 *Adam.*       Who,
Or what hath done this deed? — speak, Cain, since thou
Wert present; was it some more hostile angel,
Who walks not with Jehovah? or some wild
Brute of the forest?
 *Eve.*    Ah! a livid light
Breaks through, as from a thunder-cloud! yon brand,
Massy and bloody! snatch'd from off the altar,
And black with smoke, and red with —
 *Adam.*       Speak, my son!
Speak, and assure us, wretched as we are,
That we are not more miserable still.
 *Adah.* Speak, Cain! and say it was not *thou!*
 *Eve.*         It was.
I see it now — he hangs his guilty head,
And covers his ferocious eye with hands
Incarnadine.
 *Adah.*  Mother, thou dost him wrong —
Cain! clear thee from this horrible accusal,
Which grief wrings from our parent.
 *Eve.*       Hear, Jehovah.
May the eternal serpent's curse be on him!
For he was fitter for his seed than ours.
May all his days be desolate! May —
 *Adah.*      Hold!
Curse him not, mother, for he is thy son —
Curse him not, mother, for he is my brother,
And my betroth'd.

## ACT III.

*Eve.*            He hath left thee no brother —
Zillah no husband — me *no son!* — for thus
I curse him from my sight for evermore!
All bonds I break between us, as he broke
That of his nature, in yon — Oh death! death!
Why didst thou not take *me*, who first incurr'd thee?
Why dost thou not so now?

    *Adam.*               Eve! let not this,
Thy natural grief, lead to impiety!
A heavy doom was long forespoken to us;
And now that it begins, let it be borne
In such sort as may show our God, that we
Are faithful servants to his holy will.

    *Eve (pointing to Cain).* His will!! the will of yon incarnate
        spirit
Of death, whom I have brought upon the earth
To strew it with the dead. May all the curses
Of life be on him! and his agonies
Drive him forth o'er the wilderness, like us
From Eden, till his children do by him
As he did by his brother! May the swords
And wings of fiery cherubim pursue him
By day and night — snakes spring up in his path —
Earth's fruits be ashes in his mouth — the leaves
On which he lays his head to sleep be strew'd
With scorpions! May his dreams be of his victim!
His waking a continual dread of death!
May the clear rivers turn to blood as he
Stoops down to stain them with his raging lip!
May every element shun or change to him!
May he live in the pangs which others die with!
And death itself wax something worse than death
To him who first acquainted him with man!
Hence, fratricide! henceforth that word is *Cain*,
Through all the coming myriads of mankind,
Who shall abhor thee, though thou wert their sire!
May the grass wither from thy feet! the woods

Deny thee shelter! earth a home! the dust
A grave! the sun his light! and heaven her God!
                              [*Exit* Eve.
    *Adam.* Cain! get thee forth: we dwell no more together.
Depart! and leave the dead to me — I am
Henceforth alone — we never must meet more.
    *Adah.* Oh, part not with him thus, my father: do not
Add thy deep curse to Eve's upon his head!
    *Adam.* I curse him not: his spirit be his curse.
Come, Zillah!
    *Zillah.*     I must watch my husband's corse.
    *Adam.* We will return again, when he is gone
Who hath provided for us this dread office.
Come, Zillah!
    *Zillah.* Yet one kiss on yon pale clay,
And those lips once so warm — my heart! my heart!
                  [*Exeunt* ADAM *and* ZILLAH, *weeping.*
    *Adah.* Cain! thou hast heard, we must go forth. I am ready,
So shall our children be. I will bear Enoch,
And you his sister. Ere the sun declines
Let us depart, nor walk the wilderness
Under the cloud of night. — Nay, speak to me.
To *me — thine own.*
    *Cain.*         Leave me!
    *Adah.*              Why, all have left thee.
    *Cain.* And wherefore lingerest thou? Dost thou not fear
To dwell with one who hath done this?
    *Adah.*                 I fear
Nothing except to leave thee, much as I
Shrink from the dead which leaves thee brotherless.
I must not speak of this — it is between thee
And the great God.
    *A Voice from within exclaims*, Cain! Cain!
    *Adah.*                  Hear'st thou that voice?
    *The Voice within.* Cain! Cain!
    *Adah.*            It soundeth like an angel's tone.

ACT III.

*Enter the* ANGEL *of the Lord.*

 *Angel.* Where is thy brother Abel?
 *Cain.*        Am I then
My brother's keeper?
 *Angel.*     Cain! what hast thou done?
The voice of thy slain brother's blood cries out,
Even from the ground, unto the Lord! — Now art thou
Cursed from the earth, which opened late her mouth
To drink thy brother's blood from thy rash hand.
Henceforth, when thou shalt till the ground, it shall not
Yield thee her strength; a fugitive shalt thou
Be from this day, and vagabond on earth!
 *Adah.* This punishment is more than he can bear.
Behold, thou drivest him from the face of earth,
And from the face of God shall he be hid.
A fugitive and vagabond on earth,
'Twill come to pass, that whoso findeth him
Shall slay him.
 *Cain.*    Would they could! but who are they
Shall slay me? Where are these on the lone earth
As yet unpeopled?
 *Angel.*    Thou hast slain thy brother,
And who shall warrant thee against thy son?
 *Adah.* Angel of Light! be merciful, nor say
That this poor aching breast now nourishes
A murderer in my boy, and of his father.
 *Angel.* Then he would but be what his father is.
Did not the milk of Eve give nutriment
To him thou now see'st so besmear'd with blood?
The fratricide might well engender parricides. —
But it shall not be so — the Lord thy God
And mine commandeth me to set his seal
On Cain, so that he may go forth in safety.
Who slayeth Cain, a sevenfold vengeance shall
Be taken on his head. Come hither!
 *Cain.*       What
Wouldst thou with me?

*Angel.* To mark upon thy brow
Exemption from such deeds as thou hast done.
   *Cain.* No, let me die!
   *Angel.* It must not be.
        [*The* ANGEL *sets the mark on* CAIN's *brow.*
   *Cain.* It burns
My brow, but nought to that which is within it.
Is there more? let me meet it as I may.
   *Angel.* Stern hast thou been and stubborn from the womb,
As the ground thou must henceforth till: but he
Thou slew'st was gentle as the flocks he tended.
   *Cain.* After the fall too soon was I begotten;
Ere yet my mother's mind subsided from
The serpent, and my sire still mourn'd for Eden.
That which I am, I am; I did not seek
For life, nor did I make myself; but could I
With my own death redeem him from the dust —
And why not so? let him return to day,
And I lie ghastly! so shall be restored
By God the life to him he loved; and taken
From me a being I ne'er loved to bear.
   *Angel.* Who shall heal murder? what is done is done;
Go forth! fulfil thy days! and be thy deeds
Unlike the last! [*The* ANGEL *disappears.*
   *Adah.* He's gone, let us go forth;
I hear our little Enoch cry within
Our bower.
   *Cain.* Ah! little knows he what he weeps for!
And I who have shed blood cannot shed tears!
But the four rivers* would not cleanse my soul.
Think'st thou my boy will bear to look on me?
   *Adah.* If I thought that he would not, I would —
   *Cain.* (*interrupting her*). No,

---

* The "four rivers" which flowed round Eden, and consequently the only waters with which Cain was acquainted upon earth.

## ACT III.

No more of threats: we have had too many of them:
Go to our children; I will follow thee.

*Adah.* I will not leave thee lonely with the dead;
Let us depart together.

*Cain.* Oh! thou dead
And everlasting witness! whose unsinking
Blood darkens earth and heaven! what thou *now* art
I know not! but if *thou* see'st what *I* am,
I think thou wilt forgive him, whom his God
Can ne'er forgive, nor his own soul. — Farewell!
I must not, dare not touch what I have made thee.
I, who sprung from the same womb with thee, drain'd
The same breast, clasp'd thee often to my own,
In fondness brotherly and boyish, I
Can never meet thee more, nor even dare
To do that for thee, which thou shouldst have done
For me — compose thy limbs into their grave —
The first grave yet dug for mortality.
But who hath dug that grave? Oh, earth! Oh, earth!
For all the fruits thou hast render'd to me, I
Give thee back this. — Now for the wilderness.

[ADAH *stoops down and kisses the body of* ABEL.

*Adah.* A dreary, and an early doom, my brother,
Has been thy lot! Of all who mourn for thee,
I alone must not weep. My office is
Henceforth to dry up tears, and not to shed them;
But yet of all who mourn, none mourn like me,
Not only for thyself, but him who slew thee.
Now, Cain! I will divide thy burden with thee.

*Cain.* Eastward from Eden will we take our way;
'Tis the most desolate, and suits my steps.

*Adah.* Lead! thou shalt be my guide, and may our God
Be thine! Now let us carry forth our children.

*Cain.* And *he* who lieth there was childless. I
Have dried the fountain of a gentle race,
Which might have graced his recent marriage couch,
And might have temper'd this stern blood of mine,

Uniting with our children Abel's offspring!
O Abel!
   *Adah.* Peace be with him!
   *Cain.*                     But with *me!* —

# THE DEFORMED TRANSFORMED;

## A DRAMA.

This production is founded partly on the story of a novel called "The Three Brothers," published many years ago, from which M. G. Lewis's "Wood Demon" was also taken — and partly on the "Faust" of the great Goethe. The present publication contains the two first Parts only, and the opening chorus of the third. The rest may perhaps appear hereafter.

### DRAMATIS PERSONÆ.

STRANGER, *afterwards* CÆSAR.
ARNOLD.
BOURBON.
PHILIBERT.
CELLINI.

BERTHA.
OLIMPIA.

Spirits, Soldiers, Citizens of Rome, Priests, Peasants, &c.

# THE DEFORMED TRANSFORMED.

## PART I.

### SCENE I.

*A Forest.*

*Enter* ARNOLD *and his mother* BERTHA.

*Bert.* OUT, hunchback!
*Arn.*　　　　　　I was born so, mother!
*Bert.*　　　　　　　　　　　　　　　Out,
Thou incubus! Thou nightmare! Of seven sons,
The sole abortion!
　*Arn.*　　　　Would that I had been so,
And never seen the light!
　*Bert.*　　　　　　I would so too!
But as thou *hast* — hence, hence — and do thy best!
That back of thine may bear its burthen; 'tis
More high, if not so broad as that of others.
　*Arn.* It *bears* its burthen; — but, my heart! Will it
Sustain that which you lay upon it, mother?
I love, or, at the least, I loved you: nothing
Save you, in nature, can love aught like me.
You nursed me — do not kill me!
　*Bert.*　　　　　　　　Yes — I nursed thee,
Because thou wert my first-born, and I knew not
If there would be another unlike thee,
That monstrous sport of nature. But get hence,
And gather wood!
　*Arn.*　　　I will: but when I bring it,
Speak to me kindly. Though my brothers are
So beautiful and lusty, and as free
As the free chase they follow, do not spurn me:
Our milk has been the same.

*Bert.*                      As is the hedgehog's,
Which sucks at midnight from the wholesome dam
Of the young bull, until the milkmaid finds
The nipple next day sore and udder dry.
Call not thy brothers brethren! Call me not
Mother; for if I brought thee forth, it was
As foolish hens at times hatch vipers, by
Sitting upon strange eggs. Out, urchin, out!
                                     [*Exit* BERTHA.
   *Arn.* (*solus*). Oh mother! — She is gone, and I must do
Her bidding; — wearily but willingly
I would fulfil it, could I only hope
A kind word in return. What shall I do?
            [ARNOLD *begins to cut wood: in doing this he wounds*
               *one of his hands.*
My labour for the day is over now.
Accursed be this blood that flows so fast;
For double curses will be my meed now
At home — What home? I have no home, no kin,
No kind — not made like other creatures, or
To share their sports or pleasures. Must I bleed too
Like them? Oh that each drop which falls to earth
Would rise a snake to sting them, as they have stung me!
Or that the devil, to whom they liken me,
Would aid his likeness! If I must partake
His form, why not his power? Is it because
I have not his will too? For one kind word
From her who bore me would still reconcile me
Even to this hateful aspect. Let me wash
The wound.
            [ARNOLD *goes to a spring, and stoops to wash his hand:*
              *he starts back.*
They are right; and Nature's mirror shows me,
What she hath made me. I will not look on it
Again, and scarce dare think on't. Hideous wretch
That I am! The very waters mock me with

My horrid shadow — like a demon placed
Deep in the fountain to scare back the cattle
From drinking therein.                             [*He pauses.*
                     And shall I live on,
A burden to the earth, myself, and shame
Unto what brought me into life! Thou blood,
Which flowest so freely from a scratch, let me
Try if thou wilt not in a fuller stream
Pour forth my woes for ever with thyself
On earth, to which I will restore at once
This hateful compound of her atoms, and
Resolve back to her elements, and take
The shape of any reptile save myself,
And make a world for myriads of new worms!
This knife! now let me prove if it will sever
This wither'd slip of nature's nightshade — my
Vile form — from the creation, as it hath
The green bough from the forest.

        [ARNOLD *places the knife in the ground, with the point upwards.*

                              Now 'tis set,
And I can fall upon it. Yet one glance
On the fair day, which sees no foul thing like
Myself, and the sweet sun which warm'd me, but
In vain. The birds — how joyously they sing!
So let them, for I would not be lamented:
But let their merriest notes be Arnold's knell,
The fallen leaves my monument; the murmur
Of the near fountain my sole elegy.
Now, knife, stand firmly, as I fain would fall!

        [*As he rushes to throw himself upon the knife, his eye is suddenly caught by the fountain, which seems in motion.*

The fountain moves without a wind: but shall
The ripple of a spring change my resolve?
No. Yet it moves again! The waters stir,
Not as with air, but by some subterrane

And rocking power of the internal world.
What's hero? A mist! No more? —

> [*A cloud comes from the fountain. He stands gazing upon it; it is dispelled, and a tall black man comes towards him.*

*Arn.* What would you? Speak!
Spirit or man?
    *Stran.* As man is both, why not
Say both in one?
    *Arn.* Your form is man's, and yet
You may be devil.
    *Stran.* So many men are that
Which is so call'd or thought, that you may add me
To which you please, without much wrong to either.
But come: you wish to kill yourself; — pursue
Your purpose.
    *Arn.* You have interrupted me.
    *Stran.* What is that resolution which can e'er
Be interrupted? If I be the devil
You deem, a single moment would have made you
Mine, and for ever, by your suicide;
And yet my coming saves you.
    *Arn.* I said not
You *were* the demon, but that your approach
Was like one.
    *Stran.* Unless you keep company
With him (and you seem scarce used to such high
Society) you can't tell how he approaches;
And for his aspect, look upon the fountain,
And then on me, and judge which of us twain
Look likest what the boors believe to be
Their cloven-footed terror.
    *Arn.* Do you — dare *you*
To taunt me with my born deformity?
    *Stran.* Were I to taunt a buffalo with this
Cloven foot of thine, or the swift dromedary
With thy sublime of humps, the animals

Would revel in the compliment. And yet
Both beings are more swift, more strong, more mighty
In action and endurance than thyself,
And all the fierce and fair of the same kind
With thee. Thy form is natural: 'twas only
Nature's mistaken largess to bestow
The gifts which are of others upon man.

  *Arn.* Give me the strength then of the buffalo's foot,
When he spurs high the dust, beholding his
Near enemy; or let me have the long
And patient swiftness of the desert-ship,
The helmless dromedary! — and I'll bear
Thy fiendish sarcasm with a saintly patience.
  *Stran.* I will.
  *Arn. (with surprise).* Thou canst!
  *Stran.*      Perhaps. Would you aught else?
  *Arn.* Thou mockest me.
  *Stran.*     Not I. Why should I mock
What all are mocking? That's poor sport, methinks.
To talk to thee in human language (for
Thou canst not yet speak mine), the forester
Hunts not the wretched coney, but the boar
Or wolf, or lion, leaving paltry game
To petty burghers, who leave once a year
Their walls, to fill their household caldrons with
Such scullion prey. The meanest gibe at thee, —
Now *I* can mock the mightiest.
  *Arn.*      Then waste not
Thy time on me: I seek thee not.
  *Stran.*       Your thoughts
Are not far from me. Do not send me back:
I am not so easily recall'd to do
Good service.
  *Arn.*  What wilt thou do for me?
  *Stran.*       Change
Shapes with you, if you will, since yours so irks you;
Or form you to your wish in any shape.

*Arn.* Oh! then you are indeed the demon, for
Nought else would wittingly wear mine.
　　*Stran.*　　　　　　　　　　　　I'll show thee
The brightest which the world e'er bore, and give thee
Thy choice.
　　*Arn.*　　　On what condition?
　　*Stran.*　　　　　　　　　　There's a question!
An hour ago you would have given your soul
To look like other men, and now you pause
To wear the form of heroes.
　　*Arn.*　　　　　　　No; I will not.
I must not compromise my soul.
　　*Stran.*　　　　　　　　What soul,
Worth naming so, would dwell in such a carcass?
　　*Arn.* 'Tis an aspiring one, whate'er the tenement
In which it is mislodged. But name your compact:
Must it be sign'd in blood?
　　*Stran.*　　　　　　Not in your own.
　　*Arn.* Whose blood then?
　　*Stran.*　　　　　　　We will talk of that hereafter.
But I'll be moderate with you, for I see
Great things within you. You shall have no bond
But your own will, no contract save your deeds.
Are you content?
　　*Arn.*　　　　I take thee at thy word.
　　*Stran.* Now then! —
　　　　　　[*The Stranger approaches the fountain, and turns to*
　　　　　　　Arnold.
　　　　　　　　　A little of your blood.
　　*Arn.*　　　　　　　　　　　　　For what?
　　*Stran.* To mingle with the magic of the waters,
And make the charm effective.
　　*Arn.* (*holding out his wounded arm*). Take it all.
　　*Stran.* Not now. A few drops will suffice for this.
　　　　　　[*The Stranger takes some of* Arnold's *blood in his
　　　　　　　hand, and casts it into the fountain.*

*Stran.* Shadows of beauty!
  Shadows of power!
 Rise to your duty —
  This is the hour!
Walk lovely and pliant
 From the depth of this fountain,
As the cloud-shapen giant
 Bestrides the Hartz Mountain.\*
Come as ye were,
 That our eyes may behold
The model in air
 Of the form I will mould,
Bright as the Iris
 When ether is spann'd; —
Such *his* desire is, [*Pointing to* ARNOLD.
 Such my command!
Demons heroic —
 Demons who wore
The form of the stoic
 Or sophist of yore —
Or the shape of each victor,
 From Macedon's boy
To each high Roman's picture,
 Who breathed to destroy —
Shadows of beauty!
 Shadows of power!
Up to your duty —
 This is the hour!

[*Various Phantoms arise from the waters, and pass in succession before the Stranger and* ARNOLD.

*Arn.* What do I see?
*Stran.*      The black-eyed Roman, with
The eagle's beak between those eyes which ne'er
Beheld a conqueror, or look'd along

---

\* This is a well-known German superstition — a gigantic shadow produced by reflection on the Brocken.

The land he made not Rome's, while Rome became
His, and all theirs who heir'd his very name.

*Arn.* The phantom's bald; my quest is beauty. Could I
Inherit but his fame with his defects!

*Stran.* His brow was girt with laurels more than hairs.
You see his aspect — choose it, or reject.
I can but promise you his form; his fame
Must be long sought and fought for.

*Arn.* I will fight too,
But not as a mock Cæsar. Let him pass;
His aspect may be fair, but suits me not.

*Stran.* Then you are far more difficult to please
Than Cato's sister, or than Brutus' mother,
Or Cleopatra at sixteen — an age
When love is not less in the eye than heart.
But be it so! Shadow, pass on!
[*The phantom of Julius Cæsar disappears.*

*Arn.* And can it
Be, that the man who shook the earth is gone,
And left no footstep?

*Stran.* There you err. His substance
Left graves enough, and woes enough, and fame
More than enough to track his memory;
But for his shadow, 'tis no more than yours,
Except a little longer and less crook'd
I' the sun. Behold another! [*A second phantom passes.*

*Arn.* Who is he?

*Stran.* He was the fairest and the bravest of
Athenians. Look upon him well.

*Arn.* He is
More lovely than the last. How beautiful!

*Stran.* Such was the curled son of Clinias; — wouldst thou
Invest thee with his form?

*Arn.* Would that I had
Been born with it! But since I may choose further,
I will *look* further. [*The shade of Alcibiades disappears.*

*Stran.* Lo! behold again!

 *Arn.* What! that low, swarthy, short-nosed, round-eyed
With the wide nostrils and Silenus' aspect,    [satyr,
The splay feet and low stature! I had better
Remain that which I am.
  *Stran.*     And yet he was
The earth's perfection of all mental beauty,
And personification of all virtue.
But you reject him?
  *Arn.*     If his form could bring me
That which redeem'd it — no.
  *Stran.*     I have no power
To promise that; but you may try, and find it
Easier in such a form, or in your own.
  *Arn.* No. I was not born for philosophy,
Though I have that about me which has need on't.
Let him fleet on.
  *Stran.*   Be air, thou hemlock-drinker!
   [*The shadow of Socrates disappears: another rises.*
  *Arn.* What's here? whose broad brow and whose curly
    beard
And manly aspect look like Hercules,
Save that his jocund eye hath more of Bacchus
Than the sad purger of the infernal world,
Leaning dejected on his club of conquest,
As if he knew the worthlessness of those
For whom he had fought.
  *Stran.*    It was the man who lost
The ancient world for love.
  *Arn.*    I cannot blame him,
Since I have risk'd my soul because I find not
That which he exchanged the earth for.
  *Stran.*     Since so far
You seem congenial, will you wear his features?
  *Arn.* No. As you leave me choice, I am difficult,
If but to see the heroes I should ne'er
Have seen else on this side of the dim shore
Whence they float back before us.

*Stran.*                         Hence, triumvir!
Thy Cleopatra's waiting.
          [*The shade of Anthony disappears: another rises.*
    *Arn.*                 Who is this?
Who truly looketh like a demigod,
Blooming and bright, with golden hair, and stature,
If not more high than mortal, yet immortal
In all that nameless bearing of his limbs,
Which he wears as the sun his rays — a something
Which shines from him, and yet is but the flashing
Emanation of a thing more glorious still.
Was he e'er human only?
    *Stran.*             Let the earth speak,
If there be atoms of him left, or even
Of the more solid gold that form'd his urn.
    *Arn.* Who was this glory of mankind?
    *Stran.*                   The shame
Of Greece in peace, her thunderbolt in war —
Demetrius the Macedonian, and
Taker of cities.
    *Arn.*      Yet one shadow more.
    *Stran.* (*addressing the shadow*). Get thee to Lamia's lap!
          [*The shade of Demetrius Poliorcetes vanishes: another
           rises.*
                             I'll fit you still,
Fear not, my hunchback: if the shadows of
That which existed please not your nice taste,
I'll animate the ideal marble, till
Your soul be reconciled to her new garment.
    *Arn.* Content! I will fix here.
    *Stran.*                I must commend
Your choice. The godlike son of the sea-goddess,
The unshorn boy of Peleus, with his locks
As beautiful and clear as the amber waves
Of rich Pactolus, roll'd o'er sands of gold,
Soften'd by intervening crystal, and
Rippled like flowing waters by the wind,

All vow'd to Sperchius as they were — behold them!
And *him* — as he stood by Polixena,
With sanction'd and with soften'd love, before
The altar, gazing on his Trojan bride,
With some remorse within for Hector slain
And Priam weeping, mingled with deep passion
For the sweet downcast virgin, whose young hand
Trembled in *his* who slew her brother. So
He stood i' the temple! Look upon him as
Greece look'd her last upon her best, the instant
Ere Paris' arrow flew.

  *Arn.*    I gaze upon him
As if I were his soul, whose form shall soon
Envelope mine.

  *Stran.*   You have done well. The greatest
Deformity should only barter with
The extremest beauty, if the proverb's true
Of mortals, that extremes meet.

  *Arn.*    Come! Be quick!
I am impatient.

  *Stran.*   As a youthful beauty
Before her glass. *You both* see what is not,
But dream it is what must be.

  *Arn.*    Must I wait?

  *Stran.* No; that were a pity. But a word or two:
His stature is twelve cubits; would you so far
Outstep these times, and be a Titan? Or
(To talk canonically) wax a son
Of Anak?

  *Arn.* Why not?

  *Stran.*    Glorious ambition!
I love thee most in dwarfs! A mortal of
Philistine stature would have gladly pared
His own Goliath down to a slight David:
But thou, my manikin, wouldst soar a show
Rather than hero. Thou shalt be indulged,
If such be thy desire; and yet, by being

A little less removed from present men
In figure, thou canst sway them more; for all
Would rise against thee now, as if to hunt
A new-found mammoth; and their cursed engines,
Their culverins, and so forth, would find way
Through our friend's armour there, with greater ease
Than the adulterer's arrow through his heel,
Which Thetis had forgotten to baptize
In Styx.
   *Arn.* Then let it be as thou deem'st best.
   *Stran.* Thou shalt be beauteous as the thing thou seest,
And strong as what it was, and —
   *Arn.*                I ask not
For valour, since deformity is daring.
It is its essence to o'ertake mankind
By heart and soul, and make itself the equal —
Ay, the superior of the rest. There is
A spur in its halt movements, to become
All that the others cannot, in such things
As still are free to both, to compensate
For stepdame Nature's avarice at first.
They woo with fearless deeds the smiles of fortune,
And oft, like Timour the lame Tartar, win them.
   *Stran.* Well spoken! And thou doubtless wilt remain
Form'd as thou art. I may dismiss the mould
Of shadow, which must turn to flesh, to incase
This daring soul, which could achieve no less
Without it.
   *Arn.*      Had no power presented me
The possibility of change, I would
Have done the best which spirit may to make
Its way with all deformity's dull, deadly,
Discouraging weight upon me, like a mountain,
In feeling, on my heart as on my shoulders —
An hateful and unsightly molehill to
The eyes of happier man. I would have look'd

On beauty in that sex which is the type
Of all we know or dream of beautiful
Beyond the world they brighten, with a sigh —
Not of love, but despair; nor sought to win,
Though to a heart all love, what could not love me
In turn, because of this vile crooked clog,
Which makes me lonely.  Nay, I could have borne
It all, had not my mother spurn'd me from her.
The she-bear licks her cubs into a sort
Of shape; — my dam beheld my shape was hopeless.
Had she exposed me, like the Spartan, ere
I knew the passionate part of life, I had
Been a clod of the valley, — happier nothing
Than what I am.  But even thus, the lowest,
Ugliest, and meanest of mankind, what courage
And perseverance could have done, perchance
Had made me something — as it has made heroes
Of the same mould as mine.  You lately saw me
Master of my own life, and quick to quit it;
And he who is so is the master of
Whatever dreads to die.

  *Stran.*     Decide between
What you have been, or will be.
  *Arn.*        I have done so.
You have open'd brighter prospects to my eyes,
And sweeter to my heart.  As I am now,
I might be fear'd, admired, respected, loved
Of all save those next to me, of whom I
Would be beloved.  As thou showest me
A choice of forms, I take the one I view.
Haste! haste!
  *Stran.*  And what shall *I* wear?
  *Arn.*        Surely he
Who can command all forms will choose the highest,
Something superior even to that which was
Pelides now before us.  Perhaps *his*

Who slew him, that of Paris: or — still higher —
The poet's god, clothed in such limbs as are
Themselves a poetry.
  *Stran.*     Less will content me;
For I, too, love a change.
  *Arn.*      Your aspect is
Dusky, but not uncomely.
  *Stran.*     If I chose,
I might be whiter; but I have a penchant
For black — it is so honest, and besides
Can neither blush with shame nor pale with fear;
But I have worn it long enough of late,
And now I'll take your figure.
  *Arn.*     Mine!
  *Stran.*      Yes. You
Shall change with Thetis' son, and I with Bertha,
Your mother's offspring. People have their tastes;
You have yours — I mine.
  *Arn.*    Despatch! despatch!
  *Stran.*       Even so.

  [*The Stranger takes some earth and moulds it along
   the turf, and then addresses the phantom of Achilles.*

 Beautiful shadow
  Of Thetis's boy!
 Who sleeps in the meadow
  Whose grass grows o'er Troy:
 From the red earth, like Adam,*
  Thy likeness I shape,
 As the being who made him,
  Whose actions I ape.
 Thou clay, be all glowing,
  Till the rose in his cheek
 Be as fair as, when blowing,
  It wears its first streak!

---

\* Adam means "*red earth*," from which the first man was formed.

Ye violets, I scatter,
　Now turn into eyes!
And thou, sunshiny water,
　Of blood take the guise!
Let these hyacinth boughs
　Be his long flowing hair,
And wave o'er his brows,
　As thou wavest in air!
Let his heart be this marble
　I tear from the rock!
But his voice as the warble
　Of birds on yon oak!
Let his flesh be the purest
　Of mould, in which grew
The lily-root surest,
　And drank the best dew!
Let his limbs be the lightest
　Which clay can compound,
And his aspect the brightest
　On earth to be found!
Elements, near me,
　Be mingled and stirr'd,
Know me, and hear me,
　And leap to my word!
Sunbeams, awaken
　This earth's animation!
'Tis done! He hath taken
　His stand in creation!

[ARNOLD *falls senseless; his soul passes into the shape of Achilles, which rises from the ground; while the phantom has disappeared, part by part, as the figure was formed from the earth.*

*Arn.* (*in his new form*). I love, and I shall be beloved! Oh life!
At last I feel thee! Glorious spirit!
　*Stran.*　　　　　　　　　　Stop!
What shall become of your abandon'd garment,

Yon hump, and lump, and clod of ugliness,
Which late you wore, or were?
  *Arn.*      Who cares? Let wolves
And vultures take it, if they will.
  *Stran.*      And if
They do, and are not scared by it, you'll say
It must be peace-time, and no better fare
Abroad i' the fields.
  *Arn.*    Let us but leave it there;
No matter what becomes on't.
  *Stran.*      That's ungracious,
If not ungrateful. Whatsoe'er it be,
It hath sustain'd your soul full many a day.
  *Arn.* Ay, as the dunghill may conceal a gem
Which is now set in gold, as jewels should be.
  *Stran.* But if I give another form, it must be
By fair exchange, not robbery. For they
Who make men without women's aid have long
Had patents for the same, and do not love
Your interlopers. The devil may take men,
Not make them, — though he reap the benefit
Of the original workmanship:—and therefore
Some one must be found to assume the shape
You have quitted.
  *Arn.*   Who would do so?
  *Stran.*      That I know not,
And therefore I must.
  *Arn.*   You!
  *Stran.*     I said it ere
You inhabited your present dome of beauty.
  *Arn.* True. I forget all things in the new joy
Of this immortal change.
  *Stran.*    In a few moments
I will be as you were, and you shall see
Yourself for ever by you, as your shadow.
  *Arn.* I would be spared this.
  *Stran.*     But it cannot be.

What! shrink already, being what you are,
From seeing what you were?
  *Arn.*       Do as thou wilt.
  *Stran.* (*to the late form of* Arnold, *extended on the earth.*)
   Clay! not dead, but soul-less!
    Though no man would choose thee,
   An immortal no less
    Deigns not to refuse thee.
   Clay thou art; and unto spirit
   All clay is of equal merit.
   Fire! *without* which nought can live;
   Fire! but *in* which nought can live,
    Save the fabled salamander,
    Or immortal souls, which wander,
   Praying what doth not forgive,
   Howling for a drop of water,
    Burning in a quenchless lot:
   Fire! the only element
    Where nor fish, beast, bird, nor worm,
    Save the worm which dieth not,
   Can preserve a moment's form,
   But must with thyself be blent:
   Fire! man's safeguard and his slaughter:
   Fire! Creation's first-born daughter,
    And Destruction's threaten'd son,
    When heaven with the world hath done:
   Fire! assist me to renew
   Life in what lies in my view
    Stiff and cold!
   His resurrection rests with me and you!
   One little, marshy spark of flame —
   And he again shall seem the same;
    But I his spirit's place shall hold!
   [*An ignis-fatuus flits through the wood and rests on the brow of the body. The Stranger disappears: the body rises.*
  *Arn.* (*in his new form*). Oh! horrible!

*Stran.* (*in* ARNOLD'*s late shape*). What! tremblest thou?
    *Arn.*                                                              Not so —
I merely shudder. Where is fled the shape
Thou lately worest?
    *Stran.*            To the world of shadows.
But let us thread the present. Whither wilt thou?
    *Arn.* Must thou be my companion?
    *Stran.*                             Wherefore not?
Your betters keep worse company.
    *Arn.*                              *My* betters!
    *Stran.* Oh! you wax proud, I see, of your new form:
I'm glad of that. Ungrateful too! That's well;
You improve apace; — two changes in an instant,
And you are old in the world's ways already.
But bear with me: indeed you'll find me useful
Upon your pilgrimage. But come, pronounce
Where shall we now be errant?
    *Arn.*                        Where the world
Is thickest, that I may behold it in
Its workings.
    *Stran.*     That's to say, where there is war
And woman in activity. Let's see!
Spain — Italy — the new Atlantic world —
Afric, with all its Moors. In very truth,
There is small choice: the whole race are just now
Tugging as usual at each other's hearts.
    *Arn.* I have heard great things of Rome.
    *Stran.*                         A goodly choice —
And scarce a better to be found on earth,
Since Sodom was put out. The field is wide too;
For now the Frank, and Hun, and Spanish scion
Of the old Vandals, are at play along
The sunny shores of the world's garden.
    *Arn.*                           How
Shall we proceed?
    *Stran.*        Like gallants, on good coursers.
What ho! my chargers! Never yet were better,

Since Phaeton was upset into the Po.
Our pages too!

*Enter two Pages, with four coal-black horses.*

*Arn.*       A noble sight!
*Stran.*                       And of
A nobler breed.  Match me in Barbary,
Or your Kochlini race of Araby,
With these!
*Arn.*       The mighty steam, which volumes high
From their proud nostrils, burns the very air;
And sparks of flame, like dancing fire-flies, wheel
Around their manes, as common insects swarm
Round common steeds towards sunset.
*Stran.*                             Mount, my lord:
They and I are your servitors.
*Arn.*                            And these
Our dark-eyed pages — what may be their names?
*Stran.* You shall baptize them.
*Arn.*                          What! in holy water?
*Stran.* Why not? The deeper sinner, better saint.
*Arn.* They are beautiful, and cannot, sure, be demons.
*Stran.* True; the devil's always ugly; and your beauty
Is never diabolical.
*Arn.*             I'll call him
Who bears the golden horn, and wears such bright
And blooming aspect, *Huon;* for he looks
Like to the lovely boy lost in the forest,
And never found till now.  And for the other
And darker, and more thoughtful, who smiles not,
But looks as serious though serene as night,
He shall be *Memnon*, from the Ethiop king
Whose statue turns a harper once a day.
And you?
*Stran.* I have ten thousand names, and twice
As many attributes; but as I wear
A human shape, will take a human name.

*Arn.* More human than the shape (though it was mine
I trust.                                              (once)
  *Stran.* Then call me Cæsar.
  *Arn.*                    Why, that name
Belongs to empires, and has been but borne
By the world's lords.
  *Stran.*             And therefore fittest for
The devil in disguise — since so you deem me,
Unless you call me pope instead.
  *Arn.*                  Well, then,
Cæsar thou shalt be. For myself, my name
Shall be plain Arnold still.
  *Cæs.*                We'll add a title —
"Count Arnold:" it hath no ungracious sound,
And will look well upon a billet-doux.
  *Arn.* Or in an order for a battle-field.
  *Cæs.* (*sings*). To horse! to horse! my coal-black steed
    Paws the ground and snuffs the air!
  There's not a foal of Arab's breed
    More knows whom he must bear;
  On the hill he will not tire,
  Swifter as it waxes higher;
  In the marsh he will not slacken,
  On the plain be overtaken;
  In the wave he will not sink,
  Nor pause at the brook's side to drink;
  In the race he will not pant,
  In the combat he'll not faint;
  On the stones he will not stumble,
  Time nor toil shall make him humble;
  In the stall he will not stiffen,
  But be winged as a griffin,
  Only flying with his feet:
  And will not such a voyage be sweet?
  Merrily! merrily! never unsound,
  Shall our bonny black horses skim over the ground!

From the Alps to the Caucasus, ride we, or fly!
For we'll leave them behind in the glance of an eye.
     [*They mount their horses, and disappear.*

### SCENE II.

*A Camp before the Walls of Rome.*

ARNOLD *and* CÆSAR.

*Cæs.* You are well entered now.
 *Arn.*       Ay; but my path
Has been o'er carcasses: mine eyes are full
Of blood.
 *Cæs.* Then wipe them, and see clearly. Why!
Thou art a conqueror; the chosen knight
And free companion of the gallant Bourbon,
Late constable of France: and now to be
Lord of the city which hath been earth's lord
Under its emperors, and — changing sex,
Not sceptre, an hermaphrodite of empire —
*Lady* of the old world.
 *Arn.*    How *old?* What! are there
*New* worlds?
 *Cæs.* To *you.* You'll find there are such shortly,
By its rich harvests, new disease, and gold;
From one *half* of the world named a *whole* new one,
Because you know no better than the dull
And dubious notice of your eyes and ears.
 *Arn.* I'll trust them.
 *Cæs.*    Do! They will deceive you sweetly,
And that is better than the bitter truth.
 *Arn.* Dog!
 *Cæs.*  Man!
 *Arn.*    Devil!
 *Cæs.*      Your obedient humble servant.
 *Arn.* Say *master* rather. Thou hast lured me on,
Through scenes of blood and lust, till I am here.

*Cas.* And where wouldst *thou* be?
*Arn.* Oh, at peace — in peace.
*Cæs.* And where is that which is so? From the star
To the winding worm, all life is motion; and
In life *commotion* is the extremest point
Of life. The planet wheels till it becomes
A comet, and destroying as it sweeps
The stars, goes out. The poor worm winds its way,
Living upon the death of other things,
But still, like them, must live and die, the subject
Of something which has made it live and die.
You must obey what all obey, the rule
Of fix'd necessity: against her edict
Rebellion prospers not.
*Arn.* And when it prospers —
*Cas.* 'Tis no rebellion.
*Arn.* Will it prosper now?
*Cæs.* The Bourbon hath given orders for the assault,
And by the dawn there will be work.
*Arn.* Alas!
And shall the city yield? I see the giant
Abode of the true God, and his true saint,
Saint Peter, rear its dome and cross into
That sky whence Christ ascended from the cross,
Which his blood made a badge of glory and
Of joy (as once of torture unto him,
God and God's Son, man's sole and only refuge).
*Cæs.* 'Tis there, and shall be.
*Arn.* What?
*Cæs.* The crucifix
Above, and many altar shrines below.
Also some culverins upon the walls,
And harquebusses, and what not; besides
The men who are to kindle them to death
Of other men.
*Arn.* And those scarce mortal arches,
Pile above pile of everlasting wall,

20*

The theatre where emperors and their subjects
('Those subjects *Romans*) stood at gaze upon
The battles of the monarchs of the wild
And wood, the lion and his tusky rebels
Of the then untamed desert, brought to joust
In the arena (as right well they might,
When they had left no human foe unconquer'd);
Made even the forest pay its tribute of
Life to their amphitheatre, as well
As Dacia men to die the eternal death
For a sole instant's pastime, and "Pass on
To a new gladiator!" — Must it fall?

  *Cæs.* The city, or the amphitheatre?
The church, or one, or all? for you confound
Both them and me.
   *Arn.*     To-morrow sounds the assault
With the first cock-crow.
   *Cæs.*     Which, if it end with
The evening's first nightingale, will be
Something new in the annals of great sieges;
For men must have their prey after long toil.

  *Arn.* The sun goes down as calmly, and perhaps
More beautifully, than he did on Rome
On the day Remus leapt her wall.
   *Cæs.*      I saw him.
  *Arn.* You!
  *Cæs.*   Yes, sir. You forget I am or was
Spirit, till I took up with your cast shape
And a worse name. I'm Cæsar and a hunch-back
Now. Well! the first of Cæsars was a bald-head,
And loved his laurels better as a wig
(So history says) than as a glory. Thus
The world runs on, but we'll be merry still.
I saw your Romulus (simple as I am)
Slay his own twin, quick-born of the same womb,
Because he leapt a ditch ('t was then no wall,
Whate'er it now be); and Rome's earliest cement

Was brother's blood; and if its native blood
Be spilt till the choked Tiber be as red
As e'er 't was yellow, it will never wear
The deep hue of the ocean and the earth,
Which the great robber sons of fratricide
Have made their never-ceasing scene of slaughter
For ages.
    *Arn.* But what have these done, their far
Remote descendants, who have lived in peace,
The peace of heaven, and in her sunshine of
Piety?
    *Cæs.* And what had *they* done, whom the old
Romans o'erswept? — Hark!
    *Arn.* They are soldiers singing
A reckless roundelay, upon the eve
Of many deaths, it may be of their own.
    *Cæs.* And why should they not sing as well as swans?
They are black ones, to be sure.
    *Arn.* So, you are learn'd,
I see, too?
    *Cæs.* In my grammar, certes. I
Was educated for a monk of all times,
And once I was well versed in the forgotten
Etruscan letters, and — were I so minded —
Could make their hieroglyphics plainer than
Your alphabet.
    *Arn.* And wherefore do you not?
    *Cæs.* It answers better to resolve the alphabet
Back into hieroglyphics. Like your statesman,
And prophet, pontiff, doctor, alchymist,
Philosopher, and what not, they have built
More Babels, without new dispersion, than
The stammering young ones of the flood's dull ooze,
Who fail'd and fled each other. Why? why, marry,
Because no man could understand his neighbour.
They are wiser now, and will not separate
For nonsense. Nay, it is their brotherhood,

Their Shibboleth, their Koran, Talmud, their
Cabala; their best brick-work, wherewithal
They build more —
    *Arn.* (*interrupting him*). Oh, thou everlasting sneerer!
Be silent! How the soldiers' rough strain seems
Soften'd by distance to a hymn-like cadence!
Listen!
    *Cæs.* Yes. I have heard the angels sing.
    *Arn.* And demons howl.
    *Cæs.*                And man too. Let us listen:
I love all music.

    *Song of the Soldiers within.*

    The black bands came over
      The Alps and their snow;
    With Bourbon, the rover,
      They pass'd the broad Po.
    We have beaten all foemen,
      We have captured a king,
    We have turn'd back on no men,
      And so let us sing!
    Here's the Bourbon for ever!
      Though pennyless all,
    We'll have one more endeavour
      At yonder old wall.
    With the Bourbon we'll gather
      At day-dawn before
    The gates, and together
      Or break or climb o'er
    The wall: on the ladder
      As mounts each firm foot,
    Our shout shall grow gladder,
      And death only be mute.
    With the Bourbon we'll mount o'er
      The walls of old Rome,
    And who then shall count o'er
      The spoils of each dome?

Up! up with the lily!
  And down with the keys!
In old Rome, the seven-hilly,
  We'll revel at ease.
Her streets shall be gory,
  Her Tiber all red,
And her temples so hoary
  Shall clang with our tread.
Oh, the Bourbon! the Bourbon!
  The Bourbon for aye!
Of our song bear the burden!
  And fire, fire away!
With Spain for the vanguard,
  Our varied host comes;
And next to the Spaniard
  Beat Germany's drums;
And Italy's lances
  Are couch'd at their mother;
But our leader from France is,
  Who warr'd with his brother.
Oh, the Bourbon! the Bourbon!
  Sans country or home,
We'll follow the Bourbon,
  To plunder old Rome.

*Cæs.*      An indifferent song
For those within the walls, methinks, to hear.
  *Arn.* Yes, if they keep to their chorus. But here comes
The general with his chiefs and men of trust.
A goodly rebel!

*Enter the Constable* BOURBON *" cum suis,"* &c. &c.

  *Phil.*      How now, noble prince,
You are not cheerful?
  *Bourb.*      Why should I be so?
  *Phil.* Upon the eve of conquest, such as ours,
Most men would be so.
  *Bourb.*      If I were secure!

*Phil.* Doubt not our soldiers. Were the walls of adamant,
They'd crack them. Hunger is a sharp artillery.

*Bourb.* That they will falter is my least of fears.
That they will be repulsed, with Bourbon for
Their chief, and all their kindled appetites
To marshal them on — were those hoary walls
Mountains, and those who guard them like the gods
Of the old fables, I would trust my Titans; —
But now —

*Phil.* They are but men who war with mortals.

*Bourb.* True: but those walls have girded in great ages,
And sent forth mighty spirits. The past earth
And present phantom of imperious Rome
Is peopled with those warriors; and methinks
They flit along the eternal city's rampart,
And stretch their glorious, gory, shadowy hands,
And beckon me away!

*Phil.*      So let them! Wilt thou
Turn back from shadowy menaces of shadows?

*Bourb.* They do not menace me. I could have faced,
Methinks, a Sylla's menace; but they clasp,
And raise, and wring their dim and deathlike hands,
And with their thin aspen faces and fix'd eyes
Fascinate mine. Look there!

*Phil.*      I look upon
A lofty battlement.

*Bourb.*    And there!

*Phil.*      Not even
A guard in sight; they wisely keep below,
Shelter'd by the gray parapet from some
Stray bullet of our lansquenets, who might
Practise in the cool twilight.

*Bourb.*      You are blind.

*Phil.* If seeing nothing more than may be seen
Be so.

*Bourb.* A thousand years have mann'd the walls
With all their heroes, — the last Cato stands

And tears his bowels, rather than survive
The liberty of that I would enslave.
And the first Cæsar with his triumphs flits
From battlement to battlement.
  *Phil.*       Then conquer
The walls for which he conquer'd, and be greater!
  *Bourb.* True: so I will, or perish.
  *Phil.*        You can *not.*
In such an enterprise to die is rather
The dawn of an eternal day, than death.
      [*Count* ARNOLD *and* CÆSAR *advance.*
  *Cæs.* And the mere men — do they too sweat beneath
The noon of this same ever-scorching glory?
  *Bourb.*        Ah!
Welcome the bitter hunchback! and his master,
The beauty of our host, and brave as beauteous,
And generous as lovely. We shall find
Work for you both ere morning.
  *Cæs.*      You will find,
So please your highness, no less for yourself.
  *Bourb.* And if I do, there will not be a labourer
More forward, hunchback!
  *Cæs.*      You may well say so,
For *you* have seen that back — as general,
Placed in the rear in action — but your foes
Have never seen it.
  *Bourb.*    That's a fair retort,
For I provoked it: — but the Bourbon's breast
Has been, and ever shall be, far advanced
In danger's face as yours, were you the *devil.*
  *Cæs.* And if I were, I might have saved myself
The toil of coming here.
  *Phil.*     Why so?
  *Cæs.*       One half
Of your brave bands of their own bold accord
Will go to him, the other half be sent,
More swiftly, not less surely.

*Bourb.*                    Arnold, your
Slight crooked friend's as snake-like in his words
As his deeds.
    *Cæs.*      Your highness much mistakes me.
The first snake was a flatterer — I am none;
And for my deeds, I only sting when stung.
    *Bourb.* You are brave, and that's enough for me; and [quick
In speech as sharp in action — and that's more.
I am not alone a soldier, but the soldiers'
Comrade.
    *Cæs.* They are but bad company, your highness:
And worse even for their friends than foes, as being
More permanent acquaintance.
    *Phil.*                 How now, fellow!
Thou waxest insolent, beyond the privilege
Of a buffoon.
    *Cæs.*     You mean I speak the truth.
I'll lie — it is as easy: then you'll praise me
For calling you a hero.
    *Bourb.*             Philibert!
Let him alone; he's brave, and ever has
Been first, with that swart face and mountain shoulder
In field or storm, and patient in starvation;
And for his tongue, the camp is full of licence,
And the sharp stinging of a lively rogue
Is, to my mind, far preferable to
The gross, dull, heavy, gloomy execration
Of a mere famish'd, sullen, grumbling slave,
Whom nothing can convince save a full meal,
And wine, and sleep, and a few maravedis,
With which he deems him rich.
    *Cæs.*               It would be well
If the earth's princes ask'd no more.
    *Bourb.*               Be silent!
    *Cæs.* Ay, but not idle. Work yourself with words!
You have few to speak.
    *Phil.*           What means the audacious prater?

*Cæs.* To prate, like other prophets.
    *Bourb.*                       Philibert!
Why will you vex him? Have we not enough
To think on? Arnold! I will lead the attack
To-morrow.
    *Arn.*     I have heard as much, my lord.
    *Bourb.* And you will follow?
    *Arn.*                   Since I must not lead.
    *Bourb.* 'Tis necessary for the further daring
Of our too needy army, that their chief
Plant the first foot upon the foremost ladder's
First step.
    *Cæs.*    Upon its topmost, let us hope:
So shall he have his full deserts.
    *Bourb.*                The world's
Great capital perchance is ours to-morrow.
Through every change the seven-hill'd city hath
Retain'd her sway o'er nations, and the Cæsars,
But yielded to the Alarics, the Alarics
Unto the pontiffs. Roman, Goth, or priest,
Still the world's masters! Civilised, barbarian,
Or saintly, still the walls of Romulus
Have been the circus of an empire. Well!
'Twas *their* turn — now 'tis ours; and let us hope
That we will fight as well, and rule much better.
    *Cæs.* No doubt, the camp's the school of civic rights.
What would you make of Rome?
    *Bourb.*                That which it was.
    *Cæs.* In Alaric's time?
    *Bourb.*            No, slave! in the first Cæsar's,
Whose name you bear like other curs —
    *Cæs.*                  And kings!
'Tis a great name for blood-hounds.
    *Bourb.*               There's a demon
In that fierce rattlesnake thy tongue. Wilt never
Be serious?

*Cæs.* On the eve of battle, no; —
That were not soldier-like. 'Tis for the general
To be more pensive: we adventurers
Must be more cheerful. Wherefore should we think?
Our tutelar deity, in a leader's shape,
Takes care of us. Keep thought aloof from hosts!
If the knaves take to thinking, you will have
To crack those walls alone.
 *Bourb.* You may sneer, since
'Tis lucky for you that you fight no worse for 't.
 *Cæs.* I thank you for the freedom; 'tis the only
Pay I have taken in your highness' service.
 *Bourb.* Well, sir, to-morrow you shall pay yourself.
Look on those towers; they hold my treasury:
But, Philibert, we'll in to council. Arnold,
We would request your presence.
 *Arn.* Prince! my service
Is yours, as in the field.
 *Bourb.* In both we prize it,
And yours will be a post of trust at daybreak.
 *Cæs.* And mine?
 *Bourb.* To follow glory with the Bourbon.
Good night!
 *Arn. (to* CÆSAR). Prepare our armour for the assault,
And wait within my tent.
 [*Exeunt* BOURBON, ARNOLD, PHILIBERT, &c.
 *Cæs. (solus).* Within thy tent!
Think'st thou that I pass from thee with my presence?
Or that this crooked coffer, which contain'd
Thy principle of life, is aught to me
Except a mask? And these are men, forsooth!
Heroes and chiefs, the flower of Adam's bastards!
This is the consequence of giving matter
The power of thought. It is a stubborn substance,
And thinks chaotically, as it acts,
Ever relapsing into its first elements.
Well! I must play with these poor puppets: 'tis

The spirit's pastime in his idler hours.
When I grow weary of it, I have business
Amongst the stars, which these poor creatures deem
Were made for them to look at. 'Twere a jest now
To bring one down amongst them, and set fire
Unto their anthill: how the pismires then
Would scamper o'er the scalding soil, and, ceasing
From tearing down each other's nests, pipe forth
One universal orison! Ha! ha! [*Exit* CÆSAR.

---

## PART II.

### SCENE I.

*Before the walls of Rome.—The assault: the army in motion, with ladders to scale the walls;* BOURBON, *with a white scarf over his armour, foremost.*

*Chorus of Spirits in the air.*

I.

'Tis the morn, but dim and dark.
Whither flies the silent lark?
Whither shrinks the clouded sun?
Is the day indeed begun?
Nature's eye is melancholy
O'er the city high and holy:
But without there is a din
Should arouse the saints within,
And revive the heroic ashes
Round which yellow Tiber dashes.
Oh ye seven hills! awaken,
Ere your very base be shaken!

II.

Hearken to the steady stamp!
Mars is in their every tramp!
Not a step is out of tune,
As the tides obey the moon!

On they march, though to self-slaughter
Regular as rolling water,
Whose high waves o'ersweep the border
Of huge moles, but keep their order,
Breaking only rank by rank.
Hearken to the armour's clank!
Look down o'er each frowning warrior,
How he glares upon the barrier:
Look on each step of each ladder,
As the stripes that streak an adder.

### III.

Look upon the bristling wall,
Mann'd without an interval!
Round and round, and tier on tier,
Cannon's black mouth, shining spear,
Lit match, bell-mouth'd musquetoon,
Gaping to be murderous soon;
All the warlike gear of old,
Mix'd with what we now behold,
In this strife 'twixt old and new,
Gather like a locusts' crew,
Shade of Remus! 'tis a time
Awful as thy brother's crime!
Christians war against Christ's shrine: —
Must its lot be like to thine?

### IV.

Near — and near — and nearer still,
As the earthquake saps the hill,
First with trembling, hollow motion,
Like a scarce-awaken'd ocean,
Then with stronger shock and louder,
Till the rocks are crush'd to powder, —
Onward sweeps the rolling host!
Heroes of the immortal boast!
Mighty chiefs! eternal shadows!
First flowers of the bloody meadows

Which encompass Rome, the mother
Of a people without brother!
Will you sleep when nations' quarrels
Plough the root up of your laurels?
Ye who weep o'er Carthage burning,
Weep not — *strike!* for Rome is mourning! *

### V.

Onward sweep the varied nations!
Famine long hath dealt their rations.
To the wall, with hate and hunger,
Numerous as wolves, and stronger,
On they sweep. Oh! glorious city,
Must thou be a theme for pity?
Fight, like your first sire, each Roman!
Alaric was a gentle foeman,
Match'd with Bourbon's black banditti!
Rouse thee, thou eternal city;
Rouse thee! Rather give the torch
With thy own hand to thy porch,
Than behold such hosts pollute
Your worst dwelling with their foot.

### VI.

Ah! behold yon bleeding spectre!
Ilion's children find no Hector;
Priam's offspring loved their brother;
Rome's great sire forgot his mother,
When he slew his gallant twin,
With inexpiable sin.
See the giant shadow stride
O'er the ramparts high and wide!
When the first o'erleapt thy wall,
Its foundation mourn'd thy fall.
Now, though towering like a Babel,
Who to stop his steps are able?

---

* Scipio, the second Africanus, is said to have repeated a verse of Homer, and wept over the burning of Carthage. He had better have granted it a capitulation.

Stalking o'er thy highest dome,
Remus claims his vengeance, Rome!

### VII.

Now they reach thee in their anger:
Fire and smoke and hellish clangour
Are around thee, thou world's wonder!
Death is in thy walls and under.
Now the meeting steel first clashes,
Downward then the ladder crashes,
With its iron load all gleaming,
Lying at its foot blaspheming!
Up again! for every warrior
Slain, another climbs the barrier.
Thicker grows the strife: thy ditches
Europe's mingling gore enriches.
Rome! although thy wall may perish,
Such manure thy fields will cherish,
Making gay the harvest-home;
But thy hearths, alas! oh, Rome! —
Yet be Rome amidst thine anguish,
Fight as thou wast wont to vanquish!

### VIII.

Yet once more, ye old Penates!
Let not your quench'd hearths be Atè's!
Yet again, ye shadowy heroes,
Yield not to these stranger Neros!
Though the son who slew his mother
Shed Rome's blood, he was your brother:
'Twas the Roman curb'd the Roman; —
Brennus was a baffled foeman.
Yet again, ye saints and martyrs,
Rise! for yours are holier charters!
Mighty gods of temples falling,
Yet in ruin still appalling!
Mightier founders of those altars,
True and Christian, — strike the assaulters!

Tiber! Tiber! let thy torrent
Show even nature's self abhorrent.
Let each breathing heart dilated
Turn, as doth the lion baited!
Rome be crush'd to one wide tomb,
But be still the Roman's Rome!

BOURBON, ARNOLD, CÆSAR, *and others, arrive at the foot of the wall.* ARNOLD *is about to plant his ladder.*

*Bourb.* Hold, Arnold! I am first.

*Arn.* Not so, my lord.

*Bourb.* Hold, sir, I charge you! Follow! I am proud
Of such a follower, but will brook no leader.

[BOURBON *plants his ladder, and begins to mount.*

Now, boys! On! on!

[*A shot strikes him,* and BOURBON *falls.*

*Cæs.* And off!

*Arn.* Eternal powers!
The host will be appall'd, — but vengeance! vengeance!

*Bourb.* 'Tis nothing — lend me your hand.

[BOURBON *takes* ARNOLD *by the hand, and rises; but as he puts his foot on the step, falls again.*

Arnold! I am sped.
Conceal my fall — all will go well — conceal it!
Fling my cloak o'er what will be dust anon;
Let not the soldiers see it.

*Arn.* You must be
Removed; the aid of —

*Bourb.* No, my gallant boy;
Death is upon me. But what is *one* life?
The Bourbon's spirit shall command them still.
Keep them yet ignorant that I am but clay,
Till they are conquerors — then do as you may.

*Cæs.* Would not your highness choose to kiss the cross?
We have no priest here, but the hilt of sword
May serve instead: — it did the same for Bayard.

*Bourb.* Thou bitter slave! to name *him* at this time!
But I deserve it.

*Arn.* (*to* Cæsar). Villain, hold your peace!

*Cæs.* What, when a Christian dies? Shall I not offer a Christian "Vade in pace?"

*Arn.*     Silence! Oh!
Those eyes are glazing which o'erlook'd the world,
And saw no equal.

*Bourb.*     Arnold, should'st thou see
France — But hark! hark! the assault grows warmer — Oh!
For but an hour, a minute more of life
To die within the wall! Hence, Arnold, hence!
You lose time — they will conquer Rome without thee.

*Arn.* And without *thee!*

*Bourb.*     Not so; I'll lead them still
In spirit. Cover up my dust, and breathe not
That I have ceased to breathe. Away! and be
Victorious!

*Arn.*  But I must not leave thee thus.

*Bourb.* You must — farewell — Up! up! the world is winning.     [Bourbon *dies.*

*Cæs.* (*to* Arnold). Come, count, to business.

*Arn.*     'True. I'll weep hereafter.
[Arnold *covers* Bourbon's *body with a mantle, and mounts the ladder, crying*
The Bourbon! Bourbon! On, boys! Rome is ours!

*Cæs.* Good night, lord constable! thou wert a man.
[Cæsar *follows* Arnold; *they reach the battlement;* Arnold *and* Cæsar *are struck down.*

*Cæs.* A precious somerset! Is your countship injured?

*Arn.* No.     [*Remounts the ladder.*

*Cæs.* A rare blood-hound, when his own is heated!
And 'tis no boy's play. Now he strikes them down!
His hand is on the battlement — he grasps it
As though it were an altar; now his foot
Is on it, and — What have we here? — a Roman?
[*A man falls.*
The first bird of the covey! he has fallen
On the outside of the nest. Why, how now, fellow?

*Wounded Man.* A drop of water!
  *Cæs.*                    Blood's the only liquid
Nearer than Tiber.
  *Wounded Man.* I have died for Rome.          [*Dies.*
  *Cæs.* And so did Bourbon, in another sense.
Oh these immortal men! and their great motives!
But I must after my young charge. He is
By this time i' the forum. Charge! charge!
              [CÆSAR *mounts the ladder; the scene closes.*

### SCENE II.

*The City. — Combats between the Besiegers and Besieged in the streets. Inhabitants flying in confusion.*

              *Enter* CÆSAR.

  *Cæs.* I cannot find my hero; he is mix'd
With the heroic crowd that now pursue
The fugitives, or battle with the desperate.
What have we here? A cardinal or two
That do not seem in love with martyrdom.
How the old red-shanks scamper! Could they doff
Their hose as they have doff'd their hats, 'twould be
A blessing, as a mark the less for plunder.
But let them fly; the crimson kennels now
Will not much stain their stockings, since the mire
Is of the self-same purple hue.

  *Enter a Party fighting —* ARNOLD *at the head of the Besiegers.*
                He comes,
Hand in hand with the mild twins — Gore and Glory.
Holla! hold, count!
  *Arn.*           Away! they must not rally.
  *Cæs.* I tell thee, be not rash; a golden bridge
Is for a flying enemy. I gave thee
A form of beauty, and an
Exemption from some maladies of body,
But not of mind, which is not mine to give.
But though I gave the form of Thetis' son,

21*

I dipt thee not in Styx; and 'gainst a foe
I would not warrant thy chivalric heart
More than Pelides' heel; why then, be cautious,
And know thyself a mortal still.

  *Arn.*        And who
With aught of soul would combat if he were
Invulnerable? That were pretty sport.
Think'st thou I beat for hares when lions roar?
         [ARNOLD *rushes into the combat.*

  *Cæs.* A precious sample of humanity!
Well, his blood's up; and if a little's shed,
'Twill serve to curb his fever.
     [ARNOLD *engages with a Roman, who retires towards
      a portico.*

  *Arn.*      Yield thee, slave!
I promise quarter.
  *Rom.*    That's soon said.
  *Arn.*        And done —
My word is known.
  *Rom.*    So shall be my deeds.
      [*They re-engage.* CÆSAR *comes forward.*

  *Cæs.* Why, Arnold! hold thine own: thou hast in hand
A famous artisan, a cunning sculptor;
Also a dealer in the sword and dagger.
Not so, my musqueteer; 'twas he who slew
The Bourbon from the wall.
  *Arn.*      Ay, did he so?
Then he hath carved his monument.
  *Rom.*        I yet
May live to carve your betters.
  *Cæs.* Well said, my man of marble! Benvenuto,
Thou hast some practice in both ways; and he
Who slays Cellini will have work'd as hard
As e'er thou didst upon Carrara's blocks.
     [ARNOLD *disarms and wounds* CELLINI, *but slightly:
      the latter draws a pistol, and fires; then retires,
      and disappears through the portico.*

*Cæs.* How farest thou? Thou hast a taste, methinks,
Of red Bellona's banquet.
    *Arn. (staggers).*        'Tis a scratch.
Lend me thy scarf. He shall not 'scape me thus.
    *Cæs.* Where is it?
    *Arn.*         In the shoulder, not the sword arm —
And that's enough. I am thirsty: would I had
A helm of water!
    *Cæs.*        That's a liquid now
In requisition, but by no means easiest
To come at.
    *Arn.*    And my thirst increases; — but
I'll find a way to quench it.
    *Cæs.*        Or be quench'd
Thyself?
    *Arn.* The chance is even; we will throw
The dice thereon. But I lose time in prating;
Prithee be quick.        [CÆSAR *binds on the scarf.*
        And what dost thou so idly?
Why dost not strike?
    *Cæs.*        Your old philosophers
Beheld mankind, as mere spectators of
The Olympic games. When I behold a prize
Worth wrestling for, I may be found a Milo.
    *Arn.* Ay, 'gainst an oak.
    *Cæs.*       A forest, when it suits me:
I combat with a mass, or not at all.
Meantime, pursue thy sport as I do mine;
Which is just now to gaze, since all these labourers
Will reap my harvest gratis.
    *Arn.*        Thou art still
A fiend!
    *Cæs.* And thou — a man.
    *Arn.* Why, such I fain would show me.
    *Cæs.*        True — as men are.

*Arn.* And what is that?
*Cæs.*  Thou feelest and thou see'st.
  [*Exit* ARNOLD, *joining in the combat which still continues between detached parties. The scene closes.*

### SCENE III.

*St. Peter's — The Interior of the Church — The Pope at the Altar — Priests, &c. crowding in confusion, and Citizens flying for refuge, pursued by Soldiery.*

*Enter* CÆSAR.

*A Spanish Soldier.* Down with them, comrades! seize upon those lamps!
Cleave you bald-pated shaveling to the chine!
His rosary's of gold!
  *Lutheran Soldier.* Revenge! revenge!
Plunder hereafter, but for vengeance now —
Yonder stands Anti-Christ!
  *Cæs.* (*interposing*). How now, schismatic?
What would'st thou?
  *Luth. Sold.*  In the holy name of Christ,
Destroy proud Anti-Christ.  I am a Christian.
  *Cæs.* Yea, a disciple that would make the founder
Of your belief renounce it, could he see
Such proselytes.  Best stint thyself to plunder.
  *Luth. Sold.* I say he is the devil.
  *Cæs.*  Hush! keep that secret,
Lest he should recognize you for his own.
  *Luth. Sold.* Why would you save him? I repeat he is
The devil, or the devil's vicar upon earth.
  *Cæs.* And that's the reason: would you make a quarrel
With your best friends?  You had far best be quiet;
His hour is not yet come.
  *Luth. Sold.*  That shall be seen!
  [*The Lutheran Soldier rushes forward; a shot strikes him from one of the Pope's Guards, and he falls at the foot of the Altar.*

*Cæs. (to the Lutheran).* I told you so.
*Luth. Sold.* And will you not avenge me?
*Cæs.* Not I! You know that "Vengeance is the Lord's:"
You see he loves no interlopers.
*Luth. Sold. (dying).* Oh!
Had I but slain him, I had gone on high,
Crown'd with eternal glory! Heaven, forgive
My feebleness of arm that reach'd him not,
And take thy servant to thy mercy. 'Tis
A glorious triumph still; proud Babylon's
No more; the Harlot of the Seven Hills
Hath changed her scarlet raiment for sackcloth
And ashes! [*The Lutheran dies.*
*Cæs.* Yes, thine own amidst the rest.
Well done, old Babel!
[*The Guards defend themselves desperately, while the Pontiff escapes, by a private passage, to the Vatican and the Castle of St. Angelo.*
*Cæs.* Ha! right nobly battled!
Now, priest! now, soldier! the two great professions,
Together by the ears and hearts! I have not
Seen a more comic pantomime since Titus
Took Jewry. But the Romans had the best then;
Now they must take their turn.
*Soldiers.* He hath escaped!
Follow!
*Another Sold.* They have barr'd the narrow passage up,
And it is clogg'd with dead even to the door.
*Cæs.* I am glad he hath escaped: he may thank me for't
In part. I would not have his bulls abolish'd —
'Twere worth one half our empire: his indulgences
Demand some in return; — no, no, he must not
Fall; — and besides, his now escape may furnish
A future miracle, in future proof
Of his infallibility. [*To the Spanish Soldiery.*
Well, cut-throats!
What do you pause for? If you make not haste,

There will not be a link of pious gold left.
And *you*, too, catholics! Would ye return
From such a pilgrimage without a relic?
The very Lutherans have more true devotion:
See how they strip the shrines!
  *Soldiers.*      By holy Peter!
He speaks the truth; the heretics will bear
The best away.
  *Cæs.*   And that were shame! Go to!
Assist in their conversion.
    [*The Soldiers disperse; many quit the Church, others*
     *enter.*
  *Cæs.*     They are gone,
And others come: so flows the wave on wave
Of what these creatures call eternity,
Deeming themselves the breakers of the ocean,
While they are but its bubbles, ignorant
That foam is their foundation. So, another!

   *Enter* OLIMPIA, *flying from the pursuit — She springs*
    *upon the Altar.*

 *Sold.* She's mine!
 *Another Sold.* (*opposing the former*). You lie, I track'd her
  first; and were she
The Pope's niece, I'll not yield her.   [*They fight.*
  *3d Sold.* (*advancing towards* OLIMPIA). You may settle
Your claims; I'll make mine good.
  *Olimp.*     Infernal slave!
You touch me not alive.
  *3d Sold.*   Alive or dead!
  *Olimp.* (*embracing a massive crucifix*). Respect your God!
  *3d Sold.*    Yes, when he shines in gold.
Girl, you but grasp your dowry.
   [*As he advances,* OLIMPIA, *with a strong and sudden*
    *effort, casts down the crucifix: it strikes the Soldier,*
    *who falls.*
  *3d Sold.*    Oh, great God!

*Olimp.* Ah! now you recognize him.
*3d Sold.* My brain's crush'd!
Comrades, help, ho! All's darkness! [*He dies.*
*Other Soldiers (coming up).* Slay her, although she had a
 thousand lives:
She hath kill'd our comrade.
*Olimp.* Welcome such a death!
You have no life to give, which the worst slave
Would take. Great God! through thy redeeming Son,
And thy Son's Mother, now receive me as
I would approach thee, worthy her, and him, and thee!

*Enter* ARNOLD.

*Arn.* What do I see? Accursed jackals!
Forbear!
*Cæs. (aside, and laughing).* Ha! ha! here's equity! The
 dogs
Have as much right as he. But to the issue!
*Soldiers.* Count, she hath slain our comrade.
*Arn.* With what weapon?
*Sold.* The cross, beneath which he is crush'd; behold him
Lie there, more like a worm than man; she cast it
Upon his head.
*Arn.* Even so; there is a woman
Worthy a brave man's liking. Were ye such,
Ye would have honour'd her. But get ye hence,
And thank your meanness, other God you have none
For your existence. Had you touch'd a hair
Of those dishevell'd locks, I would have thinn'd
Your ranks more than the enemy. Away!
Ye jackals! gnaw the bones the lion leaves,
But not even these till he permits.
*A Sold. (murmuring).* The lion
Might conquer for himself then.
*Arn. (cuts him down).* Mutineer!
Rebel in hell — you shall obey on earth!
 [*The Soldiers assault* ARNOLD.

*Arn.* Come on! I'm glad on't! I will show you, slaves,
How you should be commanded, and who led you
First o'er the wall you were so shy to scale,
Until I waved my banners from its height,
As you are bold within it.
　　　　　[ARNOLD *mows down the foremost; the rest throw down
　　　　　　their arms.*
　*Soldiers.*　　　　　Mercy! mercy!
　*Arn.* Then learn to grant it. Have I taught you *who*
Led you o'er Rome's eternal battlements?
　*Soldiers.* We saw it, and we know it; yet forgive
A moment's error in the heat of conquest —
The conquest which you led to.
　*Arn.*　　　　　Get you hence!
Hence to your quarters! you will find them fix'd
In the Colonna palace.
　*Olimp.* (*aside*).　　In my father's
House!
　*Arn.* (*to the Soldiers*). Leave your arms; ye have no further
　　　　need
Of such: the city's render'd. And mark well
You keep your hands clean, or I'll find out a stream
As red as Tiber now runs, for your baptism.
　*Soldiers* (*deposing their arms and departing*). We obey!
　*Arn.* (*to* OLIMPIA). Lady, you are safe.
　*Olimp.*　　　　　I should be so,
Had I a knife even; but it matters not —
Death hath a thousand gates; and on the marble,
Even at the altar foot, whence I look down
Upon destruction, shall my head be dash'd,
Ere thou ascend it. God forgive thee, man!
　*Arn.* I wish to merit his forgiveness, and
Thine own, although I have not injured thee.
　*Olimp.* No! Thou hast only sack'd my native land, —
No injury! — and made my father's house
A den of thieves! No injury! — this temple —
Slippery with Roman and holy gore.

No injury! And now thou would preserve me,
To be — but that shall never be!
   [*She raises her eyes to Heaven, folds her robe round
   her, and prepares to dash herself down on the side of
   the Altar opposite to that where* ARNOLD *stands.*
 *Arn.*       Hold! hold!
I swear.
 *Olimp.* Spare thine already forfeit soul
A perjury for which even hell would loathe thee.
I know thee.
 *Arn.*   No, thou know'st me not; I am not
Of these men, though —
 *Olimp.*     I judge thee by thy mates;
It is for God to judge thee as thou art.
I see thee purple with the blood of Rome;
Take mine, 'tis all thou e'er shalt have of me,
And here, upon the marble of this temple,
Where the baptismal font baptized me God's,
I offer him a blood less holy
But not less pure (pure as it left me then,
A redeem'd infant) than the holy water
The saints have sanctified!
   [OLIMPIA *waves her hand to* ARNOLD *with disdain, and
   dashes herself on the pavement from the Altar.*
 *Arn.*      Eternal God!
I feel thee now! Help! help! She's gone.
 *Cæs.* (*approaches*).     I am here.
 *Arn.* Thou! but oh, save her!
 *Cæs.* (*assisting him to raise* OLIMPIA). She hath done it well!
The leap was serious.
 *Arn.*     Oh! she is lifeless!
 *Cæs.*         If
She be so, I have nought to do with that:
The resurrection is beyond me.
 *Arn.*     Slave!
 *Cæs.* Ay, slave or master, 'tis all one: methinks
Good words, however, are as well at times.

*Arn.* Words! — Canst thou aid her?

*Cæs.* I will try. A sprinkling
Of that same holy water may be useful.

[*He brings some in his helmet from the font.*

*Arn.* 'Tis mix'd with blood.

*Cæs.* There is no cleaner now
In Rome.

*Arn.* How pale! how beautiful! how lifeless!
Alive or dead, thou essence of all beauty,
I love but thee!

*Cæs.* Even so Achilles loved
Penthesilea: with his form it seems
You have his heart, and yet it was no soft one.

*Arn.* She breathes! But no, 'twas nothing or the last
Faint flutter life disputes with death.

*Cæs.* She breathes.

*Arn. Thou* say'st it? Then 'tis truth.

*Cæs.* You do me right —
The devil speaks truth much oftener than he's deem'd:
He hath an ignorant audience.

*Arn.* (*without attending to him*). Yes! her heart beats
Alas! that the first beat of the only heart
I ever wish'd to beat with mine should vibrate
To an assassin's pulse.

*Cæs.* A sage reflection,
But somewhat late i' the day. Where shall we bear her?
I say she lives.

*Arn.* And will she live?

*Cæs.* As much
As dust can.

*Arn.* Then she is dead!

*Cæs.* Bah! bah! You are so,
And do not know it. She will come to life —
Such as you think so, such as you now are;
But we must work by human means.

*Arn.* We will

Convey her unto the Colonna palace,
Where I have pitch'd my banner.
    *Cæs.* Come then! raise her up!
    *Arn.* Softly!
    *Cæs.*            As softly as they bear the dead,
Perhaps because they cannot feel the jolting.
    *Arn.* But doth she live indeed?
    *Cæs.*                   Nay, never fear!
But, if you rue it after, blame not me.
    *Arn.* Let her but live!
    *Cæs.*              The spirit of her life
Is yet within her breast, and may revive.
Count! count! I am your servant in all things,
And this is a new office: — 'tis not oft
I am employ'd in such; but you perceive
How stanch a friend is what you call a fiend.
On earth you have often only fiends for friends;
Now *I* desert not mine. Soft! bear her hence,
The beautiful half-clay, and nearly spirit!
I am almost enamour'd of her, as
Of old the angels of her earliest sex.
    *Arn.* Thou!
    *Cæs.*        I! But fear not. I'll not be your rival.
    *Arn.* Rival!
    *Cæs.*        I could be one right formidable;
But since I slew the seven husbands of
Tobias' future bride (and after all
'Twas suck'd out by some incense), I have laid
Aside intrigue: 'tis rarely worth the trouble
Of gaining, or — what is more difficult —
Getting rid of your prize again; for there's
The rub! at least to mortals.
    *Arn.*                  Prithee, peace!
Softly! methinks her lips move, her eyes open!
    *Cæs.* Like stars, no doubt; for that's a metaphor
For Lucifer and Venus.

*Arn.* To the palace
Colonna, as I told you!
*Cas.* Oh! I know
My way through Rome.
*Arn.* Now onward, onward! Gently!
[*Exeunt, bearing* OLIMPIA. *The scene closes.*

---

## PART III.

### SCENE I.

*A Castle in the Apennines, surrounded by a wild but smiling country. Chorus of Peasants singing before the Gates.*

CHORUS.

I.

 The wars are over,
  The spring is come;
 The bride and her lover
  Have sought their home:
They are happy, we rejoice;
Let their hearts have an echo in every voice!

II.

The spring is come; the violet's gone,
The first-born child of the early sun:
With us she is but a winter's flower,
The snow on the hills cannot blast her bower,
And she lifts up her dewy eye of blue
To the youngest sky of the self-same hue.

III.

And when the spring comes with her host
Of flowers, that flower beloved the most
Shrinks from the crowd that may confuse
Her heavenly odour and virgin hues.

IV.

Pluck the others, but still remember
Their herald out of dim December —

The morning star of all the flowers,
The pledge of daylight's lengthen'd hours;
Nor, midst the roses, e'er forget
The virgin, virgin violet.

*Enter* CÆSAR.

*Cæs.* (*singing*). The wars are all over,
 Our swords are all idle,
 The steed bites the bridle,
The casque's on the wall.
There's rest for the rover;
 But his armour is rusty,
 And the veteran grows crusty,
As he yawns in the hall.
 He drinks — but what's drinking?
 A mere pause from thinking!
No bugle awakes him with life-and-death call.

CHORUS.

But the hound bayeth loudly,
 The boar's in the wood,
And the falcon longs proudly
 To spring from her hood:
On the wrist of the noble
 She sits like a crest,
And the air is in trouble
 With birds from their nest.

*Cæs.* Oh! shadow of glory!
 Dim image of war!
But the chase hath no story,
 Her hero no star,
Since Nimrod, the founder
 Of empire and chase,
Who made the woods wonder
 And quake for their race.

When the lion was young,
  In the pride of his might,
Then 'twas sport for the strong
  To embrace him in fight;
To go forth, with a pine
  For a spear, 'gainst the mammoth,
Or strike through the ravine
  At the foaming behemoth;
While man was in stature
  As towers in our time,
The first-born of Nature,
  And, like her, sublime!

       CHORUS.

But the wars are over,
  The spring is come;
The bride and her lover
  Have sought their home:
They are happy, and we rejoice;
Let their hearts have an echo from every voice!

       [*Exeunt the Peasantry, singing.*

# HEAVEN AND EARTH;

## A MYSTERY.

FOUNDED ON THE FOLLOWING PASSAGE IN GENESIS, CHAP. VI.

"And it came to pass .... that the sons of God saw the daughters of men that they were fair; and they took them wives of all which they chose."

---

"And woman wailing for her demon lover." — COLERIDGE.

---

## DRAMATIS PERSONÆ.

*Angels.* — SAMIASA.
AZAZIEL.
RAPHAEL the Archangel.
*Men.* — NOAH and his Sons.
IRAD.
JAPHET.

*Women.* — ANAH.
AHOLIBAMAH.

*Chorus of Spirits of the Earth.* — *Chorus of Mortals.*

# HEAVEN AND EARTH.

## PART I.

### SCENE I.

*A woody and mountainous district near Mount Ararat. — Time, midnight.*

*Enter* ANAH *and* AHOLIBAMAH.

*Anah.* Our father sleeps: it is the hour when they
Who love us are accustom'd to descend
Through the deep clouds o'er rocky Ararat: —
How my heart beats!

  *Aho.*    Let us proceed upon
Our invocation.

  *Anah.*  But the stars are hidden.
I tremble

  *Aho.* So do I, but not with fear
Of aught save their delay.

  *Anah.*    My sister, though
I love Azaziel more than — oh, too much!
What was I going to say? my heart grows impious.

  *Aho.* And where is the impiety of loving
Celestial natures?

  *Anah.*  But, Aholibamah,
I love our God less since his angel loved me:
This cannot be of good; and though I know not
That I do wrong, I feel a thousand fears
Which are not ominous of right.

  *Aho.*     Then wed thee
Unto some son of clay, and toil and spin!
There's Japhet loves thee well, hath loved thee long:
Marry, and bring forth dust!

*Anah.*         I should have loved
Azaziel not less were he mortal; yet
I am glad he is not. I can not outlive him.
And when I think that his immortal wings
Will one day hover o'er the sepulchre
Of the poor child of clay which so adored him,
As he adores the Highest, death becomes
Less terrible; but yet I pity him:
His grief will be of ages, or at least
Mine would be such for him, were I the seraph,
And he the perishable.

*Aho.*         Rather say,
That he will single forth some other daughter
Of Earth, and love her as he once loved Anah.

*Anah.* And if it should be so, and she loved him,
Better thus than that he should weep for me.

*Aho.* If I thought thus of Samiasa's love,
All seraph as he is, I'd spurn him from me.
But to our invocation! — 'Tis the hour.

*Anah.*         Seraph!
    From thy sphere!
Whatever star contain thy glory;
    In the eternal depths of heaven
    Albeit thou watchest with "the seven,"*
Though through space infinite and hoary
    Before thy bright wings worlds be driven,
        Yet hear!
Oh! think of her who holds thee dear!
    And though she nothing is to thee,
Yet think that thou art all to her.
    Thou canst not tell, — and never be
    Such pangs decreed to aught save me, —
        The bitterness of tears.
    Eternity is in thine years,

* The archangels, said to be seven in number, and to occupy the eighth rank in the celestial hierarchy.

Unborn, undying beauty in thine eyes;
With me thou canst not sympathise,
  Except in love, and there thou must
  Acknowledge that more loving dust
Ne'er wept beneath the skies.
Thou walk'st thy many worlds, thou see'st
  The face of him who made thee great,
As he hath made me of the least
  Of those cast out from Eden's gate:
    Yet, Seraph dear!
    Oh hear!
For thou hast loved me, and I would not die
  Until I know what I must die in knowing,
That thou forget'st in thine eternity
  Her whose heart death could not keep from o'erflowing
For thee, immortal essence as thou art!
Great is their love who love in sin and fear;
And such, I feel, are waging in my heart
A war unworthy: to an Adamite
Forgive, my Seraph! that such thoughts appear,
  For sorrow is our element;
    Delight
An Eden kept afar from sight,
  Though sometimes with our visions blent.
    The hour is near
Which tells me we are not abandon'd quite. —
    Appear! Appear!
    Seraph!
My own Azaziel! be but here,
And leave the stars to their own light.

*Aho.*     Samiasa!
    Wheresoe'er
  Thou rulest in the upper air —
Or warring with the spirits who may dare
    Dispute with Him
Who made all empires, empire; or recalling
Some wandering star, which shoots through the abyss,

Whose tenants dying, while their world is falling,
Share the dim destiny of clay in this;
Or joining with the inferior cherubim,
Thou deignest to partake their hymn —
    Samiasa!
I call thee, I await thee, and I love thee.
Many may worship thee, that will I not:
If that thy spirit down to mine may move thee,
Descend and share my lot!
Though I be form'd of clay,
    And thou of beams
More bright than those of day
    On Eden's streams,
Thine immortality can not repay
  With love more warm than mine
My love. There is a ray
  In me, which, though forbidden yet to shine,
I feel was lighted at thy God's and thine.
It may be hidden long: death and decay
  Our mother Eve bequeath'd us — but my heart
Defies it: though this life must pass away
  Is *that* a cause for thee and me to part?
Thou art immortal — so am I: I feel —
  I feel my immortality o'ersweep
All pains, all tears, all time, all fears, and peal,
  Like the eternal thunders of the deep,
Into my ears this truth — "Thou liv'st for ever!"
    But if it be in joy
I know not, nor would know;
That secret rests with the Almighty giver
  Who folds in clouds the fonts of bliss and woe.
    But thee and me he never can destroy;
Change us he may, but not o'erwhelm; we are
Of as eternal essence, and must war
With him if he will war with us: with *thee*
  I can share all things, even immortal sorrow;
For thou hast ventured to share life with *me*,

And shall *I* shrink from thine eternity?
No! though the serpent's sting should pierce me thorough,
And thou thyself wert like the serpent, coil
Around me still! and I will smile,
    And curse thee not; but hold
    Thee in as warm a fold
    As — but descend; and prove
    A mortal's love
For an immortal. If the skies contain
More joy than thou canst give and take, remain!
  *Anah.* Sister! sister! I view them winging
Their bright way through the parted night.
  *Aho.* The clouds from off their pinions flinging,
As though they bore to-morrow's light.
  *Anah.* But if our father see the sight!
  *Aho.* He would but deem it was the moon
Rising unto some sorcerer's tune
An hour too soon.
  *Anah.* They come! *he* comes! — Azaziel!
  *Aho.*                                   Haste
To meet them! Oh! for wings to bear
My spirit, while they hover there,
To Samiasa's breast!
  *Anah.* Lo! they have kindled all the west,
Like a returning sunset; — lo!
    On Ararat's late secret crest
A mild and many-colour'd bow,
The remnant of their flashing path,
Now shines! and now, behold! it hath
Return'd to night, as rippling foam,
    Which the leviathan hath lash'd
From his unfathomable home,
When sporting on the face of the calm deep,
    Subsides soon after he again hath dash'd
Down, down, to where the ocean's fountains sleep.
  *Aho.* They have touch'd earth! Samiasa!
  *Anah.*                       My Azaziel!   [*Exeunt.*

PART I.

SCENE II.

*Enter* IRAD *and* JAPHET.

*Irad.* Despond not: wherefore wilt thou wander thus
To add thy silence to the silent night,
And lift thy tearful eye unto the stars?
They cannot aid thee.
  *Japh.*     But they soothe me — now
Perhaps she looks upon them as I look.
Methinks a being that is beautiful
Becometh more so as it looks on beauty,
The eternal beauty of undying things.
Oh, Anah!
  *Irad.*  But she loves thee not.
  *Japh.*       Alas!
  *Irad.* And proud Aholibamah spurns me also.
  *Japh.* I feel for thee too.
  *Irad.*     Let her keep her pride,
Mine hath enabled me to bear her scorn:
It may be, time too will avenge it.
  *Japh.*      Canst thou
Find joy in such a thought?
  *Irad.*     Nor joy nor sorrow.
I loved her well; I would have loved her better,
Had love been met with love: as 'tis, I leave her
To brighter destinies, if so she deems them.
  *Japh.* What destinies?
  *Irad.*     I have some cause to think
She loves another.
  *Japh.*   Anah!
  *Irad.*     No; her sister.
  *Japh.* What other?
  *Irad.*     That I know not; but her air,
If not her words, tells me she loves another.
  *Japh.* Ay, but not Anah: she but loves her God.
  *Irad.* Whate'er she loveth, so she loves thee not,
What can it profit thee?

*Japh.* True, nothing; but
I love.
　*Irad.* And so did I.
　*Japh.* And now thou lov'st not,
Or think'st thou lov'st not, art thou happier?
　*Irad.* Yes.
　*Japh.* I pity thee.
　*Irad.* Me! why?
　*Japh.* For being happy
Deprived of that which makes my misery.
　*Irad.* I take thy taunt as part of thy distemper,
And would not feel as thou dost for more shekels
Than all our father's herds would bring if weigh'd
Against the metal of the sons of Cain —
The yellow dust they try to barter with us,
As if such useless and discolour'd trash,
The refuse of the earth, could be received
For milk, and wool, and flesh, and fruits, and all
Our flocks and wilderness afford. — Go, Japhet,
Sigh to the stars, as wolves howl to the moon —
I must back to my rest.
　*Japh.* And so would I
If I could rest.
　*Irad.* Thou wilt not to our tents then?
　*Japh.* No, Irad; I will to the cavern, whose
Mouth they say opens from the internal world
To let the inner spirits of the earth
Forth when they walk its surface.
　*Irad.* Wherefore so?
What wouldst thou there?
　*Japh.* Soothe further my sad spirit
With gloom as sad: it is a hopeless spot,
And I am hopeless.
　*Irad.* But 'tis dangerous;
Strange sounds and sights have peopled it with terrors.
I must go with thee.

*Japh.* Irad, no; believe me
I feel no evil thought, and fear no evil.
　*Irad.* But evil things will be thy foe the more
As not being of them: turn thy steps aside,
Or let mine be with thine.
　*Japh.* No, neither, Irad;
I must proceed alone.
　*Irad.* Then peace be with thee!
　　　　　　　　　　　　　　　　[*Exit* IRAD.
　*Japh.* (*solus*). Peace! I have sought it where it should be found,
In love — with love, too, which perhaps deserved it;
And, in its stead, a heaviness of heart —
A weakness of the spirit — listless days,
And nights inexorable to sweet sleep —
Have come upon me. Peace! what peace? the calm
Of desolation, and the stillness of
The untrodden forest, only broken by
The sweeping tempest through its groaning boughs;
Such is the sullen or the fitful state
Of my mind overworn. The earth's grown wicked,
And many signs and portents have proclaim'd
A change at hand, and an o'erwhelming doom
To perishable beings. Oh, my Anah!
When the dread hour denounced shall open wide
The fountains of the deep, how mightest thou
Have lain within this bosom, folded from
The elements; this bosom, which in vain
Hath beat for thee, and then will beat more vainly,
While thine — Oh, God! at least remit to her
Thy wrath! for she is pure amidst the failing
As a star in the clouds, which cannot quench,
Although they obscure it for an hour. My Anah!
How would I have adored thee, but thou wouldst not;
And still would I redeem thee — see thee live
When ocean is earth's grave, and, unopposed
By rock or shallow, the leviathan,

Lord of the shoreless sea and watery world,
Shall wonder at his boundlessness of realm.

[*Exit* JAPHET.

*Enter* NOAH *and* SHEM.

*Noah.* Where is thy brother Japhet?
*Shem.*                              He went forth,
According to his wont, to meet with Irad,
He said; but, as I fear, to bend his steps
Towards Anah's tents, round which he hovers nightly,
Like a dove round and round its pillaged nest;
Or else he walks the wild up to the cavern
Which opens to the heart of Ararat.
    *Noah.* What doth he there? It is an evil spot
Upon an earth all evil; for things worse
Than even wicked men resort there: he
Still loves this daughter of a fated race,
Although he could not wed her if she loved him,
And that she doth not. Oh, the unhappy hearts
Of men! that one of my blood, knowing well
The destiny and evil of these days,
And that the hour approacheth, should indulge
In such forbidden yearnings! Lead the way;
He must be sought for!
    *Shem.*            Go not forward, father:
I will seek Japhet.
    *Noah.*            Do not fear for me:
All evil things are powerless on the man
Selected by Jehovah. — Let us on.
    *Shem.* To the tents of the father of the sisters?
    *Noah.* No; to the cavern of the Caucasus.

[*Exeunt* NOAH *and* SHEM.

SCENE III.

*The mountains. — A cavern, and the rocks of Caucasus.*

    *Japh.* (*solus*). Ye wilds, that look eternal; and thou cave,
Which seem'st unfathomable; and ye mountains,

So varied and so terrible in beauty;
Here, in your rugged majesty of rocks
And toppling trees that twine their roots with stone
In perpendicular places, where the foot
Of man would tremble, could he reach them — yes,
Ye look eternal! Yet, in a few days,
Perhaps even hours, ye will be changed, rent, hurl'd
Before the mass of waters; and yon cave,
Which seems to lead into a lower world,
Shall have its depths search'd by the sweeping wave,
And dolphins gambol in the lion's den!
And man — Oh, men! my fellow-beings! Who
Shall weep above your universal grave,
Save I? Who shall be left to weep? My kinsmen,
Alas! what am I better than ye are,
That I must live beyond ye? Where shall be
The pleasant places where I thought of Anah
While I had hope? or the more savage haunts,
Scarce less beloved, where I despair'd for her?
And can it be! — Shall yon exulting peak,
Whose glittering top is like a distant star,
Lie low beneath the boiling of the deep?
No more to have the morning sun break forth,
And scatter back the mists in floating folds
From its tremendous brow? no more to have
Day's broad orb drop behind its head at even,
Leaving it with a crown of many hues?
No more to be the beacon of the world,
For angels to alight on, as the spot
Nearest the stars? And can those words "*no more*"
Be meant for thee, for all things, save for us,
And the predestined creeping things reserved
By my sire to Jehovah's bidding? May
*He* preserve *them*, and *I not* have the power
To snatch the loveliest of earth's daughters from
A doom which even some serpent, with his mate,
Shall 'scape to save his kind to be prolong'd,

To hiss and sting through some emerging world,
Reeking and dank from out the slime, whose ooze
Shall slumber o'er the wreck of this until
The salt morass subside into a sphere
Beneath the sun, and be the monument,
The sole and undistinguish'd sepulchre,
Of yet quick myriads of all life? How much
Breath will be still'd at once! All beauteous world
So young, so mark'd out for destruction, I
With a cleft heart look on thee day by day,
And night by night, thy number'd days and nights:
I cannot save thee, cannot save even her
Whose love had made me love thee more; but as
A portion of thy dust, I cannot think
Upon thy coming doom without a feeling
Such as — Oh God! and canst thou —        [*He pauses.*

*A rushing sound from the cavern is heard, and shouts of laughter*
        *— afterwards a Spirit passes.*

 *Japh.*        In the name
Of the Most High, what art thou?
  *Spirit (laughs.)*     Ha! ha! ha!
  *Japh.* By all that earth holds holiest, speak!
  *Spirit (laughs.)*       Ha! ha!
  *Japh.* By the approaching deluge! by the earth
Which will be strangled by the ocean! by
The deep which will lay open all her fountains!
The heaven which will convert her clouds to seas,
And the Omnipotent who makes and crushes!
Thou unknown, terrible, and indistinct,
Yet awful Thing of Shadows, speak to me!
Why dost thou laugh that horrid laugh?
  *Spirit.*       Why weep'st thou?
  *Japh.* For earth and all her children.
  *Spirit.*        Ha! ha! ha!
          [*Spirit vanishes.*

*Japh.* How the fiend mocks the tortures of a world,
The coming desolation of an orb,
On which the sun shall rise and warm no life!
How the earth sleeps! and all that in it is
Sleep too upon the very eve of death!
Why should they wake to meet it? What is here,
Which look like death in life, and speak like things
Born ere this dying world? They come like clouds!
                    [*Various Spirits pass from the cavern.*
  *Spirit.*        Rejoice!
      The abhorred race
Which could not keep in Eden their high place,
    But listen'd to the voice
Of knowledge without power,
    Are nigh the hour
      Of death!
Not slow, not single, not by sword, nor sorrow,
  Nor years, nor heart-break, nor time's sapping motion,
Shall they drop off. Behold their last to-morrow!
    Earth shall be ocean!
      And no breath,
Save of the winds, be on the unbounded wave!
Angels shall tire their wings, but find no spot:
Not even a rock from out the liquid grave
    Shall lift its point to save,
Or show the place where strong Despair hath died,
  After long looking o'er the ocean wide
    For the expected ebb which cometh not:
      All shall be void,
        Destroy'd!
Another element shall be the lord
  Of life, and the abhorr'd
Children of dust be quench'd; and of each hue
Of earth nought left but the unbroken blue;
  And of the variegated mountain
    Shall nought remain
    Unchanged, or of the level plain;

Cedar and pine shall lift their tops in vain:
All merged within the universal fountain,
  Man, earth, and fire, shall die,
    And sea and sky
Look vast and lifeless in the eternal eye.
  Upon the foam
  Who shall erect a home?
 *Japh.* (*coming forward*). My sire!
Earth's seed shall not expire;
  Only the evil shall be put away
    From day.
  Avaunt! ye exulting demons of the waste!
Who howl your hideous joy
When God destroys whom you dare not destroy;
   Hence! haste!
  Back to your inner caves!
  Until the waves
Shall search you in your secret place,
  And drive your sullen race
Forth, to be roll'd upon the tossing winds
  In restless wretchedness along all space!
 *Spirit.*   Son of the saved!
  When thou and thine have braved
  The wide and warring element;
When the great barrier of the deep is rent,
Shall thou and thine be good or happy? — No!
 Thy new world and new race shall be of woe —
 Less goodly in their aspect, in their years
  Less than the glorious giants, who
  Yet walk the world in pride,
The Sons of Heaven by many a mortal bride.
Thine shall be nothing of the past, save tears.
  And art thou not ashamed
   Thus to survive,
  And eat, and drink, and wive?
With a base heart so far subdued and tamed,
As even to bear this wide destruction named,

Without such grief and courage, as should rather
  Bid thee await the world-dissolving wave,
Than seek a shelter with thy favour'd father,
  And build thy city o'er the drown'd earth's grave?
      Who would outlive their kind,
      Except the base and blind?
          Mine
        Hateth thine
As of a different order in the sphere,
        But not our own.
There is not one who hath not left a throne
  Vacant in heaven to dwell in darkness here,
Rather than see his mates endure alone.
          Go, wretch! and give
A life like thine to other wretches — live!
  And when the annihilating waters roar
        Above what they have done,
Envy the giant patriarchs then no more,
  And scorn thy sire as the surviving one!
        Thyself for being his son!

    *Chorus of Spirits issuing from the cavern.*
        Rejoice!
      No more the human voice
    Shall vex our joys in middle air
        With prayer;
        No more
        Shall they adore;
And we, who ne'er for ages have adored
      The prayer-exacting Lord,
  To whom the omission of a sacrifice
        Is vice;
We, we shall view the deep's salt sources pour'd
Until one element shall do the work
    Of all in chaos; until they,
  The creatures proud of their poor clay,
Shall perish, and their bleached bones shall lurk

In caves, in dens, in clefts of mountains, where
The deep shall follow to their latest lair;
   Where even the brutes, in their despair,
Shall cease to prey on man and on each other,
  And the striped tiger shall lie down to die
Beside the lamb, as though he were his brother;
   Till all things shall be as they were,
  Silent and uncreated, save the sky:
      While a brief truce
    Is made with Death, who shall forbear
  The little remnant of the past creation,
To generate new nations for his use;
   This remnant, floating o'er the undulation
    Of the subsiding deluge, from its slime,
  When the hot sun hath baked the reeking soil
    Into a world, shall give again to Time
New beings — years — diseases — sorrow — crime —
With all companionship of hate and toil,
      Until —

*Japh.* (*interrupting them*). The eternal will
    Shall deign to expound this dream
    Of good and evil; and redeem
      Unto himself all times, all things;
      And, gather'd under his almighty wings,
        Abolish hell!
    And to the expiated Earth
    Restore the beauty of her birth,
      Her Eden in an endless paradise,
    Where man no more can fall as once he fell,
    And even the very demons shall do well!

*Spirits.* And when shall take effect this wondrous spell?
*Japh.* When the Redeemer cometh; first in pain,
    And then in glory.
*Spirit.* Meantime still struggle in the mortal chain,
    Till earth wax hoary;
War with yourselves, and hell, and heaven, in vain,
    Until the clouds look gory

With the blood reeking from each battle plain;
New times, new climes, new arts, new men; but still,
The same old tears, old crimes, and oldest ill,
Shall be amongst your race in different forms;
    But the same moral storms
  Shall oversweep the future, as the waves
In a few hours the glorious giants' graves. \*

        *Chorus of Spirits.*
     Brethren, rejoice!
     Mortal, farewell!
Hark! hark! already we can hear the voice
Of growing ocean's gloomy swell;
  The winds, too, plume their piercing wings;
  The clouds have nearly fill'd their springs;
The fountains of the great deep shall be broken,
  And heaven set wide her windows; \*\* while mankind
View, unacknowledged, each tremendous token —
  Still, as they were from the beginning, blind.
    We hear the sound they cannot hear,
      The mustering thunders of the threatening sphere;
        Yet a few hours their coming is delay'd —
          Their flashing banners, folded still on high,
        Yet undisplay'd,
Save to the Spirit's all-pervading eye.
      Howl! howl! oh Earth!
Thy death is nearer than thy recent birth:
Tremble, ye mountains, soon to shrink below
        The ocean's overflow!
The wave shall break upon your cliffs; and shells,
  The little shells, of ocean's least things be
Deposed where now the eagle's offspring dwells —
How shall he shriek o'er the remorseless sea!

    \* "And there were giants in the earth in those days, and after; mighty men, which were of old, men of renown." — *Genesis.*
    \*\* "The same day were all the fountains of the great deep broken up, and the windows of heaven were opened." — *Ibid.*

And call his nestlings up with fruitless yell,
Unanswer'd, save by the encroaching swell; —
While man shall long in vain for his broad wings,
   The wings which could not save: —
Where could he rest them, while the whole space brings
   Nought to his eye beyond the deep, his grave?
        Brethren, rejoice!
And loudly lift each superhuman voice —
        All die,
Save the slight remnant of Seth's seed —
        The seed of Seth,
Exempt for future sorrow's sake from death.
        But of the sons of Cain
        None shall remain;
    And all his goodly daughters
Must lie beneath the desolating waters —
Or, floating upward, with their long hair laid
Along the wave, the cruel heaven upbraid,
        Which would not spare
      Beings even in death so fair.
        It is decreed,
        All die!
And to the universal human cry
The universal silence shall succeed!
        Fly, brethren, fly!
        But still rejoice!
          We fell!
          They fall!
        So perish all
These petty foes of Heaven who shrink from hell!
            [*The Spirits disappear, soaring upwards.*

   *Japh. (solus).* God hath proclaim'd the destiny of earth;
My father's ark of safety hath announced it;
The very demons shriek it from their caves;
The scroll* of Enoch prophesied it long

   * The book of Enoch, preserved by the Ethiopians, is said by them to be anterior to the flood.

In silent books, which, in their silence, say
More to the mind than thunder to the ear:
And yet men listen'd not, nor listen; but
Walk darkling to their doom; which, though so nigh,
Shakes them no more in their dim disbelief,
Than their last cries shall shake the Almighty purpose,
Or deaf obedient ocean, which fulfils it.
No sign yet hangs its banner in the air;
The clouds are few, and of their wonted texture,
The sun will rise upon the earth's last day
As on the fourth day of creation, when
God said unto him, "Shine!" and he broke forth
Into the dawn, which lighted not the yet
Unform'd forefather of mankind — but roused
Before the human orison the earlier
Made and far sweeter voices of the birds,
Which in the open firmament of heaven
Have wings like angels, and like them salute
Heaven first each day before the Adamites:
Their matins now draw nigh — the east is kindling —
And they will sing! and day will break! Both near,
So near the awful close! For these must drop
Their outworn pinions on the deep; and day,
After the bright course of a few brief morrows, —
Ay, day will rise; but upon what? — a chaos,
Which was ere day; and which, renew'd, makes time
Nothing! for, without life, what are the hours?
No more to dust than is eternity
Unto Jehovah, who created both.
Without him, even eternity would be
A void: without man, time, as made for man,
Dies with man, and is swallow'd in that deep
Which has no fountain; as his race will be
Devour'd by that which drowns his infant world. —
What have we here? Shapes of both earth and air?
No — *all* of heaven, they are so beautiful.
I cannot trace their features; but their forms,

How lovelily they move along the side
Of the grey mountain, scattering its mist!
And after the swart savage spirits, whose
Infernal immortality pour'd forth
Their impious hymn of triumph, they shall be
Welcome as Eden. It may be they come
To tell me the reprieve of our young world,
For which I have so often pray'd — They come!
Anah! oh, God! and with her —

*Enter* SAMIASA, AZAZIEL, ANAH, *and* AHOLIBAMAH.

*Anah.* Japhet!
*Sam.* Lo!
A son of Adam!
*Aza.* What doth the earth-born here,
While all his race are slumbering?
*Japh.* Angel! what
Dost thou on earth when thou shouldst be on high?
*Aza.* Know'st thou not, or forget'st thou, that a part
Of our great function is to guard thine earth?
*Japh.* But all good angels have forsaken earth,
Which is condemn'd; nay, even the evil fly
The approaching chaos. Anah! Anah! my
In vain, and long, and still to be beloved!
Why walk'st thou with this spirit, in those hours
When no good spirit longer lights below?
*Anah.* Japhet, I cannot answer thee; yet, yet
Forgive me —
*Japh.* May the Heaven, which soon no more
Will pardon, do so! for thou art greatly tempted.
*Aho.* Back to thy tents, insulting son of Noah!
We know thee not.
*Japh.* The hour may come when thou
May'st know me better; and thy sister know
Me still the same which I have ever been.
*Sam.* Son of the patriarch, who hath ever been
Upright before his God, whate'er thy gifts,

And thy words seem of sorrow, mix'd with wrath,
How have Azaziel, or myself, brought on thee
Wrong?

*Japh.* Wrong! the greatest of all wrongs; but thou
Say'st well, though she be dust, I did not, could not,
Deserve her. Farewell, Anah! I have said
That word so often! but now say it, ne'er
To be repeated. Angel! or whate'er
Thou art, or must be soon, hast thou the power
To save this beautiful — *these* beautiful
Children of Cain?

*Aza.* From what?

*Japh.* And is it so,
That ye too know not? Angels! angels! ye
Have shared man's sin, and, it may be, now must
Partake his punishment; or, at the least,
My sorrow.

*Sam.* Sorrow! I ne'er thought till now
To hear an Adamite speak riddles to me.

*Japh.* And hath not the Most High expounded them?
Then ye are lost, as they are lost.

*Aho.* So be it!
If they love as they are loved, they will not shrink
More to be mortal, than I would to dare
An immortality of agonies
With Samiasa!

*Anah.* Sister! sister! speak not
Thus.

*Aza.* Fearest thou, my Anah?

*Anah.* Yes, for thee:
I would resign the greater remnant of
This little life of mine, before one hour
Of thine eternity should know a pang.

*Japh.* It is for *him*, then! for the seraph thou
Hast left me! That is nothing, if thou hast not
Left thy God too! for unions like to these,
Between a mortal and an immortal, cannot

Be happy or be hallow'd. We are sent
Upon the earth to toil and die; and they
Are made to minister on high unto
The Highest: but if he can *save* thee, soon
The hour will come in which celestial aid
Alone can do so.
    *Anah.*        Ah! he speaks of death.
    *Sam.* Of death to *us!* and those who are with us!
But that the man seems full of sorrow, I
Could smile.
    *Japh.*     I grieve not for myself, nor fear;
I am safe, not for my own deserts, but those
Of a well-doing sire, who hath been found
Righteous enough to save his children. Would
His power was greater of redemption! or
That by exchanging my own life for hers,
Who could alone have made mine happy, she,
The last and loveliest of Cain's race, could share
The ark which shall receive a remnant of
The seed of Seth!
    *Aho.*        And dost thou think that we,
With Cain's, the eldest born of Adam's, blood
Warm in our veins, — strong Cain! who was begotten
In Paradise, — would mingle with Seth's children?
Seth, the last offspring of old Adam's dotage?
No, not to save all earth, were earth in peril!
Our race hath alway dwelt apart from thine
From the beginning, and shall do so ever.
    *Japh.* I did not speak to thee, Aholibamah!
Too much of the forefather whom thou vauntest
Has come down in that haughty blood which springs
From him who shed the first, and that a brother's!
But thou, my Anah! let me call thee mine,
Albeit thou art not; 'tis a word I cannot
Part with, although I must from thee. My Anah!
Thou who dost rather make me dream that Abel
Had left a daughter, whose pure pious race

Survived in thee, so much unlike thou art
The rest of the stern Cainites, save in beauty,
For all of them are fairest in their favour —
    *Aho.* (*interrupting him*). And wouldst thou have her like our
        father's foe
In mind, in soul? If *I* partook thy thought,
And dream'd that aught of *Abel* was in *her!* —
Get thee hence, son of Noah; thou makest strife.
    *Japh.* Offspring of Cain, thy father did so!
    *Aho.*                                          But
He slew not Seth: and what hast thou to do
With other deeds between his God and him?
    *Japh.* Thou speakest well: his God hath judged him, and
I had not named his deed, but that thyself
Didst seem to glory in him, nor to shrink
From what he had done.
    *Aho.*                      He was our fathers' father;
The eldest born of man, the strongest, bravest,
And most enduring: — Shall I blush for him
From whom we had our being? Look upon
Our race; behold their stature and their beauty,
Their courage, strength, and length of days —
    *Japh.*                            They are number'd.
    *Aho.* Be it so! but while yet their hours endure,
I glory in my brethren and our fathers.
    *Japh.* My sire and race but glory in their God,
Anah! and thou? —
    *Anah.*               Whate'er our God decrees,
The God of Seth as Cain, I must obey,
And will endeavour patiently to obey.
But could I dare to pray in his dread hour
Of universal vengeance (if such should be),
It would not be to live, alone exempt
Of all my house. My sister! oh, my sister!
What were the world, or other worlds, or all
The brightest future, without the sweet past —
Thy love — my father's — all the life, and all

The things which sprang up with me, like the stars,
Making my dim existence radiant with
Soft lights which were not mine? Aholibamah!
Oh! if there should be mercy — seek it, find it:
I abhor death, because that thou must die.
  *Aho.* What, hath this dreamer, with his father's ark,
The bugbear he hath built to scare the world,
Shaken *my* sister? Are *we* not the loved
Of seraphs? and if we were not, must we
Cling to a son of Noah for our lives?
Rather than thus — But the enthusiast dreams
The worst of dreams, the fantasies engender'd
By hopeless love and heated vigils. Who
Shall shake these solid mountains, this firm earth,
And bid those clouds and waters take a shape
Distinct from that which we and all our sires
Have seen them wear on their eternal way?
Who shall do this?
  *Japh.*    He whose one word produced them.
  *Aho.* Who *heard* that word?
  *Japh.*      The universe, which leap'd
To life before it. Ah! smilest thou still in scorn?
Turn to thy seraphs: if they attest it not,
They are none.
  *Sam.*  Aholibamah, own thy God!
  *Aho.* I have ever hail'd our Maker, Samiasa,
As thine, and mine: a God of love, not sorrow.
  *Japh.* Alas! what else is love but sorrow? Even
He who made earth in love had soon to grieve
Above its first and best inhabitants.
  *Aho.* 'Tis said so.
  *Japh.*   It is even so.

     *Enter* NOAH *and* SHEM.

  *Noah.*    Japhet! What
Dost thou here with these children of the wicked?
Dread'st thou not to partake their coming doom?

# PART I.

*Japh.* Father, it cannot be a sin to seek
To save an earth-born being; and behold,
These are not of the sinful, since they have
The fellowship of angels.
    *Noah.* These are they, then,
Who leave the throne of God, to take them wives
From out the race of Cain; the sons of heaven,
Who seek earth's daughters for their beauty?
    *Aza.* Patriarch!
Thou hast said it.
    *Noah.* Woe, woe, woe to such communion!
Has not God made a barrier between earth
And heaven, and limited each, kind to kind?
    *Sam.* Was not man made in high Jehovah's image?
Did God not love what he had made? And what
Do we but imitate and emulate
His love unto created love?
    *Noah.* I am
But man, and was not made to judge mankind,
Far less the sons of God; but as our God
Has deign'd to commune with me, and reveal
*His* judgments, I reply, that the descent
Of seraphs from their everlasting seat
Unto a perishable and perishing,
Even on the very *eve* of *perishing*, world,
Cannot be good.
    *Aza.* What! though it were to save?
    *Noah.* Not ye in all your glory can redeem
What he who made you glorious hath condemn'd.
Were your immortal mission safety, 'twould
Be general, not for two, though beautiful;
And beautiful they are, but not the less
Condemn'd.
    *Japh.* Oh, father! say it not.
    *Noah.* Son! son!
If that thou wouldst avoid their doom, forget
That they exist: they soon shall cease to be;

While thou shalt be the sire of a new world,
And better.

*Japh.* Let me die with *this*, and *them!*

*Noah.* Thou *shouldst* for such a thought, but shalt not; he
Who *can* redeems thee.

*Sam.* And why him and thee,
More than what he, thy son, prefers to both?

*Noah.* Ask him who made thee greater than myself
And mine, but not less subject to his own
Almightiness. And lo! his mildest and
Least to be tempted messenger appears!

*Enter* RAPHAEL *the Archangel.*

*Raph.* Spirits!
   Whose seat is near the throne,
     What do ye here?
Is thus a seraph's duty to be shown,
     Now that the hour is near
   When earth must be alone?
     Return!
   Adore and burn
In glorious homage with the elected "seven."
   Your place is heaven.

*Sam.* Raphael!
The first and fairest of the sons of God,
   How long hath this been law,
That earth by angels must be left untrod?
   Earth! which oft saw
Jehovah's footsteps not disdain her sod!
   The world he loved, and made
   For love; and oft have we obey'd
His frequent mission with delighted pinions:
   Adoring him in his least works display'd;
Watching this youngest star of his dominions;
   And, as the latest birth of his great word,
   Eager to keep it worthy of our Lord.
     Why is thy brow severe?
And wherefore speak'st thou of destruction near?

*Raph.* Had Samiasa and Azaziel been
  In their true place, with the angelic choir,
      Written in fire
    They would have seen
    Jehovah's late decree,
And not enquired their Maker's breath of me:
    But ignorance must ever be
      A part of sin;
And even the spirits' knowledge shall grow less
    As they wax proud within;
For Blindness is the first-born of Excess.
  When all good angels left the world, ye stay'd,
Stung with strange passions, and debased
By mortal feelings for a mortal maid:
But ye are pardon'd thus far, and replaced
With your pure equals. Hence! away! away!
      Or stay,
  And lose eternity by that delay.
*Aza.* And thou! if earth be thus forbidden
    In the decree
  To us until this moment hidden,
    Dost thou not err as we
      In being here?
*Raph.* I came to call ye back to your fit sphere,
In the great name and at the word of God.
Dear, dearest in themselves, and scarce less dear
  That which I came to do: till now we trod
Together the eternal space; together
  Let us still walk the stars. True, earth must die!
Her race, return'd into her womb, must wither,
  And much which she inherits: but oh! why
  Cannot this earth be made, or be destroy'd,
  Without involving ever some vast void
In the immortal ranks? immortal still
  In their immeasurable forfeiture.
Our brother Satan fell; his burning will

Rather than longer worship dared endure!
But ye who still are pure!
Seraphs! less mighty than that mightiest one,
Think how he was undone!
And think if tempting man can compensate
For heaven desired too late?
   Long have I warr'd,
   Long must I war
  With him who deem'd it hard
  To be created, and to acknowledge him
  Who midst the cherubim
Made him as suns to a dependent star,
Leaving the archangels at his right hand dim.
 I loved him — beautiful he was: oh heaven!
Save *his* who made, what beauty and what power
Was ever like to Satan's! Would the hour
  In which he fell could ever be forgiven!
The wish is impious: but, oh ye!
Yet undestroy'd, be warn'd! Eternity
 With him, or with his God, is in your choice:
He hath not tempted you; he cannot tempt
The angels, from his further snares exempt:
 But man hath listen'd to his voice,
And ye to woman's — beautiful she is,
The serpent's voice less subtle than her kiss.
The snake but vanquish'd dust; but she will draw
A second host from heaven, to break heaven's law.
   Yet, yet, oh fly!
   Ye cannot die;
   But they
   Shall pass away,
While ye shall fill with shrieks the upper sky
  For perishable clay,
Whose memory in your immortality
 Shall long outlast the sun which gave them day.
Think how your essence differeth from theirs

In all but suffering! why partake
The agony to which they must be heirs —
Born to be plough'd with years, and sown with cares,
And reap'd by Death, lord of the human soil?
Even had their days been left to toil their path
Through time to dust, unshorten'd by God's wrath,
Still they are Evil's prey and Sorrow's spoil.
  *Aho.*  Let them fly!
I hear the voice which says that all must die
Sooner than our white-bearded patriarchs died;
    And that on high
    An ocean is prepared,
    While from below
The deep shall rise to meet heaven's overflow.
    Few shall be spared,
It seems; and, of that few, the race of Cain
Must lift their eyes to Adam's God in vain.
    Sister! since it is so,
    And the eternal Lord
    In vain would be implored
For the remission of one hour of woe,
Let us resign even what we have adored,
And meet the wave, as we would meet the sword,
    If not unmoved, yet undismay'd,
And wailing less for us than those who shall
Survive in mortal or immortal thrall,
  And, when the fatal waters are allay'd,
Weep for the myriads who can weep no more.
Fly, seraphs! to your own eternal shore,
Where winds nor howl nor waters roar.
    Our portion is to die,
    And yours to live for ever:
But which is best, a dead eternity,
Or living, is but known to the great Giver.
    Obey him, as we shall obey;
I would not keep this life of mine in clay

An hour beyond his will;
Nor see ye lose a portion of his grace,
For all the mercy which Seth's race
  Find still.
  Fly!
And as your pinions bear ye back to heaven,
Think that my love still mounts with thee on high,
   Samiasa!
And if I look up with a tearless eye,
 'Tis that an angel's bride disdains to weep,—
Farewell! Now rise, inexorable deep!
 *Anah.*  And must we die?
  And must I lose thee too,
   Azaziel?
   Oh, my heart! my heart!
   Thy prophecies were true!
  And yet thou wert so happy too!
The blow, though not unlook'd for, falls as new:
  But yet depart!
   Ah! why?
  Yet let me not retain thee — fly!
My pangs can be but brief; but thine would be
Eternal, if repulsed from heaven for me.
  Too much already hast thou deign'd
   To one of Adam's race!
Our doom is sorrow: not to us alone,
But to the spirits who have not disdain'd
To love us, cometh anguish with disgrace.
The first who taught us knowledge hath been hurl'd
 From his once archangelic throne
 Into some unknown world:
   And thou, Azaziel! No —
   Thou shalt not suffer woe
For me. Away! nor weep!
 Thou canst not weep; but yet
May'st suffer more, not weeping: then forget

Her, whom the surges of the all-strangling deep
    Can bring no pang like this. Fly! fly!
Being gone, 'twill be less difficult to die.
    *Japh.* Oh say not so!
        Father! and thou, archangel, thou!
    Surely celestial mercy lurks below
That pure severe serenity of brow:
    Let them not meet this sea without a shore,
Save in our ark, or let me be no more!
    *Noah.* Peace, child of passion, peace!
If not within thy heart, yet with thy tongue
    Do God no wrong!
Live as he wills it — die, when he ordains,
A righteous death, unlike the seed of Cain's.
    Cease, or be sorrowful in silence; cease
To weary Heaven's ear with thy selfish plaint.
    Wouldst thou have God commit a sin for thee?
        Such would it be
        To alter his intent
For a mere mortal sorrow. Be a man!
And bear what Adam's race must bear, and can.
    *Japh.* Ay, father! but when they are gone,
    And we are all alone,
Floating upon the azure desert, and
The depth beneath us hides our own dear land,
    And dearer, silent friends and brethren, all
    Buried in its immeasurable breast,
Who, who, our tears, our shrieks, shall then command?
    Can we in desolation's peace have rest?
        Oh God! be thou a God, and spare
        Yet while 'tis time!
Renew not Adam's fall:
    Mankind were then but twain,
But they are numerous now as are the waves
    And the tremendous rain,
Whose drops shall be less thick than would their graves,
    Were graves permitted to the seed of Cain.

*Noah.* Silence, vain boy! each word of thine's a crime.
Angel! forgive this stripling's fond despair.
   *Raph.* Seraphs! these mortals speak in passion: Ye!
Who are, or should be, passionless and pure,
May now return with me.
   *Sam.*                It may not be:
We have chosen, and will endure.
   *Raph.* Say'st thou?
     *Aza.*              He hath said it, and I say, Amen!
   *Raph.*   Again!
Then from this hour,
Shorn as ye are of all celestial power,
And aliens from your God,
          Farewell!
   *Japh.*       Alas! where shall they dwell?
Hark, hark! Deep sounds, and deeper still,
  Are howling from the mountain's bosom:
There's not a breath of wind upon the hill,
  Yet quivers every leaf, and drops each blossom:
Earth groans as if beneath a heavy load.
   *Noah.* Hark, hark! the sea-birds cry!
In clouds they overspread the lurid sky,
And hover round the mountain, where before
  Never a white wing, wetted by the wave,
     Yet dared to soar,
Even when the waters wax'd too fierce to brave.
Soon it shall be their only shore,
   And then, no more!
   *Japh.*     The sun! the sun!
He riseth, but his better light is gone;
  And a black circle, bound
       His glaring disk around,
Proclaims earth's last of summer days hath shone!
   The clouds return into the hues of night,
Save where their brazen-colour'd edges streak
The verge where brighter morns were wont to break.

*Noah.* And lo! yon flash of light,
The distant thunder's harbinger, appears!
 It cometh! hence, away!
Leave to the elements their evil prey!
Hence to where our all-hallow'd ark uprears
  Its safe and wreckless sides!
 *Japh.* Oh, father, stay!
Leave not my Anah to the swallowing tides!
 *Noah.* Must we not leave all life to such? Begone!
 *Japh.*       Not I.
 *Noah.*             Then die
  With them!
How darest thou look on that prophetic sky,
And seek to save what all things now condemn,
  In overwhelming unison
   With just Jehovah's wrath!
 *Japh.* Can rage and justice join in the same path?
 *Noah.* Blasphemer! darest thou murmur even now?
 *Raph.* Patriarch, be still a father! smooth thy brow:
Thy son, despite his folly, shall not sink:
He knows not what he says, yet shall not drink
 With sobs the salt foam of the swelling waters;
But be, when passion passeth, good as thou,
 Nor perish like heaven's children with man's daughters.
 *Aho.* The tempest cometh; heaven and earth unite
  For the annihilation of all life.
  Unequal is the strife
Between our strength and the Eternal Might!
 *Sam.* But ours is with thee; we will bear ye far
  To some untroubled star,
Where thou and Anah shalt partake our lot:
  And if thou dost not weep for thy lost earth
Our forfeit heaven shall also be forgot.
 *Anah.* Oh! my dear father's tents, my place of birth,
And mountains, land, and woods! when ye are not,
Who shall dry up my tears?
 *Aza.*       Thy spirit-lord.

Fear not; though we are shut from heaven,
Yet much is ours, whence we can not be driven.
 *Raph.* Rebel! thy words are wicked, as thy deeds
Shall henceforth be but weak: the flaming sword,
Which chased the first-born out of Paradise,
Still flashes in the angelic hands.
 *Aza.* It cannot slay us: threaten dust with death,
And talk of weapons unto that which bleeds.
What are thy swords in our immortal eyes?
 *Raph.* The moment cometh to approve thy strength;
  And learn at length
How vain to war with what thy God commands:
Thy former force was in thy faith.

   *Enter Mortals, flying for refuge.*
    *Chorus of Mortals.*
The heavens and earth are mingling — God! oh God!
What have we done? Yet spare!
Hark! even the forest beasts howl forth their prayer!
 The dragon crawls from out his den,
 To herd, in terror, innocent with men;
And the birds scream their agony through air.
Yet, yet, Jehovah! yet withdraw thy rod
Of wrath, and pity thine own world's despair!
Hear not man only but all nature plead!
 *Raph.* Farewell, thou earth! ye wretched sons of clay,
I cannot, must not, aid you. 'Tis decreed!
        [*Exit* RAPHAEL.
 *Japh.* Some clouds sweep on as vultures for their prey,
While others, fix'd as rocks, await the word
At which their wrathful vials shall be pour'd.
No azure more shall robe the firmament,
Nor spangled stars be glorious: Death hath risen:
In the sun's place a pale and ghastly glare
Hath wound itself around the dying air.
 *Aza.* Come, Anah! quit this chaos-founded prison,
To which the elements again repair,

To turn it into what it was: beneath
The shelter of these wings thou shalt be safe,
As was the eagle's nestling once within
Its mother's. — Let the coming chaos chafe
With all its elements! Heed not their din!
A brighter world than this, where thou shalt breathe
Ethereal life, will we explore:
These darken'd clouds are not the only skies.
    [AZAZIEL *and* SAMIASA *fly off, and disappear with*
      ANAH *and* AHOLIBAMAH.
 *Japh.* They are gone! They have disappear'd amidst the
   roar
Of the forsaken world and never more,
Whether they live, or die with all earth's life,
Now near its last, can aught restore
Anah unto these eyes.
     *Chorus of Mortals.*
Oh son of Noah! mercy on thy kind!
What! wilt thou leave us all — all — *all* behind?
While safe amidst the elemental strife,
Thou sitt'st within thy guarded ark?
 *A Mother (offering her infant to* JAPHET). Oh let this child
  I brought him forth in woe,      [embark!
    But thought it joy
   To see him to my bosom clinging so.
     Why was he born?
     What hath he done —
     My unwean'd son —
To move Jehovah's wrath or scorn?
What is there in this milk of mine, that death
Should stir all heaven and earth up to destroy
    My boy,
And roll the waters o'er his placid breath?
Save him, thou seed of Seth!
Or cursed be — with him who made
Thee and thy race, for which we are betray'd!
 *Japh.* Peace! 'tis no hour for curses, but for prayer.

*Chorus of Mortals.*
For prayer!!!
And where
Shall prayer ascend,
When the swoln clouds unto the mountains bend
And burst,
And gushing oceans every barrier rend,
  Until the very deserts know no thirst?
Accursed
Be he who made thee and thy sire!
We deem our curses vain; we must expire;
  But as we know the worst,
Why should our hymn be raised, our knees be bent
Before the implacable Omnipotent,
Since we must fall the same?
If he hath made earth, let it be his shame,
  To make a world for torture. — Lo! they come,
The loathsome waters, in their rage!
And with their roar make wholesome nature dumb!
  The forest's trees (coeval with the hour
When Paradise upsprung,
  Ere Eve gave Adam knowledge for her dower,
Or Adam his first hymn of slavery sung),
  So massy, vast, yet green in their old age,
Are overtopp'd,
Their summer blossoms by the surges lopp'd,
Which rise, and rise, and rise.
Vainly we look up to the lowering skies —
  They meet the seas,
And shut out God from our beseeching eyes.
  Fly, son of Noah, fly! and take thine ease
In thine allotted ocean-tent;
And view, all floating o'er the element,
The corpses of the world of thy young days:
     Then to Jehovah raise
     Thy song of praise!

PART I.

*A Mortal.* Blessed are the dead
    Who die in the Lord!
And though the waters be o'er earth outspread,
    Yet, as *his* word,
    Be the decree adored!
He gave me life — he taketh but
    The breath which is his own:
And though these eyes should be for ever shut,
    Nor longer this weak voice before his throne
  Be heard in supplicating tone,
        Still blessed be the Lord,
          For what is past,
          For that which is:
          For all are his,
          From first to last —
Time — space — eternity — life — death —
    The vast known and immeasurable unknown.
He made, and can unmake;
    And shall *I*, for a little gasp of breath,
Blaspheme and groan?
    No; let me die, as I have lived, in faith,
Nor quiver, though the universe may quake!

        *Chorus of Mortals.*
    Where shall we fly?
      Not to the mountains high;
For now their torrents rush, with double roar,
    To meet the ocean, which, advancing still,
Already grasps each drowning hill,
    Nor leaves an unsearch'd cave.

        *Enter a Woman.*
  *Woman.* Oh, save me, save!
Our valley is no more:
  My father and my father's tent,
My brethren and my brethren's herds,
  The pleasant trees that o'er our noonday bent
And sent forth evening songs from sweetest birds,

The little rivulet which freshen'd all
    Our pastures green,
    No more are to be seen.
When to the mountain cliff I climb'd this morn,
    I turn'd to bless the spot,
And not a leaf appear'd about to fall; —
    And now they are not! —
Why was I born?
        *Japh.*          To die! in youth to die;
And happier in that doom,
Than to behold the universal tomb
            Which I
Am thus condemn'd to weep above in vain.
Why, when all perish, why must I remain?

    [*The waters rise: Men fly in every direction; many are overtaken by the waves; the Chorus of Mortals disperses in search of safety up the mountains: Japhet remains upon a rock, while the Ark floats towards him in the distance.*

www.ingramcontent.com/pod-product-compliance
Lightning Source LLC
Chambersburg PA
CBHW030400230426
**43664CB00007BB/683**